International HRM
A Cross-Cultural Approach

Terence Jackson

SAGE Publications
London • Thousand Oaks • New Delhi

© Terence Jackson 2002

First published 2002

Apart from any fair dealing for the purposes of research or
private study, or criticism or review, as permitted under the
Copyright, Designs and Patents Act, 1988, this publication may
be reproduced, stored or transmitted in any form, or by any
means, only with the prior permission in writing of the
publishers, or in the case of reprographic reproduction, in
accordance with the terms of licences issued by the Copyright
Licensing Agency. Inquiries concerning reproduction outside
those terms should be sent to the publishers.

SAGE Publications Ltd
6 Bonhill Street
London EC2A 4PU

SAGE Publications Inc
2455 Teller Road
Thousand Oaks, California 91320

SAGE Publications India Pvt Ltd
32, M-Block Market
Greater Kailash — I
New Delhi 110 048

British Library Cataloguing in Publication Data

A catalogue record for this book is
available from the British Library

ISBN 0 7619 7404 0
ISBN 0 7619 7405 9 (pbk)

Library of Congress catalog card number available

Typeset by Keystroke, Jacaranda Lodge, Wolverhampton.
Printed and bound in Great Britain by Athenaeum Press, Gateshead

To the students and staff who created and nurtured the multicultural spirit and vision of EAP European School of Management 1973–1999 in Paris, Oxford, Berlin and Madrid. Within the School nobody was a foreigner. The dedication is also to the continuation of this spirit within the new school, which combines the youth and optimism of EAP with the wisdom and maturity of ESCP.

contents

The term 'Human Resource Management', and the concept behind it, is laden with value. Values are part of the fabric of culture. The concept that human beings are a resource to further the executive ends of an organization is a concept that is contrary to the values of many non-Western cultures. Perhaps in its most instrumental conceptualization, this may also be contrary to the values of many 'Western' cultures. Certainly the ideas behind what constitute the principles, policies and practices of managing people in organizations differ even among Western European countries, and certainly between American and most Western European countries.

Since the origins of the concept in the individualistic achievement-oriented management culture of the United States, the term Human Resource Management is almost universally accepted. Particularly in writing about the management of people, it is very difficult not to use this term, even in the international context within which most managers (barring those who still keep their heads in the sand) now operate, either actively or as passive participants in the global economy. Little thought is given to the implications of its underlying concept, nor to its manifestations in the policies and practices that multinational corporations employ across different countries. Most often these policies and practices are inappropriate. Yet in many countries such as the transitional economies of the former Soviet bloc and the People's Republic of China, and the 'post-colonial' societies that make up a huge percentage of the people and land surface (as well as resources) of the globe, HRM policies and practices are often uncritically accepted, virtually 'off the shelf'.

This is not to denigrate the contributions to global managing that HRM in many of its principles, such as the competences approach, can often make. It is simply to situate it in its cultural context, and to examine its appropriateness in other cultural contexts. It is also to view this in connection with contributions from other cultural sources, as well as the multicultural (centrifugal) and strategizing (centripetal) influences acting on international organization.

In particular, Chapter 1 examines the management of people employing a 'multicultural model' of conceptualizing differences and differentiation in international organization. Chapter 2 employs an integrative conceptualization of the 'supranational organization' to look at how different formulations of international organizational strategy may influence the way cultural differences are handled. Chapter 3 explores the 'American model' of the competent organization. The competences approach takes organizational strategic and operational goals as its starting point in determining required competences for selection, development and reward: not least to determine 'international' competences. This leads into a discussion of expatriation and international careers, taking the analogy of the 'missionary organization' and the metaphor of the 'Dutch model'.

Chapters 5 to 10 look at the 'cultural' contributions of different approaches to the management of people in international organizations. Chapter 5 looks at the 'Japanese model' of the motivating organization, extending the concept of motivation to include loyalty, and examining the transferability of Japanese techniques to other countries. Chapter 6 focuses on the concept of the learning organization through the cultural lens of the 'British model'. Not all learning organizations are British, yet the British cultural setting is discussed as it is particularly conducive to the development of such a concept. This concept has been bounced back and forth across the Atlantic Ocean, and more recently has incorporated concepts of knowledge management including those from Japan. The 'flexible organization' could perhaps be relevant anywhere in the world, yet geographical as well as temporal flexibility has been especially important to developing trans-European organizations within the European Union. The European Union model is discussed in Chapter 7 as attempting to draw synergies from diversity, rather than glossing over cultural differences in the management of people in international organizations. That need for flexibility has extended to organizations and managers working more and more in joint ventures. This is no less so than in China, where because of the way foreign companies were allowed into mainland China, international joint ventures have been the norm. The 'Chinese model' is examined in Chapter 8, particularly in terms of the cross-vergence of management systems (i.e. the developing of hybrid value systems as a result of cultural interactions) and the problems involved in Western–Chinese joint ventures in relation to managing people. Both these themes are taken up in connection with the 'transitioning organization' within the 'post-Soviet model' in Chapter 9. The appropriateness of German approaches to people management in joint ventures with former Soviet bloc countries is a particular focus, as are the management systems emerging from the remnants of Soviet systems of management and control. Many of the issues that confront countries in transition also confront the post-colonial countries of Africa and South Asia. Chapter 10 focuses on the 'post-colonial organization' within a 'stakeholder model', and looks at the humanistic regard for people, in contrast to the instrumental one of many Western companies operating in post-colonial countries.

This is a book primarily for advanced students, including those on MBA-type courses taught in English around the globe. It is for students and managers of international management and 'human resource management' in an international context. On such courses there is a major problematic of maintaining and conveying a high level of academic rigour, while ensuring that the theories and material are relevant to the day to day decision-making activities of real managers doing real and demanding jobs. The approach of this book is to discuss issues as far as possible within the context of real companies and real cultures. Each chapter therefore provides a real-life case or cases. Each chapter also provides, by way of conclusion, a section on management implications together with sample questions that will help readers to draw conclusions from the cases, and a section on developing a research agenda. It is hoped that this will be useful for readers who are developing research projects and writing dissertations in these particular areas, and sample questions are provided. These may help in formulating specific research questions.

The text does not aim to be comprehensive in coverage in terms of industries, but to illustrate the activities and approaches of international organizations. Also, the coverage of different cultures is not intended to include all the different and diverse cultures of the world, simply to enable sufficient understanding of the cultural contexts from which many of the approaches are derived, and to provide background on the appropriateness of different aspects of managing people in international organizations. A conceptual map at the end of this preface should help readers navigate through the chapters. It is further discussed in the Introduction.

Terence Jackson
Centre for Cross Cultural Management Research,
ESCP-EAP European School of Management

A conceptual map of international organization and human resource management

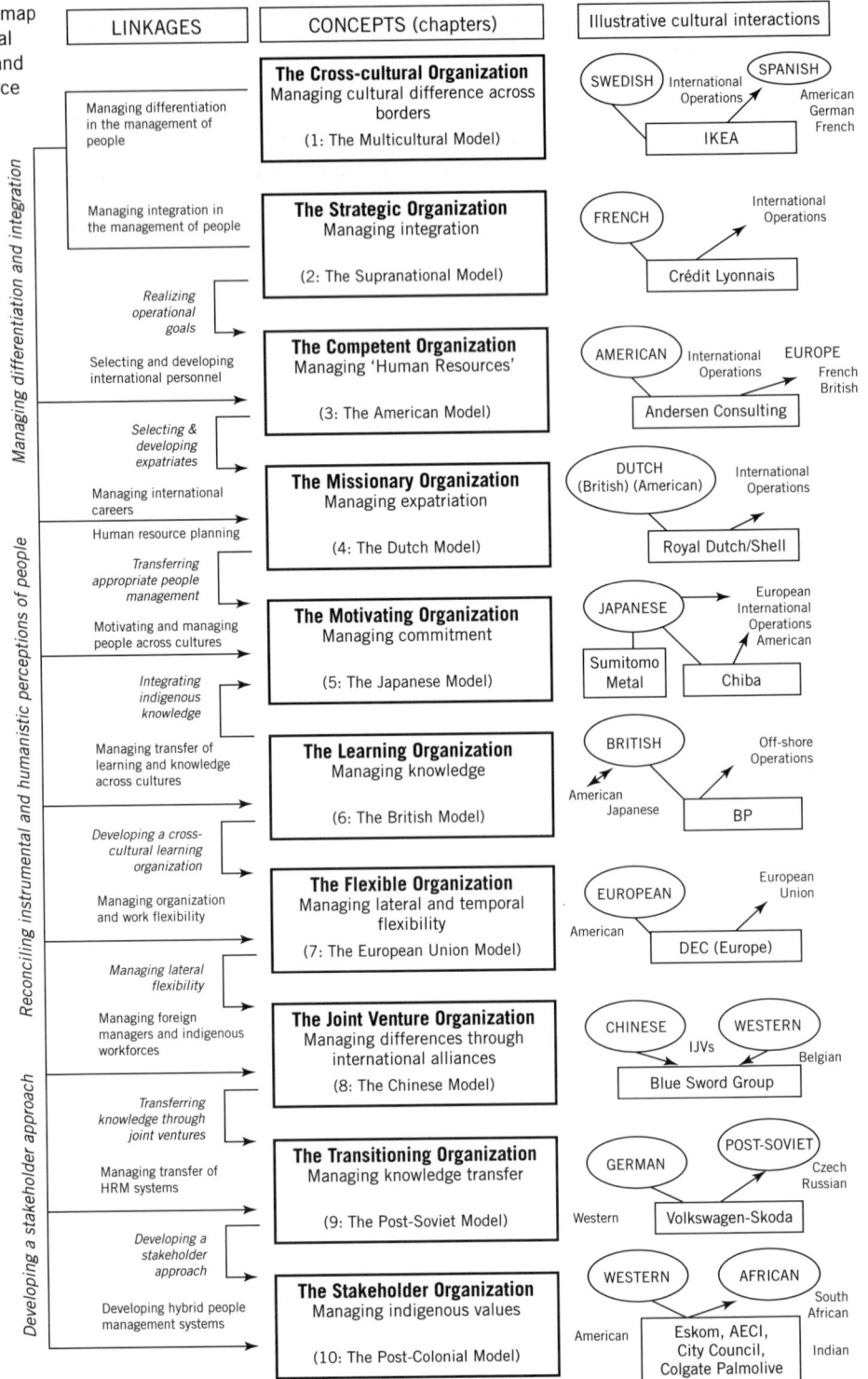

LINKAGES	CONCEPTS (chapters)	Illustrative cultural interactions

Managing differentiation and integration

Managing differentiation in the management of people

The Cross-cultural Organization
Managing cultural difference across borders

(1: The Multicultural Model)

SWEDISH — International Operations → SPANISH / American German French
IKEA

Managing integration in the management of people

The Strategic Organization
Managing integration

(2: The Supranational Model)

FRENCH → International Operations
Crédit Lyonnais

Realizing operational goals

Selecting and developing international personnel

The Competent Organization
Managing 'Human Resources'

(3: The American Model)

AMERICAN — International Operations → EUROPE French British
Andersen Consulting

Reconciling instrumental and humanistic perceptions of people

Selecting & developing expatriates

Managing international careers

Human resource planning

The Missionary Organization
Managing expatriation

(4: The Dutch Model)

DUTCH (British) (American) → International Operations
Royal Dutch/Shell

Transferring appropriate people management

Motivating and managing people across cultures

The Motivating Organization
Managing commitment

(5: The Japanese Model)

JAPANESE → European International Operations / American
Sumitomo Metal — Chiba

Integrating indigenous knowledge

Managing transfer of learning and knowledge across cultures

The Learning Organization
Managing knowledge

(6: The British Model)

BRITISH — Off-shore Operations
American Japanese — BP

Developing a cross-cultural learning organization

Managing organization and work flexibility

The Flexible Organization
Managing lateral and temporal flexibility

(7: The European Union Model)

EUROPEAN → European Union
American — DEC (Europe)

Developing a stakeholder approach

Managing lateral flexibility

Managing foreign managers and indigenous workforces

The Joint Venture Organization
Managing differences through international alliances

(8: The Chinese Model)

CHINESE — IJVs — WESTERN / Belgian
Blue Sword Group

Transferring knowledge through joint ventures

Managing transfer of HRM systems

The Transitioning Organization
Managing knowledge transfer

(9: The Post-Soviet Model)

GERMAN → POST-SOVIET / Czech Russian
Western — Volkswagen-Skoda

Developing a stakeholder approach

Developing hybrid people management systems

The Stakeholder Organization
Managing indigenous values

(10: The Post-Colonial Model)

WESTERN — AFRICAN / South African
American — Eskom, AECI, City Council, Colgate Palmolive — Indian

Introduction: beyond human resource management

Avoiding disasters

On 6 March 1987, the *Herald of Free Enterprise*, a roll-on/roll-off passenger and vehicle ferry, capsized and sank in five minutes off the coast of Zeebrugge, Belgium, with the loss of 193 lives. The incident was caused by a combination of factors, including the actions or lack of actions of both line staff and senior management. The report of the formal investigation allocated responsibilities for the disaster among the top management, including the board of directors and the junior superintendents. The disaster's immediate cause was the ferry's having put to sea with the bow doors open. The assistant bosun had opened the doors. He acknowledged it was his duty to close them. He had previously been released from duty by the bosun, fell asleep and had not been woken by the call of 'harbour stations'. But, although the assistant bosun was nominally in charge, he was not the only person in charge, and not the only person who ever closed the doors. There was no clear system.

The system of checking the doors was the responsibility of the chief officer, but the system required him to be in two places at the same time: checking the bow doors and taking up his position on the bridge. The bosun was the last person to leave the area of the bow doors and could have closed them. He said that it had never been part of his duties to close them. Nor did the Master of the vessel check with the chief officer if the ship was secure when he came onto the bridge, and the chief officer did not make a report to that effect.

The standing orders of the company were that 'Heads of departments are to report to the Master immediately they are aware of any deficiency which is likely to cause their departments to be unready for sea in any respect at the due sailing time. In the absence of any such report the Master will assume, at the due sailing time, that the vessel is ready for sea in all respects'. This therefore accepts that negative reporting is sufficient to count for a positive information transmission. That is, no report is considered to convey positive information. So if there is a failure to make a report for other reasons, the wrong communication may be transmitted. This does not give the Master any responsibility to request the information: absence of information is regarded as sufficient to put to sea. This does not, however, preclude bottom-up responsibility. Whilst standing orders were interpreted so that no checks were made on whether the bow doors were actually closed or not, managers (e.g. the bosun) could also be held responsible for not questioning these ambiguous orders and the interpretations of these orders by senior managers (captain and superintending captain).

It is Allinson (1993) who recounts this disaster. He suggests that it may be understood in terms of dysfunctional management: there was a total lack of safety priority for crew and passengers; a non-assignment of responsibilities and issuing of unclear orders; an apparent lack of ethical consciousness and lack of understanding of the responsibilities of a manager; and a lack of proper management structure.

Allinson suggests that a safety-first consciousness could have been implemented by a clear attribution of domains of responsibilities for specific officers; by issuance of clear orders and instructions; by safety not being seen to be an add-on, but an intrinsic feature of good business management; by shared responsibility (perhaps bottom-up and horizontally as well as top-down); and by the will to communicate, including respectful listening. A similar disaster had been averted in 1983 when the assistant bosun of the *Pride of Free Enterprise* had fallen asleep. Some masters had requested a light on the bridge to indicate that the door had been closed. These requests were ignored until after its sister ship *Herald* went down.

Allinson focuses on this, and on other major disasters: the launch of the *Challenger* space shuttle, the King's Cross underground station fire in London, and the crash of the Air New Zealand DC10, flight TE 901 on Mount Erebus. He concludes that above all management ethics is a respect for persons. He suggests that applying some of the principles that appear to pertain in Japanese management systems might have led to the avoidance of technological disasters. These include intra-departmental cooperation, for example, between the manager (who may see her job as cost cutting and therefore safety cutting) and the engineer (who may propose safety features); and the understanding that one dissenting voice can stop disasters (the will to communicate: in such as the *ringi* system).

One of the main messages that Allinson (1993) conveys is that people should be treated as an end in themselves, and not as a means to an end. It seems to have been the practice of such ferry companies to maximize returns by turning ferries around as quickly as possible (similar disasters have taken place more recently, such as the ferry *Estonia* capsizing in the Baltic Sea with the loss of many lives). Other stakeholders, apart from shareholders such as staff and customers, were not given due attention, and hence safety was disregarded. They were simply seen as a means to an end.

Human resource management and beyond

Instrumental attitudes to people in organizations do not always lead to disasters, although they have the potential to do so in certain combinations of circumstances. However, contained within any managerial decision making are attitudinal values that can determine the outcome of decisions. Decisions that managers make in organizations can affect people's lives.

The importance of the contribution to the bottom-line and to shareholder value is a key issue in many Western-based human resource management systems (Becker et al., 1997). Yet the underlying values basis for this approach may become a major impediment to the successful transfer of management policies and practices internationally. The cultural perception of human beings as a resource used in the pursuit of shareholder value may be challenged by the perception that people have a value in their own right (Jackson, 1999). Hence, a developmental approach towards people, as an integral part of the organization, and as a direction of its objectives, may be implicit within, for example, Japanese approaches to managing people (Allinson, 1993).

Certainly since Allinson's book was published there has been an increasing emphasis in Western literature on the stakeholder approach to managing organizations, and a hard instrumental approach had already been challenged in a limited way within the context and conceptual framework of Western human resource management (Legge, 1989; Ellig, 1997). A distinction has been made in the strategic human resource management literature between the 'hard' perspective reflecting utilitarian instrumentalism which sees people in the organization as a mere resource to achieving the ends of the organization, and the 'soft' developmental approach which sees people more as valued assets capable of development, worthy of trust, and providing inputs through participation and informed choice (Beer and Spector, 1985; Tyson and Fell, 1986; Hendry and Pettigrew, 1990; Storey, 1992; Vaughan, 1994).

Yet Tayeb (2000) quite rightly states that the concept of human resource management is itself a product of a particular Anglo-American culture. It is likely that the 'hard' and 'soft' approaches taken within Western organizations both reflect an inherent cultural concept that perceives human beings in organizations as a means to an end (Blunt and Jones, 1997, uses the term 'functionalism'). They are simply two poles of a continuum from high to low instrumentalism.

If managers and human resource professionals are unable to break out of this paradigm, it is likely that when they, or managers educated in the Western tradition, try to implement 'Western' human resource practices in cultures which have a different concept of people, and a different regard for people in organizations, then incompatibilities will be manifested in lack of motivation and alienation, leading to low productivity and labour strife. This is of particular importance because of the extent of internationalization (see Chapters 2 and 4 below).

The importance of cultural values to the conduct of organizational life is well established in the literature (this is explored in more detail in Chapter 1). Yet the way that cultural values influence the regard for people in organizations, whilst implicit in the cross-cultural values literature, has been insufficiently articulated. There is, in particular, a growing interest in the relationship between indigenous and foreign (mainly Western) cultures in the practice and development of management and organization in the transitional economies of the former Soviet bloc (Shekshnia, 1998; Koubek and Brewster, 1995; Lawrence, 1994; and Chapter 9 this text), in China (Wang, 1994; Sergeant and Frenkel, 1998; Jackson and Bak, 1998; Huo and von Glinow, 1995; and Chapter 8) and to a lesser extent in the so-called 'developing' countries of South Asia, Africa and Latin America (Jaeger and Kanungo, 1990; Blunt and Jones, 1992; and Chapter 10). These issues have also been explored in the newly industrialized countries of East Asia (Chen, 1995; and Chapter 5), as well as in the 'hybrid' East/West cultures of the economies of Hong Kong (Priem et al., 2000) and Singapore (Gill and Wong, 1998; and Chapter 8). This literature by and large challenges the assumptions upon which human resource management is based in the Western world, and its applicability to managing people in countries whose economies have more recently been launched into the global market place.

3

The differences in perspectives on the value of people in organizations, and the validity of human resource management, particularly in non-Western countries, may be best understood in terms of the concept of locus of human value.

Locus of human value

It is possible to define 'humanism' as a regard for people as an end in themselves, and as having a value in themselves within an organizational context. Hence the locus of value, or the worth attributed to persons in a work organization is orientated towards those persons in themselves rather than towards organizational objectives as appropriate ends (for conceptual roots see Jackson, 1999; Koopman, 1991; Lessem, 1994 and Saunders, 1998). 'Instrumentalism' is defined as a regard for people as a means to an end, where the locus of value or the worth attributed to persons is towards the ends (objectives) of the organization.

Conceptually it may be tempting to subsume 'instrumentalism-humanism' under an *individualism–collectivism* dimension. There seems to be a simple split between the individualistic Western cultures where individuals are brought up in nuclear families and where individual achievement is often stressed, and collectivistic non-Western cultures where people are more likely to be part of an extended family and group involvement is stressed (see Chapter 1). The lifetime protection of people which collectivism affords would seem to indicate a valuing of people in their own right, and as part of a collective. The expectation that people in individualistic cultures will look after themselves (Hofstede, 1980a) would indicate a more instrumental view of people in organizations.

Confounding this simplistic view is first the target-specific and obligatory nature of collectivism (Hui, 1990). Japanese men may be more psychologically involved with their organizations, and Chinese more involved with their families, but at the expense of those outside the collective. Hence those outside the in-group may be regarded instrumentally. Secondly the work of Schwartz (1994) and Smith, Dugan and Trompenaars (1996) contrasts 'conservatism' and 'egalitarian commitment': the former correlating negatively with Hofstede's (1980a) individualism, and the latter correlating positively with it (these concepts are dealt with specifically in Chapter 1).

Whilst the socio-centric values attached to 'conservatism' are those that would be expected to be associated with collectivism, 'egalitarian commitment' expresses a transcendence of selfish interest (loyalty, social justice, responsibility and equality: Schwartz, 1994), but places a voluntary aspect on this rather than an obligatory one towards the in-group.

It may be that instrumentalism and humanism do not relate in a direct way to the level of individualism and collectivism in a society, as there may be different propelling cultural influences in different societies that lead to a diminution of a humanistic locus of human value within the organization and/or a softening of an instrumental locus.

For example, Australia is an individualistic (Hofstede, 1980a), 'Western' culture, yet has also been seen as having a 'humanistic' orientation (England, 1975, 1978) which Westwood and Posner (1997) argue leads to a concern for the well-being of the workforce and for quality of work life. More accurately this may reflect a moderately high level of egalitarian commitment (Schwartz, 1994,

Smith et al., 1996) and the 'mateship' of Australian society often identified in the literature (Encel, 1970). More recent research has suggested that Americans are not as individualistic as Hofstede's (1980a) study has suggested (Bond et al., 2001).

This view is reflected in the moderately high scores on Schwartz's (1994) and Smith et al.'s (1996) egalitarian commitment (see Chapter 1). Yet with Australia's higher historical levels of protectionism of both business and of the labour market, American work culture may be expected to exhibit a higher level of achievement orientation than that of Australia. However, both countries have similar moderately high scores on Hofstede's (1980a) masculinity dimension, which in part measures the level of competitiveness and results focus, and Australia has more recently gone through a phase of economic liberation and increase in competitiveness and freer labour markets (Edwards et al., 1997; Tixier, 2000; Boxall, 1999).

Both Australian (Karpin, 1995) and American (Wheeler and McClendon, 1998) organizations have been shown to have a command and control orientation with a top-down management approach. Again this may be a factor which promotes the view that employees may be used instrumentally towards the objectives of the organization's executive.

Yet there are other reasons, apart from the recent conceptualization of 'egalitarian commitment' in the cross-cultural values literature, why the harder forms of instrumentalism are being modified and 'softened' in the Anglo-Saxon countries and probably also in Western Europe; but also why the 'harder' versions may be being adopted uncritically in the rather short-term orientation of transitional countries in the former Soviet bloc (see Chapter 9), and in the newly industrialized countries of East Asia (see Chapter 8).

Influences from both cross-vergence of cultural systems (for example, the continued influence of Japanese policies on Western management thought and practices since the time of Pascale and Athos' 1981, and Ouchi's 1981, ground-breaking work), and the maturity of HRM systems under these and Western 'indigenous' influences such as human relations theory (from Roethlisberger and Dickson, 1939 and Likert, 1961), may give rise to the 'softer' instrumentalism in terms of policy and practice manifestation.

Similarly, with cross-vergence operative on 'hybrid' management cultures such as that of Hong Kong (a study of cross-vergence in Hong Kong by Priem, Love and Shaffer, 2000 found Hong Kong respondents to be closer to those from America than respondents from Guangzhou in their values), a humanistic locus of human value in organizations may take on 'harder' manifestations, or instrumental approaches to managing people may also feature.

For example, Hui (1990) notes the differential treatment of employees of in-group members and out-group members in Chinese family firms as conceptualized by McGregor's theory Y and theory X respectively. Hong Kong society is culturally complex, having been at the interface of Eastern and Western society for many years. The evidence in the literature in terms of its level of individualism–collectivism and the way it is changing is contradictory (Ho and Chiu, 1994; and see Chapters 1 and 8). Hence, as a result of both cross-vergence (Priem et al., 2000), and differential treatment of employees within a 'hybrid' collectivist management, both instrumentalism and humanism will be modified by the influence of the other.

5

The influence of instrumentalism on transitional and newly industrialized countries should also be taken into account (see Chapters 8 and 9). For example May, Bormann Young and Ledgerwood (1998) identify in Russia a tendency of corporations to adopt uncritically imported HRM solutions, stating that there is an underestimation of the complexities of the free market economy in the context of the Russian situation. They also note the lack of commitment to the organization, a lack of managerial responsibility, disregard for health and safety issues, and strained labour–management relations. This would seem indicative of a high level of instrumentalism. Srica (1995) also indicates that this may be the case in Eastern and Central European post-Soviet countries.

Yet countries such as the Czech Republic and Poland, which historically are different from Russia, have traditions of pre-Soviet industrialization and entrepreneurship, and relative efficiency under the Soviet system (Koubek and Brewster, 1995). They may be far closer to Western Europe than Russia in their cultural orientation, yet suffer from a lack of maturity of their 'HRM' systems.

Russia also has a stronger tradition of collectivization, and perhaps even 'Asiatic' humanistic orientations, than Poland and the Czech Republic. In Smith et al.'s (1996) conservatism–egalitarian commitment dimension, Russia is much higher on conservatism and lower on egalitarian commitment than Poland.

The newly industrialized countries in East Asia are also likely to come under the influence of the older industrialized countries to adopt short-term measures that have been successful elsewhere in order to compete effectively in the global economy. In the case of Korea (and distinguishing it from the transitional countries of the former Soviet bloc) these may be influences from both Japanese models of industrialization as well as from American models (Chen, 1995).

Bae and Chung (1997) have shown Korean organizations to be different from those of Japan in terms of the level of solidarity shown towards co-workers (see Chapter 5). Although Korean employees expect a higher level of commitment from their companies towards them, and from them to the company, the corporation shows a lower level of solidarity with workers than either their Japanese or their American counterparts. Chen (1995) depicts Korean people management as less consultative than that of Japanese firms, and as having a lower loyalty downwards, yet with loyalty expected upwards, and as representing a more authoritarian system than that of Japan. Hard instrumentalism may therefore be a feature in the newly industrialized countries of East Asia as well as of transitional countries. However, there will also be humanistic influences on such countries.

If organizations are regarded as fulfilling collective social needs such as providing full employment (as in the case of the former Soviet bloc: Koubek and Brewster, 1995), or serving the needs of people as part of a collective in-group (as in the case of Japan and Korea: Chen, 1995), this may be reflected in the extent to which people see their organization as fulfilling the needs of its people. A perception of contractual obligations only within individualistic societies may militate against this type of view. In a society with such collectivistic socio-cultural values, individuals may be valued as part of the wider collective.

This may be different from the values implicit within 'egalitarian commitment' and the 'human relations school' in Western society where a consideration of the 'valuing' of people may still be oriented towards a particular end that is separate from the individual. In a collectivist society, the 'end' may not be separate from the individual. It may also be that the relationship between the cultural antecedent of collectivism and a humanistic locus in organizations is more straightforward than the relationship between individualism and instrumentalism.

Managers in Japan, Korea and Hong Kong in Smith et al.'s (1996) study are all relatively high in loyal involvement on the dimension utilitarian involvement/loyal involvement. This is a dimension associated with individualism–collectivism, and it contrasts a contractual involvement with a moral involvement with the organization (see Chapter 1). The difference noted in the literature between the lower loyalty of the Korean corporation and the higher loyalty of the Japanese corporation has already been discussed. This may impact on the extent that managers regard employees as having a value in themselves. Unlike in other collectivist cultures, such as India (Rao, 1996) and Africa (Jackson, 1999; Blunt and Jones, 1992; and Chapter 10), Japanese corporations have been successful in harnessing societal collectivism to the corporation, by 'utilizing social and spiritual forces for the organization's benefit, and in accepting the responsibilities to their employees' (Pascale and Athos, 1981: 25). Although people management practices emanating from this (e.g. lifetime employment, payment by seniority) have come under increasing pressure (Chen, 1995), there still seems to be a people and relationship focus that is important in obtaining employees' moral commitment to the organization (Gill and Wong, 1998). This relationship focus is also found in Chinese business organizations where familial relations are important both internally and in *guanxi* relations or personal connections or networking in business dealings (Chen, 1995). Although there are differences in the ways corporations capture this societal collectivism in people identifying with the corporation and the corporation identifying with its people, the mindset or locus of human value is still likely to be humanistic in a collectivist society. Where corporations cannot or do not harness this, alienation is likely to ensue between people's 'home' culture and the alien culture they step into when they go to work in the morning.

Implications for human resource management

Despite the complex socio-cultural antecedents to these concepts of people in organizations, an understanding of the way people are seen, and see themselves, in organizations, is fundamental to effective people management across different cultures. This is particularly relevant to management in transitional and newly industrialized economies where conflicts between indigenous and foreign practices (based on conflicting views of human beings) may come to the fore. A premise in this is that there are inherent tensions between an instrumental locus and a humanistic locus of human value that are manifested differently in different cultures.

The contradiction between life outside and inside the world of work organizations has been investigated in various guises since the Industrial Revolution in the West: from the concept of alienation in the Marxian literature through to Etzioni's (1975) concepts of moral, calculative, compliant and alienative involvement (see Chapter 5).

Organizations in different cultural settings may have different responses to this contradiction: from the calculative/contractual responses of American

HRM systems (see Chapter 3) which recognize and work within the instrumental relationship between employer and employee (attempting to humanize this through quality of work life initiatives and employee involvement, whilst firmly focusing on the bottom-line: Ellig, 1997; Ehrlich, 1997), to the moral, spiritual (Pascale and Athos, 1981) and obligatory responses (such as creating an internal labour market: Chen, 1995) of traditional Japanese organizations which capture the collectivistic and humanistic orientations of the wider society (see Chapter 5).

There seems little doubt that between these different approaches, which have been represented here as humanism and instrumentalism, policies and practices are being shared across cultures through the processes and activities of firms who are internationalizing using different types of strategies (see Chapter 2), and expatriates' activities and functions in host countries (see Chapter 4). This may not be through convergence (the coming together of value systems), but by cross-vergence (developing of hybrid value systems as a result of cultural interactions: see for example Priem et al., 2000). Hence raw Taylorism with high levels of control may not be a feature of the mature HRM systems in, for example, the United States as a result of the influences discussed above, but may be evident in the policy manifestations of organizations in Russia and other post-Soviet countries. Lawrence (1994) identifies in the post-Soviet system a move towards greater efficiency, higher workforce discipline, less paternalism and more instrumentalism and a decline in human contact, while Srica (1995) notes a short-termism and deterioration in employee–manager relations (see Chapter 9).

In HRM practice this means borrowing from the West. Hence in Russia Shenkshnia (1998) notes that HRM systems are built more explicitly around business objectives, with formal systems of staffing, career planning, management development, skills training and appraisal systems with Management by Objectives (MBO). This may also be evident in policy manifestations in Korea. For example, Chen (1995) notes that Korean workers put a strong emphasis on extrinsic rather than intrinsic factors of motivation, and some organizations have MBO systems and focus more on wages and conditions, with performance being seen as an important factor. Yet there is retention of seniority systems. Appraisal systems for formally assessing performance are also represented, but include other considerations apart from performance, and an emphasis on harmony militating against negative judgements, and reflecting tolerance and appreciation of people's best efforts (Chapter 5).

The manifestations of an instrumental locus are best explained by the competences approach to human resource management (see Chapter 3). Constable (1988) following Boyatzis' (1982) definition of a skill defines competence as 'the ability to demonstrate a system or sequence of behavior as a function related to attaining a performance goal'. As such the required competences are determined by operational objectives, which are related to strategic objectives, and link the various human resource functions such as selection, training and reward, in seeking organizational objectives (Jackson, 1991). An instrumental locus is also underpinned by a systems concept of organization (Silverman, 1970), where people (as resources) are organized in the best way, and have the best skills, to ensure efficient throughput in the system. For example, job descriptions would identify appropriate persons for particular positions within the system, ensuring that they had the required competences.

This may be one of the more fundamental implications and manifestations of an instrumental locus of control, which may predominate although certain features of a 'softer' instrumentalism (e.g. quality of work life) may resemble features of a 'harder' humanism. This may be an appropriate response of HRM policies with the aim of obtaining higher levels of mutual contractual involvement of employees in cultures that exhibit an instrumental locus of human value.

In cultures that have a humanistic locus of human value, the development of a moral commitment may be more appropriate. Hence Japanese firms may exhibit a higher commitment to people and community welfare by retaining (in-group) employees through economic downturns, which in turn encourages stability, commitment and a sense of belonging (Gill and Wong, 1998; Beardwell, 1994). This element of social welfare and responsibility was also exhibited in the Soviet countries, which also gained the commitment of workers through ideological means (Kornai, 1992; Koubek and Brewster, 1995; and Chapter 9). However, it is likely that the two systems diverge on the level of commitment to developing people, although the same opportunity may have presented itself through longer term planning and a lack of pressure from shareholders in the case of Japan (Chen, 1995) and the Soviet economy (Kossov and Gurkov, 1995).

Rather than a competences approach which links individuals into the operational and strategic objectives of the organization, a developmental approach, based on job flexibility and rotation (rather than fitting a person to a job) and promotion based on experience through seniority (Kuwahara, 1998), seems to reflect a more holistic approach to the person. The organization, and experience within this, is geared to developing the person as a committed part of the human organization.

The concept of locus of human value may therefore be helpful in understanding an inherent contradiction between the world outside work organizations and life inside. The differing attempts at reconciling these two worlds, and the possible effects of cross-vergence through global cultural interaction, may bring the two loci into conflict or contradiction. Yet they may meld into a hybrid people management system. Through cross-vergence, management systems may be borrowed and adapted, rather than the cultural orientations of those being managed substantially changing. It is the managers from emerging and transitional economies who are trained and influenced by Western traditions, rather than the workers who staff the enterprises. Similarly, the literature on international and comparative HRM practices in different countries reflects those policies and practices being introduced, rather than telling us very much about how employees react to such policies, and how successful they might be in the long term. The wholesale adoption of Western HRM methods in Russia for example may ultimately be ineffective as an inappropriate way to manage people within a culture that may reflect a humanistic locus of human value. This is currently suggested by May et al.'s (1998) work on Russia.

This view is currently illustrated by the growing management literature in at least two parts of the world, South Africa and India. In practice this is embodied in the *ubuntu* movement in South Africa (e.g. Mbigi, 1997), where enlightened corporations are attempting to integrate indigenous African approaches with their people management systems, and in India (e.g. Rao, 1996) where an Indian approach to Human Resource Development provides a synthesis of Western and Indian approaches (Chapter 10). It may also be that the so-called K-type management of Korea (Chen, 1995) represents an effective synthesis of indigenous Korean with Japanese and American approaches.

In developing effective international and cross-cultural systems, managers should learn to think outside the parochial box of HRM. Developing lateral flexibility across cultures may be one approach to this, and this is discussed in the context of Europe in Chapter 7; integrating some of the concepts of the learning and knowledge organization discussed in Chapter 6 may also offer a way forward, as we see in the concluding chapter. Blindly introducing Western HRM practices that reflect an instrumental view of people may be ineffective, if not an affront to the humanity of people outside Western tradition. Yet managing globally goes further than simply adapting effectively practices from one culture to another. Managers should ask themselves what could be learned from the humanism of South Asia and from Africa in managing global enterprises successfully. What can be learned from the attempts to reconcile instrumental and humanistic approaches in the countries where this is becoming more successful?

Towards a conceptual approach to managing people internationally

From the above, it is possible to draw three interdependent conceptual threads that need to be considered in managing people internationally: stakeholder consideration; locus of human value; and multicultural/strategizing oppositions.

An understanding and a consideration of stakeholders are important in any enterprise. The ferry disaster described in the opening pages of this Introduction is an example of the disregard of the stakeholder perspective. Within the context of corporate life two categories of stakeholder may be identified: corporate and community. In many societies these two sets of stakeholders may be quite distinct. For example, a high regard for shareholder value in societies stressing a free market economy may regard the local community within which it operates as only a source of labour. Where there is a high governmental or institutional involvement in the finances and control of enterprises, government and local communities may be high profile stakeholders in the enterprise.

One of the major tasks of the management of people within the enterprise is to reconcile the distinctions between these two groups, and between the lives of people in the community, and their lives in the enterprise. Across cultures, there are different ways in which this is approached. One major cultural influence is the way in which people are perceived in organizations (locus of human value). An instrumental cultural perspective may therefore give rise to a contractual relationship with the employee who provides his or her time in exchange for wages. A humanistic cultural perspective may give rise to an obligatory relationship of commitment among members of the corporation.

As a result of the often competing centrifugal and centripetal forces in international management, which on the one hand lead to local cultural adaptation and adoption, and on the other to universalization of management principles through international strategizing, there are different combinations of solutions to this issue: some highly adaptive and successful, and some not so successful. Hence hybrid solutions adopted in Korea may be regarded as successfully reconciling corporate and community life, whereas solutions in many sub-Saharan African countries have been maladaptive.

These themes are taken up in the following chapters, which offer examples of different approaches to managing the international integration–differentiation dilemma, and which reconcile corporate and community life in different ways by considering cultural variations in the way people are perceived in organizations. These themes, and the linkages between aspects of HRM/people management are encapsulated in the conceptual map at the end of the Preface. They are illustrated by cultural interactions mediated by corporations such as IKEA, Crédit Lyonnais, Andersen Consulting, Royal Dutch/Shell, Chiba International, BP, DEC and Volkwagen–Skoda. Chapters 1 and 2 focus on differentiation and integration respectively. The reconciling of these two influences is a dynamic that is taken up in subsequent chapters. Chapter 3 involves a concern with converting strategic objectives to operational objectives, and realizing these through a competences approach for selecting and developing key people. Often this has a universalizing effect, and is based on instrumental perceptions of people in organizations. Yet it is possible to see the influence of differentiation by distinguishing different types of management competences required in different countries' contexts. The competences approach can also be challenged from a cross-cultural perspective, and evidence is provided that it is not a universal approach to HRM.

These aspects have to be taken into consideration when looking at expatriation (Chapter 4) where often the competences approach is used to select and develop expatriates. Expatriates (often known as 'missionaries') transfer know-how, appropriately or inappropriately. Again this involves the interplay of the influences of differentiation and integration in a process that includes the management of individual careers as well as a corporation's planning of its deployment of human resources: making sure it has the requisite skills and knowledge in the right place at the right time. Not least, expatriate–local interaction, and the transfer of people management principles and practices, have major implications for the motivation of the workforce. The way this is undertaken from a Japanese perspective is looked at in Chapter 5, with an examination of the cultural transferability of principles and techniques. This is an altogether more holistic approach to motivation, taking account of employee/corporate commitment, but may be context dependent.

The concept of the learning organization (Chapter 6), although emanating itself from a particular culture, might be useful in understanding and managing the transfer of knowledge across cultural contexts, and integrating indigenous knowledge with imported know-how. An important aspect of this is the appropriate motivation of an indigenous workforce. These aspects are taken up in later chapters that look at international joint ventures (Chapters 8 and 9). Organizational learning is particularly important where there is a need for organizations and work practices to be flexible across geography and across time (Chapter 7). Hence, in times of rapid technological, social and economic change there is a need for temporal flexibility. Working across borders and cultures there is a need for lateral flexibility and to adapt work practices and organizational forms appropriately. Again the interplay of the need to differentiate across cultures and to integrate through international strategizing comes to the fore. This is especially the case in international joint ventures.

There appears to be a high failure rate among such joint ventures in China (Chapter 8 illustrates one such failure). This may well be a question of the poor management of differentiation–integration, the lack of organizational learning, and the lack of developing appropriately flexible organizational forms and work practices. The way knowledge (including the cultural perception of people in organizations) is transferred in joint ventures is relevant to a consideration of people management in post-Soviet countries (Chapter 9). So much of this involves the transfer of knowledge through joint ventures. The wholesale adoption of Western HRM systems in Russia, for example, has been problematic. As discussed above, this may be a result of taking up a 'hard' instrumental approach. One suggestion for the successful transfer of know-how across cultures is that corporations take a stakeholder approach (Mills, 1997). This is no less relevant in post-colonial countries (Chapter 10) than in post-Soviet societies. By taking such an approach, some of the antitheses discussed above, may be reconciled. The sometimes contradictory influences of local differentiation and global integration may be reconciled by taking account of the perception, expectations and needs of all stakeholders. It may be possible to manage the often opposing perceptions of people as a resource for the organization, by seeing that people have a value in their own right. The two worlds of work and community may be reconciled through managing these oppositions by developing appropriate hybrid organizational forms and processes. This is a particularly appropriate aim in post-Soviet and post-colonial countries, where so often people feel alienated from the world of work. It is hoped that this text can shed some light on these issues.

The cross-cultural organization: the multicultural model

The problem of transferring management techniques from one culture to the other is often viewed as a problem of the lack of transferability of American techniques to the rest of the world (Hofstede, 1980b). Differences in power distance, different levels of achievement-based incentives, and differences in work-related attitudes such as centrality of work and values associated with Hofstede's concept of masculinity–femininity seem to explain some of the problems encountered by Americans in their management of people in some northern European countries. When a Swedish company extends operations into cultures that are generally more hierarchical, more rule bound, and more status conscious than Swedish culture, what problems are encountered? There is a need not only to be cross-culturally aware. A facility for cross-cultural management of people and organizations is suggested.

The objective of this chapter is to focus on the management of differentiation across cultures in an international operation and to consider the issue of transferability of people management styles and techniques across cultures. In order to do this it is necessary to consider the current cross-cultural management literature. To place this in the context of real cultures and real management issues, the company IKEA is considered as a corporate mediator between Swedish people management culture, and other cultures (American, French and German), and especially Spanish culture and the issues arising and solutions adopted.

Swedish culture and people management

According to Hofstede (1980a) Swedish organizational and management culture is low in power distance, which means that organizations tend not to be hierarchical. It is high in individualism, very high (the highest in Hofstede's study) on femininity and low in uncertainty avoidance. Economic and political democracy, within the Swedish social democratic political model, stresses six fundamental values: equality, freedom, democracy, solidarity, security and efficiency (Furness and Tilton, 1979). Even though economic contingencies have required a decrease in state planning and welfare, and a move towards more economic competition, this particular model of social democracy is still very prominent. It relies on close collaboration between business, government and labour. Gannon and Associates (1994) have remarked that this has created a society which is free from the inequalities of capitalism and the inefficiencies of the authoritarian central planning of communism, and is indicative of the Swedish word *lagom*, meaning a combination of 'middle road' and 'reasonable'. They suggest that Swedes are unemotionally practical, believing that problems can be solved rationally through the application of reason. This results in a uniquely sensible way of life which is calm, well ordered, part welfare, part technological advance, part economic innovation and part common sense.

Gannon and Associates (1994) outline three main facets of Swedish culture:

- *Love of nature.* Sweden was late to develop as an industrial nation but this industrialization was rapid from the beginning of the 1900s with only 2 per cent of the population employed on the land, the tie with farming and unspoiled nature being implicit. This industrialization with an emphasis on engineering has given international prominence to such companies as Volvo, Saab, Scania, Ericsson, ASEA, SKF and Electrolux. The low power distance may reflect the traditions of village life, and a low uncertainty avoidance may reflect an outlook which is not threatened by the ambiguity of living with nature. A strong practicality and rationality may also reflect the closeness which is felt to the farming community. This practicality, Gannon and Associates suggest, may also be shown in the strong commitment to a welfare state, yet without nationalizing industry.

- *Individualism through self-development.* Individualism is connected to a person's own self-development and time to him/herself, rather than the competitive thrust of corporate life (as perhaps is the case for American individualism). It can lead to insularity, but can also encourage self-dependency. Work centrality is not high, and managers complain about an unwillingness of employees to do overtime (a factor involved in Hofstede's femininity). Five weeks' holiday is the norm, and absenteeism and excessive sick leave is an issue, with an average of 27 sick days per year, which is more than five times the US average. Quality of life is important, and the achievement orientation of Swedes is often directed towards jobs which can help them develop as individuals, that are intrinsically interesting or allow them to spend time away from work. Decentralized decision making may be part of this quality which encourages interest in the job and independence. Yet often corporate life involves making decisions through groups, working towards group goals, and conforming to the group.

- *Equality.* This is quite often expressed through complex systems of welfare and other state mechanisms designed to provide the same service to everybody: health service, child benefits, maternity/paternity leave, pensions, and so on. Taxation is high in order to support these systems, and also serves as a leveller of social inequalities. Commitment is high to overseas aid, and to the government's integration policies towards immigrants, many of whom have sought humanitarian and political refuge in Sweden. There are indications that these systems have come under both economic and political pressure in recent years. In corporate life this quest for equality has been reflected in lower hierarchies and participation in decision making.

Parkum and Agersnap (1994) suggest that such equality is reflected in society and corporate life by: equality between men and women (75 per cent of women are in the workforce, the largest female participation rate of any OECD country: Hammarström and Nilsson, 1998); slight class differences, with education, job status and income making a difference; and narrow income differentials. Education is important as is competence in one's occupation. Lawrence and Spybey (1986) further indicate that egalitarianism in the workplace precludes authoritarian management and a 'them and us' attitude; facilitates communication both vertically and laterally; and is a prerequisite for the operation of industrial democracy and co-determination. Most employees are members of unions (90 per cent blue-collar and 80 per cent white-collar employees: Hammarström and Nilsson, 1998) largely because a number of social benefits, including unemployment benefit, are administered by the trade unions, and the degree of union influence achieved through the long period of Social Democratic government and the close government–union relations. The Act of Co-determination at Work (*Medbestämmandelagen*) was passed in 1976, and this prescribed that management should be a joint effort of capital and labour, between managers and union representatives, both having equal rights to information, and managers having to consult the unions before any major decision on changes in the company, including restructuring and introduction of new technology. Local unions also have the right to representation on companies' boards of directors (Hammarström and Nilsson, 1998). In recent times, since the end of the 1980s, there has been a move towards blurring distinctions between blue- and white-collar workers in 'associate' agreements, which cut across trade unions' representation in the workplace and treat all employees as associates. There has also been a growth in the service industries, and in economic problems which have weakened union influence. Joining the European Union in 1994 may also be leading to a more European model of fragmentation of bargaining structures and consequent weakening of the unions.

From the outside, the structure and processes of Swedish organization may be seen as ambiguous by foreign managers: with matrix structures, overlapping of reporting systems, decision-making processes which seem long and diffuse, and a lack of visibility of these processes, with unclear objectives and a possible perception that management is indecisive and has difficulties in establishing when a decision has actually been made. Relations with foreign subsidiaries are often informal, with control being implicit yet still compelling, as well as a tendency to seek consensus and avoid conflict. Feedback may be clear, but corrective action against poor performers is exceptional with authority not usually exercised on the basis of formal power (Parkum and Agersnap, 1994).

IKEA: managing cultural differences

Since its inception in the 1950s and its subsequent internationalization, IKEA has had to deal with the problem of maintaining its unique 'Swedishness' as a competitive advantage, but at the same time having to adapt this to the different national cultures in which it has been working.

IKEA (Grol et al., 1998) has over the last 25 years become a global player: this is unusual in the furniture distribution industry, which often remains national in character. It has established itself all over Europe including the South and East, and in North America. Its biggest single markets are Germany, Sweden and France. It also has a presence in the Middle East, Singapore and Hong Kong, and is looking to enter the mainland Chinese market. It has recently taken over

15

Habitat, its main rival in the UK and France. Its founder, Ingvar Kamprad's business philosophy has been to supply low-priced (30 to 50 per cent lower than traditional distributors), reasonable quality furniture with no delays in supply. This has attracted strong reactions from the company's competitors over the course of IKEA's development. IKEA's logistics, sourcing and retailing strategies have reflected this. Producers are consided as major stakeholders and together with IKEA work to reduce costs through long production runs and other means. Flat-pack self-assembly of simple Swedish design is what IKEA offers its customers. This is combined with a distinctive store design which aims to attract customers and hold them. This has created a strong Swedish character, which is used throughout IKEA's markets to sell the company and its products: furniture which is durable, easy to live with, and which represents a natural and youthful free lifestyle (its recent advertising campaign in England extols its potential customers to stop being so English). Products are designed by Swedish designers in its Swedish and international headquarters in Almhult. This Swedish character is also strongly represented in its internal organization. Hence management style is seen as informal, open and caring. Hierarchy is relatively flat, with three levels of responsibility at store level between store manager and 'co-workers' (employees or 'associates').

Decision making by consensus is embedded in management practice and co-workers are encouraged to take initiatives. Making mistakes is seen as an aspect of learning by doing, and pragmatic problem solving is encouraged. Managers are expected to share information with employees, as well as their knowledge and skills. Hence employees are considered important and encouraged to feel responsible for improving working practices. Bureaucratic procedures and status barriers are disparaged, and managers are expected to be close to co-workers, and not to take themselves too seriously. This apparently egalitarian approach (titles are not given on managers' business cards, and economy model cars are the same for all who need them) has encouraged employees to work their way up the organization with little formal training.

This organizational culture is propagated by discussion and explanation rather than through training programmes and detailed rules and regulations. The founder's 'Testament of a Furniture Dealer' which sets out his philosophy is distributed throughout the organization. Managers are encouraged to act as 'missionaries' to communicate this culture by example and explanation, as can be seen by the strong presence of expatriate managers in international operations. Managers who have not been directly exposed to the founder's way of doing business are provided with a one-week seminar at Almhult. Typically, a new store is opened in a foreign market by a tight-knit group of well trusted 'missionaries' who solve problems and make decisions. They run the store until it is turned over to local managers, while keeping most of the key national positions in the hands of Swedes until the market and operation has reached maturity.

Human resource management practices have reflected this strong Swedish approach, with a belief that people like to participate in decision making, like to be respected and take on responsibility. People are recruited on the basis of their good communication skills, open minds, positive work attitudes and good potential without necessarily having formal qualifications. They are expected to favour cooperative informal relations, be independent with a high toleration of others, know how to listen and be able to communicate their knowledge to others, while not feeling they are any better than anyone else. IKEA appears to offer a pleasant working environment, job security and a caring attitude to its employees.

Swedish managers are expected to be ambassadors, and explain the IKEA way to non-Swedish co-workers in overseas operations. This has proved relatively easy in the Netherlands, but not so in Germany and France. In the United States older workers seem more at ease with Swedish managers than American managers. Younger American managers show a lack of egalitarian spirit towards employees.

There is generally a lack of Swedish managers within IKEA willing to work long periods out of the country, and the company has had to hire Swedish managers from outside IKEA. Although there is progression within store management for non-Swedes, they have found it difficult to work their way up the promotion ladder in production and the international organization. This is centred on the headquarters at Almhult, a remote location where only Swedish is spoken. There is no formal career path, and apart from a good understanding of the product range and the IKEA way, working through the informal network is essential, yet hard for outsiders. The culture itself is difficult: humbleness is not seen as a weakness, and learning from experience, which takes time and patience, is viewed as a prerequisite for moving up the ladder, which is seen in itself as something which cannot be rushed.

Grol et al.'s (1998) research on problems encountered by IKEA's management of people in Germany, France and the USA, although producing some national stereotypes, indicates that in Germany there were problems of addressing managers using first name and undermining managers' authority; doing exactly as the manager asks and not using one's own initiative. IKEA concepts were regarded as too vague, while managers' suggestions were interpreted as orders; there were also problems with regarding Swedes as more results oriented but without properly assessing risks before taking action; and with the lack of formal rules and the need to reduce bureaucracy. In France there were problems of informality being seen as a sign of weakness or indecisiveness, meaning that employees could do what they liked; a problem with keeping subordinates informed; with the lack of a formal job description and written procedures as well as general flexibility; with status not being recognized, causing identity problems and being lost in the crowd; and trade union distrust of IKEA's consensus management approach. In the United States people felt uncomfortable with the Swedish lack of showing emotion; avoiding conflict and not setting themselves apart by avoiding self-promotion. There were also problems with instructions by managers not being spelt out, and the longer-term Swedish management approach of explaining why things are done: this is seen as indecision. There was a perception that individual achievement is not rewarded in view of a Swedish avoidance of discrimination in pay increases. As a consequence they lost key American managers because of slow progression and not being sure of their role or future in the organization.

How can these problems and issues be understood in a sensitive way by employing concepts from the cross-cultural management literature? What are the implications for people management practices in multicultural organizations?

The multicultural model

In this chapter, and in the book generally, a multicultural model is used. This suggests that the interesting aspect of working internationally is that we have to work with people who have different cultural heritages. Cultural differences should be taken into account when communicating and interacting across nations and across cultures within nations. Although multinational companies are supranational in operations and strategy (this is the subject of Chapter 2), people within them do not necessarily share the same cultural values and views on people and life. The multicultural model is built on the premise that it is necessary to understand cultural differences, rather than trying to smooth them over or override them. For example, companies like IBM may have a strong corporate culture, but one of the aspects that the work of Hofstede (1980a) demonstrated was that within IBM there is wide cultural variation across nations.

Cultural values

Hofstede's (1980a) empirically derived theory on cultural values and how they relate to organizational life instituted a conceptual framework and methodology some two decades ago which has provided a standard for subsequent studies. Although this has attracted some criticism over the years, and has been at least partially superseded, it has gone a long way in guarding against the approach of pure 'description' of a national culture. Such descriptions abound in a myriad of publications on how to do business in specific countries (one of the more intelligent of these being Harris and Moran, 1989). This type of approach often leads to stereotyping, and to expectations about a different culture which might hamper cross-cultural communication.

Stereotyping is a common way of perceiving different nationalities, and it is necessary to be aware of the implications of this and the difficulties which may be encountered as a result of relying too heavily on such caricatures. The approach taken in this text is not to add to these 'potted' descriptions of different nationalities, but to try to transcend such a 'commonsense' approach by building frameworks which provide a means of analysing and thinking about the differences and similarities among different cultures. This can be described as 'thin' description. 'Thick' description should also be used to understand a specific culture (often in relation to one's own), but should not be based on 'travellers' tales' or other anecdotal information. Throughout this book, thick descriptions are constructed of specific illustrative cultures, such as Sweden and Spain in this chapter. These are built on conceptual frameworks of cultural differences drawing attention initially to values (e.g. Hofstede, 1980a; Schwartz, 1994; and Smith, 1996), for example the 'cultural metaphor' approach of Gannon and Associates (1994), and on specific work in the literature on management and human resource practices in the specific country.

Hofstede (1980a) was one of the first to attempt to develop a universal framework for understanding cultural differences in managers' and employees' values based on a worldwide survey, although not the only one (see e.g. Haire et al., 1966; England, 1975). The argument here is that this work was a starting point, both for serious academic research, and for managers working across cultures to make a first estimate of the differences in organizational values which may exist among different countries.

Hofstede's work (which is already well documented; for a synopsis see Hofstede, 1994) focuses on 'value systems' of national cultures which are represented by four dimensions (five in Hofstede, 1991):

- **Power distance**. This is the extent to which inequalities among people are seen as normal. This dimension stretches from equal relations being seen as normal to wide inequalities being viewed as normal. Hofstede's (1980a) sample of Swedish managers and organizational employees scored very low (31) on this scale (maximum 104, minimum 11). Spanish managers and employees scored higher (57). Of the other countries referred to in this chapter, (former West) Germany scored a relatively low 35, USA a relatively low to medium 40 and France a relatively high 68.

- **Uncertainty avoidance**. This refers to a preference for structured situations versus unstructured situations. This dimension runs from being comfortable with flexibility and ambiguity to a need for extreme rigidity and situations with a high degree of certainty. Sweden scored a very low 29 on this scale (maximum 112, minimum 8), with Spain a high 86. The former West Germany scored a medium 65, France a high 86 on a level with Spain, and Hofstede's (1980a) sample of US managers and organizational employees scored a relatively low 46.

- **Individualism**. This looks at whether individuals are used to acting as individuals or as part of cohesive groups, which may be based on the family (more the case with Chinese societies) or the corporation (as may be the case in Japan: Hui, 1990). This dimension ranges from collectivism to individualism. Spain is relatively weak on individualism, scoring a medium 51 (maximum 91, minimum 6), while Sweden is relatively high, scoring 71. USA is the highest (91). France has the same score as Sweden (71), and managers and organizational employees from Hofstede's (1980a) sample of the former West Germany scored at around the same level (67).

- **Masculinity**. Hofstede (1980a) distinguishes 'hard values' such as assertiveness and competition, and the 'soft' or 'feminine' values of personal relations, quality of life and caring about others, where in a masculine society gender role differentiation is emphasized. Sweden is the lowest on this dimension, scoring 5 (maximum 95, minimum 5) indicating a very high level of femininity. Spain has a medium to low score of 42, and France 43. The US samples scored a medium to high 62, with the former West Germany at 66.

Hofstede (1980a) factor-analysed his questionnaire data to derive his four cultural values dimensions. From this Hofstede (1980a, 1991), drawing on prior literature, extrapolated from his data and, drawing on other studies since his own, he derived detailed descriptions of these dimensions. Power distance is polarized into small and large and comprises attitudes which people within the culture have about the acceptable inequalities between people in the society or organization.

In small power distance cultures there is a belief that inequalities among people should be minimized, that parents should treat children as equals and that teachers expect student initiative in the classroom. Hierarchies in work organizations are established as a convenience intended only to manage inequality of roles. Decentralization is popular, subordinates expect to be consulted, and privileges are frowned upon in a small power distance society. Conversely, in a large power distance culture, inequalities are expected and desired, parents teach children obedience and teachers are expected to take the initiative in the classroom. Hierarchies in organizations reflect the natural order of inequalities between the higher-ups and the lower-downs, centralization is popular and subordinates expect to be told what to do. Privilege and status symbols are also expected.

Weak uncertainty avoidance cultures accept uncertainty as a feature of everyday life, there is generally low stress and people feel comfortable in ambiguous situations. People are curious about what is different. Students are happy with open-ended learning situations, and teachers can say 'I don't know'. Rules should be kept to a minimum, people may be lazy and may work hard only when necessary. Punctuality has to be learned, and people are motivated by achievement and esteem or by belonging to a group.

Strong uncertainty avoidance is characterized by the threat of uncertainty which is always present but must be fought. It is characterized by high stress and a fear of ambiguous situations and unfamiliar risk. There is a feeling that what is different must be dangerous. Students are more comfortable in a structured learning situation and like to be told the right answer: teachers are supposed to know the answers. There is an emotional need for rules, even when these may not work. There is a need to be busy, and a feeling that time is money: an inner urge to work hard. Punctuality is natural, and people are motivated by security, esteem or belongingness.

A study which supplements this, building on concepts both of uncertainty avoidance and of power distance, is that of Laurent (1986). In an international study one item provided a statement 'It is important for a manager to have at hand precise answers to most of the questions that his subordinate may raise about their work'. Only 13 per cent of managers from the United States and Sweden agreed with this, 18 per cent from the Netherlands, 27 per cent from Denmark, 30 per cent from Britain, 40 per cent from the former West Germany and from Switzerland, 49 per cent from Belgium, 59 per cent from France and from Italy, 67 per cent from Indonesia and 77 per cent from Japan.

In individualist societies people look after themselves and the immediate nuclear family. A person's identity is based on him or her as an individual. Speaking one's mind is respected. Education is aimed at learning to learn, and academic and professional diplomas increase self-respect and potential economic worth. The employer–employee contract is assumed to be based on mutual advantage, and hiring decisions are supposed to be based on individual competence. Managers manage individuals, and tasks are more important than relationships.

In collectivistic societies people are born into and protected by extended families, to which they give loyalty. One's identity is based on belongingness to a social group or network. Children are taught to think of 'we' not 'I'. Rather than speaking one's mind, harmony should be maintained and direct confrontation avoided. The purpose of education is to learn how to do this, and diplomas provide entry into higher status groups. Rather than purely a contract, the employer– employee relationship is seen as a moral one such as a family relationship, and when hiring or firing, the employee's in-group is considered. Managers manage groups, and relationships are more important than tasks.

In a 'masculine' society values are based on material success, money and possessions. Men are expected to be assertive and ambitious, and women tender and concerned with relationships. The father deals with facts and the mother with feelings. There is sympathy for the strong and the best student is the norm: failing in school is seen as a disaster. People live in order to work. Managers are expected to be decisive and assertive, and there is a stress on competition, performance and resolution of conflict by direct means. In contrast, the 'feminine' society has values of caring for others and preservation rather than progress. People and good relationships are more important than money and things, and people are expected to be modest. Both men and women are expected to be concerned with rela-tionships, and both mother and father should deal with feelings and facts. There is sympathy for the weak, and the average student is the norm. Failing in school is a minor accident. People work in order to live. Managers use intuition and try to gain consensus. There is a stress on equality, solidarity and quality of work life. Conflicts are resolved by compromise and negotiation.

A study which relates to the dimensions is the Meaning of Working study (MOW, 1987) which investigated the related value of work centrality. This study supported the assumption that national cultures vary in the extent to which organizational employees see work as central to their lives. Japanese employees were discovered to have a higher work centrality than those in the USA, who had a higher work centrality than those in the former West Germany.

Other cultural dimensions

Although Hofstede's (1980a, 1991) work has been influential in the formation of a sub-area of management theory – cross-cultural management – some criticism has been directed at his work over the years, mostly methodological but also conceptual in nature. For example, some commentators have suggested that because collectivism is target specific, an appropriate emphasis of study is not on the degree to which individuals are concerned with each other, but on the way this involvement is distributed in society (Hui, 1988; Hui and Triandis, 1986). Hofstede's (1980a) original factor analysis generated a first factor which was a combination of individualism and power distance. His subsequent conceptual separation of these two dimensions (which correlate at –0.67) was justified by their low correlation when variation due to national wealth was controlled for (Berry et al., 1992). Uncertainty avoidance, although based only on three questionnaire items, does have a reasonably well-developed conceptual background based in a concept of tight–loose cultures (Peltro, 1968; Triandis, 1990). The masculinity–femininity construct is not extensively supported in the literature (but see Eagly, 1978, who discusses gender differences in social behaviour). The power distance dimension is constructed from only three questionnaire items, and appears to be related to collectivism. Again, this is generally not well supported in the subsequent literature.

Hofstede's (1980a, 1991) definitions of the four dimensions are far broader than perhaps justified by the limited number of items which comprise at least two of the dimensions (Berry et al., 1992). Some criticism has also been directed at the fact that the study was undertaken entirely within IBM (although Hofstede, 1991, himself argues that this enabled differences due to organizational culture to be controlled for, while enabling the study to focus on national cultural differences). Other studies have failed to corroborate Hofstede's dimensions (IDE, 1981; Williams and Best, 1982).

A fifth dimension was added by Hofstede (1991) to the original four. This was developed through the Chinese Cultural Connection study (CCC, 1987), and in part justified by Hofstede's (1991) warning of the dangers of developing constructs from a Western point of view. The Chinese Cultural Connection was an attempt to counter this by introducing an Eastern perspective and values. The study reinforced three out of the four dimensions in Hofstede's (1980a) study: the Chinese dimension of 'human-heartedness', which incorporates values such as kindness, courtesy and social consciousness, correlates negatively with masculinity; 'integration' which encompasses the cultivation of trust, tolerance and friendship correlates negatively with power distance; 'moral discipline', including values of group responsiveness, moderation, adaptability and prudent behaviour, correlates negatively with individualism (CCC, 1987). None of the new dimensions correlated with uncertainty avoidance, but a new dimension was added, termed Confucian dynamism (Hofstede and Bond, 1988) and then long term orientation (Hofstede, 1991), with values of persistence and perseverance, ordering relationships by status and observing order, thrift and having a sense of shame (Hofstede and Bond, 1988). Uncertainty avoidance is concerned with absolute truth, which may not be a relevant value in Chinese society and other Eastern cultures which are more concerned with virtue. Of particular relevance is the virtue of working hard and acquiring skills, thrift, patience and perseverance: all values connected with this fifth dimension which may replace uncertainty avoidance as a relevant Eastern concept (Hofstede, 1991). On a scale from a minimum score of 0 to a maximum 118, Pakistan scores 0 and China 118. The Chinese societies of Hong Kong (96) and Taiwan (87) are towards the top of the scale with Japan (80) and South Korea (75) next. India scores 61, Singapore 48 and the Netherlands 44. Sweden (33), Poland (32) and the former West Germany (31) follow. The USA scores a relatively low 29, with Britain at 25. Of African countries, Zimbabwe (25) scores the same as Britain, and Nigeria is second from bottom with 16. This seems to bear out an assumption that the Eastern 'tiger' countries which have done well economically are high on this dimension, with the Anglo-Saxon countries relatively low, and African countries with a short-term economic perspective scoring very low.

Other studies have been undertaken which in part have taken a lead from Hofstede's seminal work. It is important to understand this work in relation to the management of people in international organizations. Despite severe limitations of methodology and academic rigour, the work of Trompenaars (1993) has been used extensively, particularly in connection with cross-cultural management development activities. It is necessary to consider its conceptual relevance to understanding the management of people in international organizations, while bearing in mind its limitations, and focusing on the reanalysis of Trompenaars' extensive database (Smith et al., 1996).

Trompenaars' (1993) work was conceptually built on Parsons and Shils (1951) and Kluckholn and Strodtbeck's (1961) formulations of cultural differences, and other dimensions drawn from Rotter (1966) and Hall (1959). These are: regard for rules or relations (universalism–particularism), individualism–collectivism, neutral–affective expression of emotions, low and high context societies (specific–diffuse) and the way status is accorded (achievement–ascription). Trompenaars (1993) also considers attitudes to time (synchronic–sequential) and relation to nature (external–internal locus of control). His results are presented in terms of the percentage of positive (or negative) responses to each of several questions for each of some 50 different nationalities. His information was gathered through administering a questionnaire to attendees of management seminars in the various countries surveyed.

Smith, Dugan and Trompenaars (1996) reanalysis provides two major value dimensions (through multidimensional scaling). Positions of countries on two axes representing scores on the two dimensions are provided in Figure 1.1.

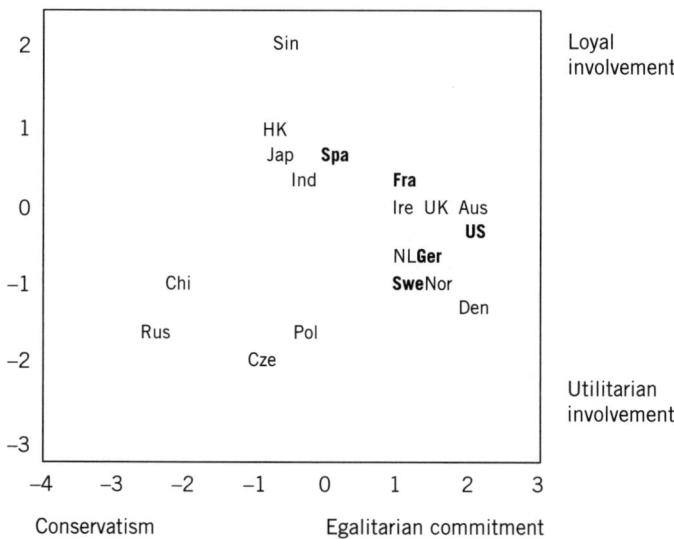

Note: Approximate locations of illustrative countries referred to in the current text, with those referred to in this chapter emboldened: Aus (Australia), Chi (China), Cze (former Czechoslovakia), Den (Denmark), Fra (France), Ger (former West Germany), HK (Hong Kong), Ind (India), Ire (Ireland), Jap (Japan), NL (Netherlands), Nor (Norway), Pol (Poland), Rus (former Soviet Union), Sin (Singapore), Spa (Spain), Swe (Sweden), UK (United Kingdom), US (United States). See Smith et al. (1996) for details on other countries. Numbers on axes represent relative positions on MDS plot and are used in this adapted figure as guides only.

A summation of these dimensions comprising value elements which are composites of each dimension, and those which correlate with each dimension, is provided in Table 1.1.

The concepts which Trompenaars' (1993) items are purported to capture, and which are referred to in Table 1.1, are as follows:

- *Universalism–particularism.* In some cultures people see rules and regulations as applying universally to everyone, regardless of who they are. In cultures which are more particularist, people see relationships as more important than applying rules that are the same for everyone. There is an inclination to apply

23

the rules according to friendship and kinship relations. This has implications for recruitment and promotion policies in organizations in some Asian countries, which may be at variance with practices in countries such as the United States and Britain. However, there are differences in European countries. Greece, Spain and France are seen as more particularist, and Sweden, former West Germany and Britain as more universalist. One of Trompenaars' questionnaire items asks respondents to assume they are a passenger in a car which a friend is driving in an urban area above the speed limit. He hits a pedestrian. His lawyer says that it will help him considerably if you swear in court that he was driving below the legal speed limit. Helping your friend indicates particularism, not helping him indicates universalism.

- *Achievement–ascription.* Status is accorded to people on the basis of what they achieve in their jobs and their lives (achievement) or who they are and where they come from such as family background, their school or some other prior factor (ascription). Quite often more traditional societies accord status according to the latter precept. Again, this may influence recruitment and promotion policies which may be at variance with practices in some (but not all) Western cultures. On some measures Austria, Belgium, Spain and Italy are more ascription oriented, and Denmark, Britain and Sweden more achievement oriented.

- *Locus of control.* People tend to believe that what happens to them in life is their own doing (internal locus of control), or they have no or little control over what happens to them (external locus of control), the causes of which are external to them.

Table 1.1   Composition and correlates of Smith et al.'s (1996) cultural dimensions

	Conservatism	Egalitarian commitment	Utilitarian involvement	Loyal involvement
Comprises:	Ascribed status favoured	Achieved status favoured	Aspects of individualism which stress individual credit and responsibility	Aspects of collectivism which stress loyalty and obligation to group, and corporate loyalty and obligation
	Particularistic Paternalistic employers Formalized hierarchy	Universalistic Non-paternalistic Functional hierarchy		
Correlates with:	Hofstede's collectivism Hofstede's high power distance Schwartz's conservatism falls just short of significant correlation External locus of control	Hofstede's individualism Hofstede's low power distance Schwartz's egalitarian commitment Internal locus of control	Hofstede's individualism Hofstede's low power distance	Hofstede's collectivism Hofstede's high power distance

Paternalism is also an important concept in cross-cultural research and management, and is more thoroughly investigated elsewhere (see Aycan et al., 1999: 504), who define it as 'people in authority assuming the role of parent and considering it an obligation to provide support and protection to others under their care', and Redding, 1994). Also referred to in Table 1.1 is Schwartz's (1994) global study of cultural values. Dimensions were derived from his data by smallest space analysis, and are shown with scores of those countries discussed in this chapter in Table 1.2 (with the exception of Sweden, which was not included in this study; Denmark is the only Scandinavian country included).

The scores shown in Table 1.2 are for samples derived from schoolteachers. Schwartz (1994) argues that these are good representatives as they are custodians of culture and it is they who pass this on to the next generation. He also takes a sample from university students, which corroborates results from schoolteachers. It is likely that because of the way the constructs and the variables comprising them have been tested among various cultural groups, at both individual level and group level, that they may be claimed to be universally representative of values which may occur anywhere in the world. They also provide a more up-to-date cross-cultural study of values than the Hofstede study, as well as accessing former Soviet countries and China. Omissions, particularly from the point of view of the current text, include Sweden, UK, India. The inclusion of Zimbabwe is of interest, as little information of this sort exists on the sub-Saharan African countries.

Some reflections on the cross-cultural organization

In management, a clear analysis and understanding of an issue should lead to implementation. If it is possible to understand the implications of culture for the management of people, what do we then do with that information in a practical situation? For example, if we know that a high power distance culture prevails in a particular country, do we make sure that our people management practices reflect accepted and expected high levels of inequality? Do we adopt authoritarian behaviour because this is what employees expect? Or, do we bring to the situation ideas of participative management and employee empowerment? Sometimes the answer is not simple. Let us take the example of organizations in emerging regions where, as in the case of Africa, management practices have been regarded as fairly authoritarian and power distance regarded as high (Blunt and Jones, 1992). Perhaps employees expect and accept this level of power inequality at work, yet workers are alienated from their places of work. Traditional African cultures reflect a high level of participation and lower levels of absolute authority (Reader, 1997) and this is shown in the levels of mutual cooperation found in the informal economic sector in African countries (Brown, 1995). Entrepreneurs like Koopman (1991) have obtained good business results from developing more participative methods in South Africa, and the movement towards more democratic employment relations is also growing in that country (Jackson, 1999).

Mostly, IKEA has had to operate outside Sweden, in countries that may be seen as having a higher power distance. So, how did IKEA adapt to the need to keep its essentially Swedish management philosophy, while making its people

Table 1.2 Schwartz's (1994) cultural values with scores of selected countries

Conservatism

Conservatism

Values which support the status quo and likely to be important in societies based on close-knit harmonious relations. Interests of the person are same as the group. Stresses security, conformity and tradition. Correlates positively with Hofstede's power distance and negatively with individualism

	+
Singapore	4.38
Taiwan	4.31
Poland	4.31
Zimbabwe	4.21
Hong Kong	4.04
China	3.97
United States	3.90
Japan	3.87
Netherlands	3.68
Denmark	3.64
East Germany	3.50
West Germany	3.42
Spain	3.42
France	3.35

Hierarchy

Stresses power relations and authority, and the legitimacy of using power to attain individual or group goals (not the legitimacy of inequalities). Correlates negatively with Hofstede's individualism

	+
China	3.70
Zimbabwe	3.14
Japan	2.86
Taiwan	2.85
Hong Kong	2.83
Singapore	2.75
East Germany	2.69
Poland	2.53
United States	2.39
West Germany	2.27
Netherlands	2.26
France	2.16
Spain	2.03
Denmark	1.86

Self-enhancement

Mastery

Mastery of the social environment through self-assertion, and to get ahead of people. Positively correlates with Hofstede's masculinity

	+
China	4.73
Zimbabwe	4.62
United States	4.34
Japan	4.27
Hong Kong	4.18
East Germany	4.16
Spain	4.11
Taiwan	4.11
West Germany	4.07
Poland	4.00
Netherlands	3.98
Denmark	3.97
Singapore	3.93
France	3.89

Automony

Intellectual autonomy

The individual pursues own interests and desires in the intellectual area (intellectual self-direction). Correlates positively with Hofstede's individualism and negatively with power distance

	+
France	5.15
Spain	4.90
West Germany	4.75
Japan	4.68
Denmark	4.58
East Germany	4.47
Netherlands	4.44
China	4.27
United States	4.20
Poland	4.09
Hong Kong	4.08
Taiwan	3.93
Zimbabwe	3.82
Singapore	3.68
	−

Affective autonomy

The individual pursues own interests in the affective domain (stimulation and hedonism). Correlates positively with Hofstede's individualism and negatively with power distance

	+
France	4.41
East Germany	4.16
West Germany	4.03
Denmark	4.01
Spain	3.97
Zimbabwe	3.85
United States	3.65
Japan	3.54
Netherlands	3.51
China	3.32
Taiwan	3.21
Poland	3.13
Hong Kong	3.11
Singapore	3.04
	−

Self-Transcendence

Egalitarian commitment

Transcending selfish interests, voluntary commitment to promoting the welfare of other people, rather than through obligation and kinship ties. Correlates positively with Hofstede's individualism

	+
Spain	5.55
Denmark	5.52
France	5.45
Netherlands	5.39
West Germany	5.37
East Germany	5.29
United States	5.03
Hong Kong	4.85
Poland	4.82
Singapore	4.79
Japan	4.69
Taiwan	4.68
China	4.49
Zimbabwe	4.48
	−

Harmony
Stresses harmony with nature as
opposed to assertion and dominance
over the environment. Correlates
positively with Hofstede's
uncertainty avoidance

	+
Spain	4.53
West Germany	4.42
France	4.31
Taiwan	4.17
Denmark	4.16
Poland	4.10
East Germany	4.08
Japan	4.07
Netherlands	3.98
Singapore	3.72
China	3.71
United States	3.70
Zimbabwe	3.42
Hong Kong	3.34

management practices more compatible with employees' expectations in the other countries of operation? Firstly in France, the company has provided clear communication in facts and figures of IKEA's benefits compared with its competitors. Formal training programmes have been developed as a more credible alternative to learning by doing. Management has also taken a more affirmative attitude towards employees, headed by a Frenchman (who has a Swedish wife) who has worked at the IKEA headquarters at Almhult, and has developed better relations with trade unions.

While Grol et al. (1998) note no significant changes in Germany in IKEA's people management policies, in the United States changes have been made. Not only has the company adapted its marketing and business practices, IKEA has given more autonomy to local management. An American style performance review procedure has been initiated, requiring the documenting of performance strengths and weaknesses (something with which the senior Swedish managers feel uncomfortable because of its formality, and the negative feedback it gives, and in practice this has resulted in little pay discrimination). The question remains: can IKEA maintain its particular Swedish approach to managing people in view of its expanding international and multicultural operation? And how can it develop a truly cross-cultural approach to managing and developing people? These questions can be answered, at least in part, by now focusing on IKEA's operations in Spain.

Spanish culture and work values

Spain is depicted by Hofstede's (1980a) data as being of medium power distance, but far higher than Sweden and on a par with Taiwan and Pakistan; less individualistic than Sweden and close to India and Japan on this dimension.

Masculinity is not high, but somewhat higher than in Sweden and on a par with Peru, France and Iran; and with Peru, France, Chile, Costa Rica, Panama and Argentina it is very high on uncertainty avoidance, with Sweden being very low. Gannon and Associates (1994) remark that it is this high uncertainty avoidance that is reflected in the tendency to work in the same organization for many years and sometimes for life. This may also be part of the clustering together in both rural and urban habitations, a need generally for close proximity as an act of self-defence, and the love of communal festivals (rather than as an indication of collectivism). Loyalty, however, does not extend to the larger collective, but to the smaller units of family, friends, town and region, with a protective instinct towards these and especially towards children.

Although the nurturing role of women at the centre of the household and the authority of the man was enshrined in a number of laws under Franco, things have changed considerably since his death in 1975, yet still few women attain high level jobs. Gannon and Associates' (1994) assertion that Spanish culture is one of proud individualism also mirrors Schwartz's (1994) findings that Spain is high on intellectual and affective autonomy and low on conservatism, as well as being high on egalitarian commitment. It is based on a fierce self-sufficiency, but is anarchic and inorganic, with no cohesive and unified goal (Crow, 1985), which can lead to a difficulty in cooperating. Work centrality is also low, although 'moonlighting' (taking on a second job) is common in order to make financial ends meet: perhaps as a result of jobs not being well paid. There is a social orientation rather than a task orientation, with an emphasis on the quality of life. Self-expression may be more important than material success (Gannon and Associates, 1994), and emotional expressiveness may reflect the Spanish score on Schwartz's (1994) affective autonomy, and an ability to act genuinely and hospitably towards colleagues and associates. With a long break in the middle of the day which extends the working day well into the evening, socializing with family and friends often goes on late into the night. Yet Hofstede's (1980a) score for Spain for power distance reflects a subordination to authority and an acceptance of inequality, with work organizations being hierarchical. Work relationships between managers and employees can be paternalistic and are often formal (Diaz and Miller, 1994). This perhaps reflects a gulf between rich and poor in the wider society.

People management in Spain

Spain has changed, and is changing fast. A high rate of foreign direct investment including the presence of large operations run by such American multinationals as General Motors and Hewlett Packard, and Japanese giants such as Nissan, Sanyo and Sony has had an effect on human resource practices as well as production techniques. This is accompanied by a growing internationalization of Spanish companies (Diaz and Miller, 1994). While the majority of businesses are small and medium sized, and under-unionized, the larger privately owned and prominent state enterprises (which have increasingly come under privatization plans) are heavily unionized with a power sharing balance. Although only 10 per cent of the working population is unionized and the unions have relatively weak organizational structures, they do have power in negotiations through collective bargaining and sometimes mobilization of workers. As a result of negotiation, job security is good, and severance can be expensive for employers. This has all contributed to a need to balance economic activity with social interest. The government is directly involved in the redistribution of industrial wealth, and in correcting regional economic imbalances. Spain is a strong supporter of the European Social Chapter (Diaz and Miller, 1994), and workers' committees are a legal feature in all enterprises larger than 50 employees. Apart from these committees, there is still little worker participation in the decision making of the company and a lack of two-way communication between directors and workers.

Despite improvements in worker productivity, as a result of declining employment opportunities and better vocational training, productivity levels are still lower than than those achieved by countries such as Japan and the United States. Although things are changing towards more formal job descriptions and specified criteria and methods for selection, this is often still absent in small and medium-sized firms (Diaz and Miller, 1994). Training has grown in importance, particularly since the 1980s, although it can still be lacking in perceived importance in some areas. In areas such as staff planning and development training, Spain has lagged behind other EU countries and investment in such areas is amongst the lowest in Europe. The concept of career progress and remuneration in relation to employee performance was not part of corporate culture, but this has changed drastically in recent years. This has accompanied a belief that investment in training people within the company rather than bringing them in from the outside is more effective. Again there have been major changes in pay systems from quite rigid salary structures to very flexible ones.

IKEA in Spain[1]

Communicating the organization culture

IKEA entered Spain almost as a complete unknown. It has since been involved in communicating and instilling its Swedish character and the IKEA culture into the Spanish subsidiary. It has sought to do this in a number of ways:

- A network of Swedish managers was sent as a build-up team with the main objectives to pass on their know-how and the IKEA culture to the local management. This is one of the items evaluated in the latter's annual performance appraisal, and is regarded as extremely important. This is because at the lower levels of the organization the 'IKEA world' is limited to the local stores. It is through the day to day interaction between managers and 'co-workers' at store level that the culture develops.

- Employment of the 'right' people is regarded as one of the key means of preserving the IKEA culture. These are young co-workers who can keep up the enthusiasm; people who have not been 'contaminated' by another company culture and whose values correspond to the IKEA ones. IKEA does select on the basis of competences, which were defined by taking as the starting point the 'glossary of terms' used in the IKEA 'Little Dictionary'. These competences are then used as the basis for evaluation of co-workers during their 'Development Talks'.

29

- Awareness is created through introductory programmes for new co-workers; through 'IKEA Way' seminars during which participants are given lectures on IKEA's history, human resource ideas, and so on; and by official 'scriptures', handbooks and other IKEA documents.

Adapting the organizational culture

Although co-worker awareness is high, many are rather sceptical towards the culture. The Swedish style of management with its avoidance of formal planning and unwritten manuals, informality in recruitment, the search for unconventional solutions, cost consciousness, team spirit, and informal and egalitarian relationships, differs from what would be regarded as the 'normal style' in Spain. For most of the co-workers hierarchy is something natural, they need to have clear responsibilities and to know who is in charge of what. It is also important for them to move up the promotion ladder. The management realized that because the co-workers question the idealized description of the company, they had to address this by becoming more 'structured' and taking a more conscious approach to developing the organization and to generally adapting to local needs. The first way this was done was to recruit a Spanish human resource manager. Other steps that were taken are as follows:

- Running 'Cultural Seminars' to help everyone to discuss their experience and opinions about the culture and how it is put into practice. By using the managing director and the human resource manager as facilitators, a message about its importance is sent out. It is also stressed that participation is vital in order to improve the organization. Participants go through the 'IKEA words' in the 'Little Dictionary' and create a debate by using the 'four room apartment model' and working in groups on the IKEA words. They agree on which stage of the model IKEA Spain is at the moment (satisfaction, inspiration, denial or confusion). This then leads to conclusions about the 'hot issues' or areas in which problems are being perceived. Participants are also asked to formulate realistic and feasible proposals of changes, and are encouraged to follow up on these.

- Development programmes have come into focus to ensure the retention of talent within the company, offering possibilities for making a career in IKEA. Co-workers with potential to become group leaders go through the Aspirant Programme (year 1). Group leaders with potential to become departmental heads are invited to participate in the Selling in the IKEA Store Training Programme. To meet the needs of further expansion in Spain, the Leadership Development Programme has also been designed.

- In association with these development programmes there is succession planning from group leader level upwards. The stated intention is that by 2001 80 per cent of the management should be Spanish.

- Annual training plans are formulated which include a number of off-the-job training courses. These are strongly demanded by co-workers and regarded as an important benefit. Such off-job training programmes also comply with the

National Agreement with Trade Unions which requires companies to provide employees with general skills they can use outside their company in order for them to have a value on the job market.

- A flexible salary structure is being developed in order to attract and retain competent employees. IKEA salaries are mostly fixed, and this does not conform to what Spanish workers have become used to. There is a movement towards a compensation package which reflects the performance level of co-workers, as opposed to current IKEA rules.

Implications for managers

The use of wide-scale studies on cultural values is useful as a good first guess of the nature of management and organization in different countries. They should be regarded as a starting point for managers working across cultures. For example, this may have helped the management of IKEA in making decisions about adapting its culture to the expectations of its Spanish employees. Such studies of course have limitations, and should be supplemented with detailed knowledge about management systems in the respective countries. A summary follows of the main cultural dimensions in common use (both academically and in management development circles in English speaking countries), and their implications for managing people across cultures.

- **Power distance** (Hofstede, 1980a): the extent to which participative or paternalist management is appropriate. Many theories of people management are based on Western perceptions drawn from what works in a medium to low power distance culture. Participative management does not have universal currency throughout the world. More paternalistic or even autocratic methods of managing people may be more appropriate (or expected) where there is a higher power distance.

- **Individualism/collectivism** (Hofstede, 1980a): the extent to which group or individual results are appropriate; the extent to which Management by Objectives-type systems are appropriate. Western methods of human resource management (HRM) focus on individual incentives and on the performance and results of individuals. The encouragement of such individualism may not be appropriate in more collectivist countries.

- **Masculinity and work centrality** (Hofstede, 1980a; MOW, 1987): the extent to which results-focused approaches are appropriate; the centrality of work to employees. Work is not seen as equally central to people's lives in every culture. Results-focused HRM systems do not always work successfully in other cultures.

- **Uncertainty avoidance** (Hofstede, 1980a): the degree of control, rules and regulations needed over employees. There is a move away from control and regulation in Western HRM. Particularly in the management of change, people are encouraged to take ownership of the change through communication and decision-making groups. This may increase uncertainty, so may not be appropriate in cultures that seek to decrease uncertainty. It may be more

31

appropriate to decrease the risk and uncertainty by introducing rules of operation to affect change.

- **Universalism** (Trompenaars, 1993): the use of 'nepotism' and its appropriateness and logic. Why employ someone you do not know when you can employ someone you do know? You can put pressure on the employee's family if they do not perform as expected. You can also trust them in a way that you cannot trust a stranger. Nepotism is often seen from a Western perspective as negative, but this may need reconstruing in the context of a particularistic culture.

- **Ascription** (Trompenaars, 1993): the extent to which recruiting and promotion policies are based on prior factors (education, family) or achievement factors. Not all cultures place equal emphasis on achievement. Prior consideration of education and family standing may be more important in the recruitment of people. Ideas and policies on recruitment, pay and promotion may need modifying when managers move from an achievement to an ascription society.

- **Locus of control** (Trompenaars, 1993): the extent to which fatalism is a factor in what people can achieve and do; the extent to which individuals feel they have control over their working lives; the extent to which planning is seen as effective. If you reward people on the basis of results, and those results are felt to be beyond the control of the individual, then the HRM system may be out of line with the culture. This may also influence other aspects like the feasibility and success of training and development.

- **Long-term orientation** (Hofstede, 1991): the extent to which employees may be given short-term targets in the case of short-term orientation (e.g. quarterly sales targets), or where long-term perspectives are seen as more appropriate. Western (particularly American) targets may be quite short term (monthly, quarterly, annually). Management in longer-term-oriented cultures may require a greater commitment to developing relationships, and steadily developing market shares.

- **Egalitarian commitment** (Schwartz, 1994; Smith et al., 1996): the extent to which employee welfare is seen as a right and obligation, or as a voluntary commitment. The levels of 'collegiality' or allegiance to co-workers varies from culture to culture. This should be taken into consideration when focusing on the nature of the work process, as well as relative commitment (and nature of that commitment) to the organization and co-workers.

Questions for managers

1   How could the cultural dimensions listed above have helped the Swedish IKEA management to better prepare itself for managing people in Spain? What are the major differences and similarities between the two cultures on these dimensions, and what are their implications for management? What are their shortcomings, and what additional information would have been useful for the IKEA management?

2   What advice would you give to the management of IKEA if it were planning to set up operations in your country?

3 How could IKEA have better adapted itself to the expectations of its local management and workforce in the United States?

An agenda for research

It may be concluded from the case of IKEA that research by companies on culture as it affects work values and management techniques is neglected, and that consumer research and product development is regarded as more pressing when entering a new country. Within the academic literature, there is a lack of research on the connections between culture, work values and people management practices which may ultimately inform such practices in organizations such as IKEA, as well as in the many American (and other Western) multinational companies which operate across national borders but seem to be blind to cultural differences (Boyacigiller and Adler, 1991): a blindness which must have implications for their effectiveness.

One approach that points the way for future research is the model of cultural fit which is proposed by Kanungo and associates (Kanungo and Jaeger, 1990; Mendonca and Kanungo, 1994; Aycan et al., 1999). This postulates that the socio-cultural environment affects internal work culture and ultimately human resource management practices (being mediated by internal work culture). It is this connection which is particularly pertinent to the approach taken in this chapter: the discussion in the above section 'Implications for Managers' may be regarded as setting out a number of hypotheses regarding the connection between cultural values in the literature and the effective management of people in different cultures. The model of cultural fit, for example, proposes a connection between 'socio-cultural' dimentions, 'internal work culture' and 'human resource management practices'. 'Socio-cultural dimensions' include paternalism, power distance, masculinity, uncertainty avoidance, loyalty to community and self-reliance. 'Internal work culture' includes task-driven assumptions (such as profit versus social gain, process versus results and pragmatic versus normative competitive orientation), employee-related assumptions (futuristic orientation, locus of control, malleability, proactivity, obligation towards others, responsibility seeking and participation). 'Human resource management practices' are concerned with job design (feedback, autonomy, skills variety, task significance), concerned with supervisory practices (goal setting, empowerment and control) and concerned with reward allocation (performance-reward and contingency).

In a study that sought to test this model in Canada and India (Aycan et al., 1999) the assumptions of the model were supported by the findings. In particular, paternalism and loyalty to community were predictive of variation in work culture and HRM practices. The study found that paternalism, power distance and uncertainty avoidance seemed to create a dependent relationship between subordinate and boss, leading to an assumption of lower employee proactivity, and consequently not encouraging employee autonomy on the job. It also found that HRM practices involving joint goal setting seemed to be a result of managers' perceptions about employee reactivity and obligation towards others, which in turn seemed to be influenced by the socio-cultural values of paternalism, loyalty to the community and self-reliance. Also, HRM practices involving feedback, empowerment and performance–reward contingencies seem to be a function of

33

managers' assumption that employees can change and control the outcomes of their actions. These beliefs in malleability and internal locus of control seem to be adversely influenced by the socio-cultural values of community loyalty and paternalism. Finally, from this study, masculinity seems negatively to influence futuristic orientation, which in turn inhibits goal-setting practices. This, the authors suggested might indicate a connection between masculinity and short-term materialistic gains, and femininity and longer-term investment in developing enduring relations.

This study points the way to further research, which could encompass other countries. However, even though research may produce information about the connection between cultural values and people management practices, this still does not answer the question about how managers who wish to introduce more participative techniques may do so (if this is socially desirable and ethically sound). This may require additional research on the effectiveness of attempts to do so, and may necessitate case study research.

This chapter has pointed to the relationship between diverse culture in a multicultural organizational situation, and the implications for the management of people in international organizations. The implications are that cultural values should be taken into account when managing people across cultures, yet the connections proposed in this chapter are still under-researched. The work of Kanungo and associates suggests an avenue for future research that may inform managerial practice. The case of IKEA illustrates the issues and problems of one international organization with a strong corporate culture derived from its Swedish origin, and its attempts to both communicate this culture and to adapt this to the local cultures of its international operations.

Succeeding chapters look more specifically at culture-specific aspects of people management. First, Chapter 2 places this within the context of inter-national organizations operating supranationally. It explores the strategic aspects of this, and the relationship to effective management of people in international organizations.

Questions for researchers

1   What is the relationship between cultural values and people management practices? What are the shortcomings of this approach in understanding people management practices in different countries? What additional information is needed?

2   What are the main causes of cultural clashes between managers from Sweden and employees in Spain? What can be done to lessen the negative aspects and to strengthen the synergies between the two country cultures, as manifested in people management practices? What would happen if Spanish managers operated in Sweden with Swedish employees?

3   What measures can a management team take to successfully set up operations in another country, where the local culture is different from their own?

Note

1. I am grateful to Pilar Guitian Gonzalez and Richard Hynes of IKEA Spain for this information.

The strategic organization: the supranational model

There are two ways to look at an international organization. The first is to see it as a set of relationships between national units, each of which exists within its national culture. Apart from its people having different cultural values, as was discussed in Chapter 1, the organization will also work within the local conditions of the host country. This includes legal, social, economic and political circumstances. In this view, the headquarters organization in the home country will have to adapt its human resource management practices to the circumstances in the host country. This will lead to a differentiation of practices among the subsidiary countries, and between the headquarters and the subsidiaries (affiliates). The other view is that the international organization will have a set of objectives which can be achieved only by integrating the various geographical functions. Hence an overall strategy will have to be formulated in order to achieve objectives. Following from this, an overall, international human resource management strategy will be formulated and a policy will be implemented throughout the international organization.

If the last chapter was about differentiation by culture, this chapter is about integration across cultures or nations. However, no company which operates across borders is simply 'international' in the sense of having no national identity, but purely an international presence which cuts across national cultures. All corporations are rooted in the national culture and identity from which they grew, although some have made great strides towards the 'transnational' model discussed by Bartlett and Ghoshal (1989) which is discussed later. Crédit Lyonnais is a company firmly rooted in its French origins and identity. By its nature banking is an international business, yet national banks often find it difficult to become truly international in concept and in scope, and particularly in organizational culture. The quest of IKEA to maintain its unique Swedishness as a competitive advantage is not so much an issue when it comes to banking. Finance is the same, given local differences in legislation, all over the world. Market makers and bond dealers do the same things in London as they do in Frankfurt or in Hong Kong or in New York. New products are copied rapidly, and adapted to different national markets. The banking industry has undergone massive changes in the last decade, with liberalization of the marketplace, intense competition from institutions not previously direct competitors, and a more discerning customer who can shop around for the best deals. Through market liberalization has come more intense competition on the home front from foreign institutions. Innovation in technology over the last decade has ensured that financial markets effectively ignore national borders. The internationalization of Crédit Lyonnais may be firmly placed within the context of these developments of banking whilst being firmly rooted within its French cultural context (Chevalier and Segalla, 1996).

The objective of this chapter is therefore to explore the issue of integration of international organization across borders by looking at the way different strategies influence the management of people throughout the international operation. In order to do this, the literature on international strategy and human resource management is examined. To position this within a real culture and focusing on real issues, Crédit Lyonnais is provided as an example of a French bank struggling with internationalization. French management culture is discussed in order better to understand the types of approaches the bank has taken.

French culture and people management

Trouvé (1994) outlines the factors influencing culture in France. Firstly, France is a Catholic country, which, according to Weber, explains the distrust of the business world, and the attachment to the rural community, particularly in the south. A sense of honour in being able to serve the state and one's fellow men, since the time of Louis XIV, may have been at the expense of industrial development. D'Iribarne (1989) has observed that within traditional French organizations an 'honour system' still operates which is different from the 'contract system' of the United States, or the 'consensus system' which may be more typical of the Netherlands or Scandinavian countries. The state is important in France (Trouvé, 1994): it plays a positive and active role in both economy and society. From Louis XIV, through the Jacobins of the Revolution and the *code civil* of Napoleon, the tradition of centralization has been maintained in recent times. Since the Second World War the state has played a major role in financing the revitalization of the economy, with ownership of energy, the main deposit banks and insurance companies and the car industry.

These traditionally high levels of centralization and involvement of the state are perhaps reflected in France's high levels of power distance and uncertainty avoidance (Hofstede, 1980a). This may also be seen in the education system, often said to be elitist, inegalitarian, discriminatory and exclusive (Trouvé, 1994), and the associated means of identifying and developing high potential in traditional French organizations, with the management cadre traditionally being recruited from the exclusive *grandes écoles*. This type of background has been more important than the results individuals are able to achieve in the job. Self-made managers are still not common in traditional French organizations. These organizations generally have many hierarchical levels, with each level restricting managers to a narrow range of activities and responsibilities. Autonomy within these well-defined areas is guarded against encroachment (d'Iribarne, 1997). Roussillon and Bournois (1997) outline the main features of French management which pertain in the literature:

- excessive importance of the elitist education systems which guarantee top posts for young graduates, with an established hierarchy of diplomas which contribute heavily to preconceived career patterns;

- highly responsible posts given straight away to young graduates from prestigious schools, despite lack of practical experience;

- an emphasis on the theoretical, with young executives in 'consultancy' positions with conceptualizing responsibility rather than in an operational capacity;

- considerable influence of public sector practices in career management on the private sector, particularly on those firms which work closely with the public sector or have been recently privatized. Hence Crédit Agricole has set up competitive examinations like those in the public sector, to select top executives;

- moving those from careers in government administration directly to top jobs in private enterprise. This practice of 'pantouflage' allows top managers to move back to their former positions in public administration if they desire;

- exclusivity of 'old boy networks' in French business life.

Workers' attitudes to their organizations has been largely instrumental: they consider work as a necessity and have a low involvement in the well-being of the company. Human resource management has mainly focused on the connection between the objectives of employee and organization during the 1980s and 1990s (Chevalier and Segalla, 1996). However, this, and the sometimes negative portrayal of French management in descriptions such as that of Roussillon and Bournois (1997), needs further comment and analysis. Barsoux and Lawrence (1990), after Michel Crozier, see the impersonality of French work relations as reflecting a need to separate personal and professional relations, to maintain a distance from the role and the person occupying the role, in order to protect one's independence. Authority is vested in the role not the person, and this is how a French manager gets things done. The pattern of interpersonal relations at work is therefore formal. Work is done in isolation, punctuated by formal meetings, excluding the need for personal involvement. Barsoux and Lawrence (1990) suggest that French cadres are specialists in 'meetings', where much of organizational life comes together in a microcosm (Barsoux and Lawrence, 1990).

The impersonality and formal nature of relations characterizes the hierarchy, but segregation and partitioning in organizations is also horizontal. This may all be part of the protection of one's territory and independence from one's role. Hence French work relations may be more highly structured and detached than the Anglo-Saxon model which may disparage the French system. Yet the lesser involvement of the self may be seen as a means of preserving personal choice, independence and individual dignity (Barsoux and Lawrence, 1990). Attempts to introduce more informality into organizations have often been unpopular and seen as a means of subordinating the interests of the individual to the interests of the company. Preserving one's independence through detachment of the persona from the role is important to preserving human dignity. It could be suggested that this avoids some of the problems of the extreme instrumentalism in the Western model of human resource management, by detaching the self from the means of achieving the organization's ends. This may be an alternative solution to the influence of the human relations school in the Anglo-Saxon world which attempts to soften the effect of instrumentalism on individuals, and may reflect the Weberian stance. Catholic countries have historically had a mistrust of commerce and industry, whilst the Protestant ethic has engendered an identification with work in enterprises.

The state has also been used in France to protect against the extremes of a free market economy, through major investment in industry, and has sought to ensure that companies invest in people through training. There is an obligation on companies to devote 1.4 per cent of their salary budget to training, and they are required to draw up a training scheme in consultation with works councils (Trouvé, 1994; Tregaskis and Dany, 1996). The state is involved in collective bargaining through legislation which, for example, requires all companies to prepare a 'social plan' before implementing layoffs. Works committees were established as early as 1945, and employee participation is a feature enshrined in legislation (Goetschy and Jobert, 1998). People are protected by the state in other ways, such as by the high levels of public medical care and state pensions, which are paid for by higher social charges on employers and employees.

Crédit Lyonnais: The Internationalization Process

The requirement for French banks to assist in the development of industry was established by Napoleon II, who set up two national banks to this end (Garrison, 1994). The main French banks either are or have been in state hands. Apart from state ownership, the government also plays a key role in employment relations, and itself is a major employer with its salary budget representing some quarter of GNP. Employment relations have tended to be confrontational. Although French trade unions have much political and economic power they actually represent directly less than 10 per cent of the workforce. Through collective agreements, conditions negotiated generally apply to all employees in a particular industry. This situation applies in the banking industry.

This has perhaps been important as banks have struggled to refocus both their business and their 'human capital' over this period. Both banks and their employees have had to focus more on being competitive, client focused and more international. Chevalier and Segalla (1996) specify these challenges as:

- needing to grow through acquisition, in order to dominate niche markets such as personal, investment or small business banking;

- becoming a universal bank offering a full range of financial services in all major markets;

- defending domestic markets by developing client relations;

- selling more services such as insurance and financial advice.

This has had implications for the management of 'human capital' in changing a surplus of 'old style' generalist banking personnel to new style personnel who can address the needs outlined above. This has meant some retrenchment, retraining and recruiting of new employees who fit these needs.

Crédit Lyonnais was privatized in 1999, with the government retaining a 10 per cent share. With assets of $214 billion it is a profitable business and has new management and a market value of $9.6 billion. This followed a state bailout which segregated most of the bank's previous bad debts into a separate entity, and follows a major fraud scandal which caused *Forbes* magazine to dub Crédit Lyonnais the 'dirtiest bank in the world' (*Forbes*, 13 December 1999). Yet in September 2000 the bank (France's third largest) reported it had overcome its previous difficulties by doubling its half-yearly profits and its return on equity (*Financial Times*, 8 September 2000).

Founded in 1863, Crédit Lyonnais became a major universal and global bank, headed by a chairman appointed by the government after nomination by the board of directors and fulfilling the role of chief executive officer. Separate operating divisions of the bank comprise those responsible for the domestic banking network, international affairs, capital markets, relations with major corporates, and real estate. Administrative processing, group financial management, marketing and human resources each have their own divisions. Other specialized divisions include legal services, inspectorate and research.

The Europe network had been expanded during the decade to 1991, and the bank had 630 offices in Europe and 610 offices outside Europe, including foreign branches, subsidiaries with major shareholdings and associated companies with minority shareholdings. The bank had two growth strategies: organic growth (increasing the activities of its branches and subsidiaries or opening new units); and acquisition or merger (take-overs or purchasing minority interests in local banks). It had also expanded its capital market activity in the major financial centres of the world (coordinated through its Capital Markets Division).

There was a perceived need (according to Chevalier and Segalla's 1996 research) for better integration of this expanding international network in terms of common products and management of clients who themselves are operating internationally. This was from a position of dominance of French management in its traditional form and foreign operations that had been centralized around an international division of the bank based in France. Human resource management had been characterized by pragmatic career management, different systems of career management for French and foreign managers, and by using expatriation as the main link between the headquarters and foreign operations. Its main characteristics and influences appear to have been as follows:

- Its tradition as a deposit bank with reliance on general rather than specific skills, and promotion based on seniority. With increasing attention to commercial activities this had been somewhat reversed, with specialist and commercial expertise being brought in and promoted.

- Historically being based on a worldwide organization with local managers being delegated large amounts of power, and respect for this personal power of fiefdom being ingrained in the organization. This local autonomy had been protected, and this resulted in internal competition where local managers are reluctant to share customers with colleagues in other countries militating against the need to service clients who operate across borders. This had been addressed partly by increasing professional mobility and changes in the organization chart, but coordination remained a problem.

- A corporate identity which instilled pride in working for a world leader and which extended to foreign employees, and a caution which acted both positively

41

when taking on innovation and technical improvements, but also negatively in a distrust of the new and the foreign.

- A career management system that was strongly oriented towards the bank's French managers. At local level across the international network human resource practice was seen as a local responsibility with different rules and procedures. At the group level there are two systems of career management: one for French and a less well developed one for non-French. Promotion was based largely on where vacancies exist, and favoured managers in touch with the right personal network and associated with prestigious projects. This militated against strategic career and human resource planning. Local career development was managed locally and was generally restricted to opportunities within the particular country.

- French expatriates provided the link between the Paris headquarters and the foreign subsidiaries. Whilst this may have maintained and transmitted the corporate culture and ways of doing things, it also isolated subsidiaries from the centre.

- Crédit Lyonnais could be seen as essentially a French bank with an international dimension. Cooperation and exchanges between subsidiaries were limited; information flows from headquarters to subsidiaries were vertical, with subsidiaries feeling they were not involved in strategic development. Career opportunities within the group were limited for foreign executives.

Crédit Lyonnais is an example of a French bank struggling with its internationalization process. Before looking at different strategies which involve the use of people internationally through formulated human resource strategies, policies, plans and practices, it is worth looking at a model of globalization which takes up the main theme of this chapter: the integration of multinational organizations through cutting across national (as well as cultural) boundaries.

The supranational model

In 1977 Alvin W. Wolfe, an anthropologist, identified the main features of

> a supranational system encompassing multinational corporations and states . . . a modern supranational structure that is more than just international . . . a cultural-ecological system that is above the level of the nation-state and above the level of the multinational firm . . . the system of our concern is different from an international organization and different from a cartel formed by corporations . . . a qualitatively disinctive sociocultural system at a higher level of integration. . . . Involving states, corporations and networks of corporations and states and persons, systematically processing information in such a way that the higher-order system exerts significant control over the elements organized at a lower level of integration. (Wolfe, 1977: 631)

He was suggesting that the international production system through multinational enterprises was in effect working beyond and above the level of the

nation state.

> Once a legal fiction recognized by a state government for a strictly
> limited purpose, the corporation has developed to the point that some
> of its variants are operating multinationally, with virtually unlimited
> purposes of their own and identities quite unrelated to their origins
> and to the identities of their shareholders, and controlling in some
> sense more resources than most states. (Wolfe, 1977: 619)

The extraction industry is an example of how this has developed, for
example across African states, often with government involvement: 'The new
states are weak, their governments poor, so they tend to take their places among
the companies in the system rather than try to upset it. An advantage of the
circuitous, acephalous character of the supranational system is that no coup d'état
on that plateau is possible' (Wolfe, 1977: 619).

Early multinational organizations such as the British and Dutch East India
Companies were able to maintain their own armies, and to govern countries in
which they did business. Latter-day multinationals, perhaps more subtly, work
across nations through the movement of capital and finance, often with the
involvement of nation states and major corporations within different countries.
The United Nations Centre for Transnational Corporations estimates that there
are some 37,000 transnational companies in the world with 170,000 affiliates
(subsidiaries), with the top 100 companies owning about a third of the worldwide foreign direct investment stock (UNCTC, 1993). In many senses, they
transcend nation states, and can often have an influence on events, particularly
in 'developing' countries, which far exceeds any intervention that other nations'
governments might make. At least a third of all world trade takes place inside such
companies (UNCTC, 1993).

One of the implications for the multicultural model discussed in Chapter 1
is that here is an approach which tries to diminish the effects of national cultures
on the operation of the organization, although the degree to which this may
happen is largely dependent on the nature of the internationalizing strategy of
the organization. Using the supranational concept as an analogy, the purpose
of this chapter is to explore the ways organizations have internationalized (often
ignoring national and cultural differences), and the implications for the management and development of people within the international context. In so doing,
two frameworks are introduced for classifying organizations: Perlmutter's 1969
geocentric model and Bartlett and Ghoshal's (1989) transnational model. These
frameworks are used to cut across most of the confusion in describing cross-border
organizations and its relation to human resource policy in the international
context.

Strategies for international organizations

A great deal has been written on the need to develop new and more adaptive
forms of organizations as a result of increased internationalization. Particularly
the changes in Europe, and the needs of cross-border operations have prompted
discussion on these issues (see also Chapter 7). Van Dijck (1990) has pointed to the
tendency towards transnationalization as evidenced in Europe by an increase
in cross-border operations, investment and strategies in Europe. This has also

included an increased international mobility of young graduates, professional and managers. There has also been more inter-company competition in Europe than between countries. Within multinational companies, there is a need to balance international strategy with local conditions and needs; and move towards new organizational structures. This may be away from development and direction from the headquarters, towards 'managing diversity' by networking structures which take account of the efforts and initiatives from all operating countries.

There is an indication that old structures will not be sufficient to deal with these changes. Smiley (1989) some years ago identified a shift from 'multi-domestic' organizations to global organizations that operate across borders to meet converging consumer tastes. This signifies a need for more flexible, temporary organizational forms that can adapt quickly to a changing marketplace. He even suggests that the word 'structure' will have to be conceived in its scientific form as meaning a 'union of parts'. So rather than talking about the structure we will in future be talking about the 'form' of an organization.

Integration and differentiation

One of the key aspects of the strategic management of modern organizations is the balance between differentiation and integration (Lawrence and Lorsch, 1967). While flexibility is required in the way business is conducted differently in different locations, there is a need to integrate activity and coordinate not only business activity, but the way people are developed and deployed within the international organization. Generally the more complex an operating environment the more differentiation is required.

In domestic operations this may require a high level of professional specialization. Banks such as Crédit Lyonnais have been through phases of developing generalist bankers in times of relative stability, but have focused on the employment and training of specialists over the last decades in times of extreme competition, increased use of complex technology, information systems and financial products, where there is a need to have a thorough specialized knowledge of markets and products. In international situations diversity of national markets and a requirement to meet the needs of a diverse and discriminating national customer base, as well as different legislation may require a great deal of local autonomy. Combined with this may be a need to utilize specialist technical assistance from the centre, to propagate and instil a sense of corporate identity, and retain financial control over operations.

These aspects require a level of integration, and the attempt to balance this level of integration with differentiation has been evident within Crédit Lyonnais (for example, the local autonomy of subsidiary managers versus the use of French expatriates in subsidiaries). Doz and Prahalad (1986) have called this 'controlled' variety: where there is a need to combine strategic variety and strategic control in multinational enterprises. They depict the requirement for differentiation by type of business, type of subsidiary and type of ownership.

Hence the level of strategic control needed in an international operation is depicted along three axes: the type of subsidiary operating in each country; the type of international business strategy employed; and the type of ownership. Export platforms need tight controls as they are managed directly from a home headquarters, while large self-contained subsidiaries, especially those prevented from being integrated fully into a global enterprise through protectionist measures, do not require heavy control. The types of international business strategy used by enterprises also influences the levels of control used.

Those that see the world as a single market, and centralize research, product development and production tend to have strong international control over their subsidiaries. Some, with highly localized business and differentiated markets may organize internationally in a loose federation of enterprises and hence have very loose controls. Different types of ownership will also influence the levels of control. At the loosely controlled end of the continuum are collaborative agreements, for example multigovernment-funded technology projects such as nuclear fusion projects, and intergovernmental aerospace projects involving consortia of private sector enterprises. Through the various organizational forms being extensively employed in difficult and restrictive markets such as joint ventures, fully owned subsidiaries at the other end of the continuum are more likely to be directly controlled from the central organization in the home country.

Although Crédit Lyonnais' main activities were through fully owned or partially owned subsidiaries in the early 1990s, increasingly the banking industry sought other types of international organization such as the strategic alliance between the French Banque Nationale de Paris and German Dresdner Bank in 1993 (ul-Haq, 1995), and in 1999 Crédit Lyonnais was negotiating a three-way joint venture with a Spanish and an Italian bank to set up a pan-European investment bank. This would indicate a lessening of control for its subsidiaries and consequent altering of human resource policies to better suit the new organizational form. These types of business strategies are more fully taken up by Perlmutter.

Perlmutter's model

In the late 1960s Perlmutter (1969) suggested different internationalizing strategies that organizations tend to fit, which influence personnel practices within the global context. The ethnocentric approach is probably closest to Doz and Prahalad's (1986) global organization, where control is tight from the centre, with subsidiaries having little autonomy, and where key positions are held by home-country nations and there is a high degree of management by expatriates. The polycentric approach sees each subsidiary as a separate entity (purely local in Doz and Prahalad's terms). Although subsidiaries are managed by locals, these same local managers are unlikely to have a career in the international group or at headquarters. The 'ideal' approach is seen as the geocentric organization (see Table 2.1).

This goes beyond Doz and Prahalad's conception in the sense that it is not merely a multifocal organization but one which is able to identify and utilize talent anywhere in the world. The regiocentric approach (added later by Perlmutter) reflects this, but on a regional basis only. It is more likely that the geocentric (and to a certain extent the regiocentric) organization will have a strong integrating culture in order to develop a certain amount of uniformity and coherence in the way people work, so that good managers can be developed for key positions anywhere. The organization then may be shaped either by the home cultures or (theoretically at least) by international interaction among the national units. This

45

Table 2.1 Perlmutter's model of international strategies

	Ethnocentric	Polycentric	Regiocentric	Geocentric
Prevailing organizational culture	Home country	Host country	Regional	Global
Finance	Repatriation of profits to home country	Retention of profits in host country	Redistribution within region	Redistribution globally
Strategy	Global integration	National responsiveness	Regional integration and national responsiveness	Global integration national responsiveness
Marketing	Product development determined mostly by needs of home country customers	Local product development based on local needs	Standardized within region, but not across regions	Global products, with local variation
Personnel practices	People of home country developed for key positions everywhere in the world	People of local nationality developed for key positions in their own country	Regional people developed for key positions anywhere in the region	Best people everywhere developed for key positions everywhere in the world

Source: Adapted from Chakravarthy and Perlmutter, 1985

may in fact not differ too much from the strong culture of the ethnocentric organization that is propagated by the centre. It is more likely that the polycentric organization will not have this overriding strong culture, as a result of a lack of interaction among the subsidiaries, and between the subsidiaries and the headquarters. In terms of staffing the international organization, the strategy of Crédit Lyonnais may be conceptualized as ethnocentric in the sense of propagating a strong (French) culture from the centre, and staffing some key jobs by expatriates. The fact that banks such as Crédit Lyonnais can also be regarded as polycentric in that local management has a certain amount of autonomy (control may be mainly financial, with subsidiaries being sold off if they do not perform), and local managers may have a career locally and be promoted to key, but not expatriate, careers, may indicate a weakness in such categorization of international strategies.

Bartlett and Ghoshal's model

In 1989 Bartlett and Ghoshal offered the 'transnational' as the ideal type. They distinguish: multinational organizations; global organizations; international organizations; and, transnational organizations. By reference to their model of cross-border organizing it is possible to gain insight into the environmental influences pressing hard on organizations, and how their consequent structures may influence behaviour within them.

Multinational This type of organization responds to the need to exploit national diversity and recognizes that, for example, consumer tastes and needs of technology may be based on local conditions and national culture. This type of organization will therefore have a strong national presence and can respond to national diversity. It will be decentralized and nationally self-sufficient, sensing and exploiting local opportunities, and developing and retaining knowledge within each national unit. There is very little direct influence from the parent company, and interpersonal communication among representatives from the different cultures may be quite limited. An example of this type of organization is the American ITT, which needs to respond on a local basis to specific regulations, requirements and formats in the telecommunications switching industry.

Global Here the organization exploits the cost advantages of centralized global-scale operations based on knowledge development that is retained at the centre, and on the implementation of the parent company's strategies. It responds to the trends of growing globalization of tastes, fashions and consumer demand generally. This type of organization is globally scaled. An example of a global enterprise is the Japanese Matsushita (see also Chapter 5), which exploits and promotes the globalization of taste in consumer electrics, being export-based with research and development, manufacturing and branding concentrated at the centre.

International Here, the organization exploits the parent company's knowledge and adapts it worldwide. Sources of core competences are centralized, but other competences may be decentralized. The role of overseas operations is to adapt the parent company's competences to the local environment. Knowledge is developed at the centre and then transferred to the overseas subsidiaries. Procter and Gamble is a good example of an international organization. Many of its research and development functions are centralized, but branding and packaging of products is undertaken at local level to meet the needs of national tastes and legislation.

Transnational This type of organization is an ideal type in the eyes of Bartlett and Ghoshal (1989) and is put forward as something towards which many cross-border companies ought to be striving. It seeks to integrate the separate forces operating in the international marketplace, which each of the three organizational forms described above addresses only partially. These three forces are:

- *global integration*: the trend towards greater integration of global tastes. Product trends such as Coca-Cola and McDonald's are examples, as is the demand for the same consumer electric goods around the world. Global organizations address this particular market force.

- *local differentiation*: the demand of local and national tastes, and of protectionism from national governments tend towards multinational organizational structures, and to an extent international organizational structures.

47

- *worldwide innovation*: the cost of innovation is great and it is more cost-effective, usually, if research and development is centralized, and such products emanating from the centre are marketed globally, or are adapted internationally in local centres around the world. The corollary of this is that centralized research and development functions may not take account of the expertise and resources available in local centres, and may in fact be missing opportunities to maximize efficiencies in new product development.

Transnational organizations (according to Bartlett and Ghoshal, 1989) address these issues by deploying dispersed, interdependent and specialized capabilities and assets, by facilitating differentiated contributions from national units in order to integrate worldwide operations, and by developing knowledge jointly and sharing it worldwide. In order to achieve these organizational characteristics management has a role to play in legitimizing and encouraging diverse perspectives and capabilities, developing multiple and flexible coordinating processes, and building shared vision and individual commitment.

Bartlett and Ghoshal (1989: 61) describe the transnational model as an 'integrated network' which

> emphasizes the very significant flow of components, products, resources, people, and information that must be managed in the transnational. Beyond the rationalization of physical facilities, the company must integrate tasks and perspectives; rich and complex communication linkages, work interdependencies, and formal and informal systems are the true hallmark of the transnational.

Implications for human resource management policy

Adler and Ghadar (1990) provide an account of the implications of different phases of internationalization for human resource management. Their framework and typology are similar in concept to previous ones (discussed above), yet in common with other theorists such as Negandhi (1987) they view organizational forms as representative of stages in the development of international enterprises. The four phases identified are: *domestic*, with a focus on home markets and export; *international*, with a focus on local responsiveness and the transfer of learning, and most closely resembling Perlmutter's polycentric approach and Bartlett and Ghoshal's multinational and international models; *multinational*, with a focus on global strategy and price competition, and resembling Perlmutter's ethnocentric approach and Bartlett and Ghoshal's global model; and *global* with a focus on both local responsiveness and global integration. This most resembles Perlmutter's geocentric approach and Bartlett and Ghoshal's transnational model.

Adler and Ghadar's (1990) model particularly looks at the relationship of culture and responses within human resource management. In the first phase, domestic, there is a denying or ignoring of other cultural contexts with foreigners simply being offered a product developed in the home country. This is reflected in the brief visits of sales, or sometimes technical, personnel to foreign offices, with technical competence the only priority. In the second phase, international, it is important to take the cultural component into consideration, as firms are moving into foreign markets in which they need to operate more fully and take account of local conditions. There is a greater need for longer-term assignments, with a priority on technical and managerial skills, but also on cultural adaptation. There is also a need to recruit from the host country for lower level managerial functions in areas such as sales, marketing and personnel. The third phase, multinational, is characterized by a globalization of products and services in order to compete on price, and therefore culture is not such a major factor, but through necessity there is a recognition of cultural differences among the countries of operation. In order to utilize cost advantage around the world it is necessary to recruit from other countries, yet key positions would remain in the hands of home managers. In the fourth phase, global, there is a more complete adaptation to local markets of global products, and cultural sensitivity becomes a crucial issue. Cultural diversity is seen more as an opportunity than an inconvenience, and the international human resource function attempts to provide managers from anywhere with the opportunities to develop in order to develop the organization itself.

An integrated strategic framework

Schuler, Dowling and De Cieri (1993) suggest the need for an integrated framework of strategic international human resource management that brings together a number of the aspects already discussed above. They propose that there are two major multinational enterprise components that impact on strategic international HRM issues: the inter-unit linkages and internal operations (Figure 2.1). The former involves the organization's mechanisms for managing the differentiation and integration of its operating units; the latter involves the need for each

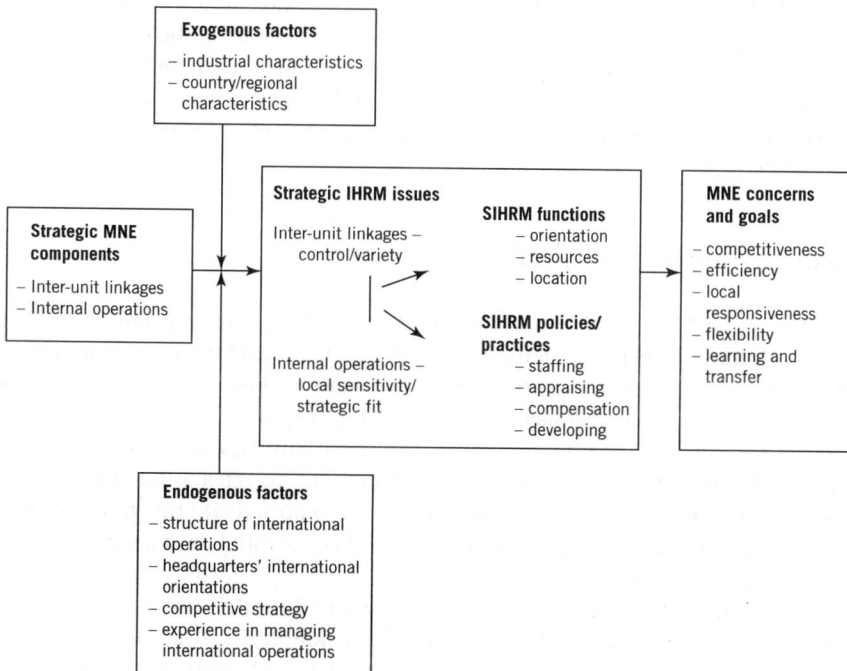

Figure 2.1
Schuler, Dowling and De Cieri's (1993) integrated strategic framework

operating unit (e.g. subsidiary) to function effectively within its own (national or market) environment. The strategic international human resource issues in their framework are concerned with these two components and with the need to manage the international organization by balancing differentiation and integration and balancing the autonomy of local units against the need to coordinate and control them.

These issues impact on strategic international functions, that is, the way human resources are managed: the resources put into its managing of functions, the location of function and the balance between centralized and decentralized functions. Some companies have large centralized human resource functions for selecting and repatriating expatriate staff, training and compensation. Others devolve many functions to the subsidiaries either as well as this central function or instead of it. These issues also impact on policies and practices, including the general guidelines on how staff are managed and the development of particular practices. Again this may involve the extent to which local practices may be developed. If general guidelines are formulated by the centre that refer only to the need to develop a system for rewarding individual performance, subsidiaries may then be free to develop their own incentive schemes.

Factors both outside and inside the organization influence strategic issues of human resource management functions and policies and practices. Exogenous factors include industry characteristics such as the type of business and technologies available, the nature of the competition and the nature and extent of change; and country characteristics such as political, economic and socio-cultural conditions, and legal requirements. Endogenous factors include the structure of operations, international orientation of the headquarters, the competitive strategies being used, and the company's experience in managing international operations. All these factors influence the company's effort to be responsive to local factors and to be adaptable and globally coordinated and controlled.

Functions and policies are aimed ultimately at meeting the concerns and goals of the multinational organization. These include global competitiveness, efficiency, local responsiveness, flexibility, and organizational learning and transfer of information. These concerns, of course, vary from company to company (Schuler et al., 1993).

Crédit Lyonnais Revisited[1]

Since the mid-1990s, Crédit Lyonnais, has largely emerged from problems which severely damaged the image of the bank, both in France and internationally, with the associated difficulty that employees were unable to show pride in working for the bank. In some ways this has strengthened the corporate identity. People still with the bank now, and who were working there during that period, are now committed to the bank as they feel they supported it through a difficult time. This may be less true for newer staff, but they seem to appreciate the general calm atmosphere of the bank which reflects a spirit of cooperation and a lack of direct competition with their colleagues.

Internationally, subsidiaries are still relatively autonomous, often with competition between Paris and a subsidiary. For example, Paris and London share the same region (Europe, Africa and the Middle East). Although theoretically they have different clients, this often engenders competition between the two centres. However, the matrix structure of the international organization creates links between Paris and the subsidiaries. For example, in project finance (a product line) the management of each subsidiary participates in regular conference calls organized by the head of the product line in Paris. This ensures that through discussion of prospects and strategy, the subsidiaries are included, and have influence. For example the American subsidiary is particularly strong within the bank's international operations.

It is still the case that it is easier for French managers to become expatriates, compared with their non-French counterparts. It would seem that selection for such positions is based mainly on connections with the right people, as there is still an absence of career plans, and specific competency requirements. Yet more and more non-French people are working in Paris. For example, expatriates from London come as specialists to work in Paris. Increasingly in the subsidiaries key people are recruited locally. This is seen as particularly important in the Asian subsidiaries such as Hong Kong and Singapore, where local languages and contacts facilitate business with local clients. However, the top management is always French.

Attitudes towards the role of expatriation are also changing. It used to be a central element in developing management (from the parent) for an employee to have experience in a broad cross-section of functions, including a period of expatriation. Specialization is now seen as far more important. However, the bank still has difficulties with this, because of entrenched attitudes. People are often keen to change their jobs after about five years, rather than stay in the same specialization, as they feel that their qualities are not recognized if they are not proposed for a change in job in the bank. This attitude is slowly changing, but there is still some way to go.

Implications for managers

The extent to which the need for internal consistency (integration) across national borders contends with forces for local isomorphism (differentiation) is examined by Rosenzweig and Nohria (1994). Their study of subsidiaries of foreign companies operating in the United States suggested that in general HRM practices closely follow local practices, with differences among specific practices. It may be that their empirical study can be generalized to subsidiaries within the United States, and here their conceptual framework is more significant than their findings. The variables that they investigate, which are associated with different levels of local adaptation, are valuable for a consideration of the implication for practising managers, and these can be related to factors affecting the internationalization of Crédit Lyonnais, and indeed, to IKEA (see Chapter 1).

Local embeddedness

Method of founding Greenfield investments are more likely to reflect the characteristics of the multinational company, whereas acquisitions may remain similar to local companies. Rosenzweig and Nohria's (1994) findings support this assumption. Crédit Lyonnais' main method of expansion into the early 1990s was through acquisition. With other factors, such as a management that is orientated towards autonomy of function within the different levels of the hierarchy (d'Irabarne, 1997), it is likely that this would provide subsidiaries with a higher level of local differentiation. This is quite the opposite for IKEA, whose international expansion has mainly been through greenfield investment. With other factors such as the importance attached to corporate culture (not a key consideration for Crédit Lyonnais), IKEA's subsidiaries are not likely to be afforded a high level of differentiation.

Age of subsidiary Over the years subsidiaries should come to resemble more closely the local situation. Certainly, IKEA has had to adapt its practices to local conditions as it has become more entrenched in a country such as Spain, as was seen in Chapter 1. The opposite may be true of Crédit Lyonnais, as its acquired subsidiaries may increasingly be influenced by French expatriation, and other connections with the home country. In fact, Rosenzweig and Nohria's (1994) findings do not support a relationship between age of subsidiary and local embeddedness.

Size of subsidiary Among other factors, larger subsidiaries will be more dependent on employees and resources within the locality and therefore more likely to resemble local company HRM practice. This was certainly a factor for IKEA, which had to recruit staff locally and had to conform more to local practices and agreements with unions. With the acquisition of subsidiaries Crédit Lyonnais is likely to have acquired use of local resources, including employees, although this may be related more to the next factor considered below. Rosenzweig and Nohria's findings do not support this relationship among their sample of subsidiaries in the United States.

Local resource dependency The more it depends on local resources, the more likely the subsidiary is to emulate local practices. Both IKEA and Crédit Lyonnais are dependent on local resources, and this is reflected in their need to conform to local requirements, with this being more painful for the former. Rosenzweig and Nohria's (1994) findings support this relationship.

Level of unionization The higher the level of unionization, the more likely it is that local practices will prevail. This varies from country to country, and among industries, which means that Rosenzweig and Nohria's (1994) study is not a good predictor of the influence of this factor (their findings offer some support for this in the United States). Both banking and retail sectors tend to be highly unionized in some countries and not in others. Although the level of unionization in Spain is not high, the presence of collective bargaining agreements means that IKEA has had to conform to local training and development practices.

Local regulatory and other pressures Conformity to local practices may be influenced by government regulations, interest and pressure groups within the local community as well as by trade associations and consumer groups (although Rosenzweig and Nohria's findings in the United States did not confirm such a relationship). Although banking may be a similar activity through the world, it is subject to a complexity of laws in different parts of the world. This is another factor contributing to the pressure on Crédit Lyonnais' subsidiaries to adopt local practices, with a higher autonomy enjoyed by managers in IKEA's subsidiaries.

Parent company characteristics

Parent country culture Based on the cross-cultural literature which suggests that national culture has a strong influence on company practice, it is likely that the bigger the cultural distance between the parent country and subsidiary country, the less likely it is that subsidiary practice will resemble local practice. Rosenzweig and Nohria's findings provided some evidence for this. For IKEA its 'Swedishness' is seen as an important factor permeating its business and personnel practices. This is heavily protected within its subsidiary operations, and adapted to local conditions only when necessary. Crédit Lyonnais does not market its 'Frenchness' and is not protecting it in the same way as IKEA. However, it is likely that the French culture influences its international operations and the way its subsidiaries are managed from the centre. Hence the autonomy of subsidiaries, yet their tendency towards higher levels of centralization in financial control, career planning and expatriation, and levels of one-way communication from the centre.

International experience of the parent With greater international experience, it is more likely the parent will develop a more cosmopolitan and less parochial perspective. Therefore, the less international experience, the less likely that the subsidiary will adopt and resemble local practices. With greater experience of working internationally, IKEA has become more adept at adapting to local culture and practices while maintaining its essential 'Swedishness'. Crédit Lyonnais has many years' experience of operating internationally, but perhaps not of thinking internationally. This, as in many other international companies, has enabled it to successfully operate fairly autonomous subsidiary units, but not to have drawn to any great extent expertise, talent and other ways of working into its global pool of resources and knowledge. Rosenzweig and Nohria's findings do not provide any evidence of a relationship between length of international experience of the parent and local embeddedness.

Level of control-orientation of the parent Subsidiaries with greater autonomy are more likely to adopt local practices. However, the way that control is exerted is more likely to result in a lack of local embeddedness. IKEA is not overly control-oriented in its management culture, yet its strong organizational culture, together with expatriate start-up teams, and top management in subsidiaries means that the parent exerts a strong influence over the subsidiary. Crédit Lyonnais' management culture is control-oriented, but allows for autonomy of function within its units. Rosenzweig and Nohria's (1994) findings do not support a relationship between control-orientation and a lack of local embeddedness.

Flows between parent company and subsidiary

Presence of expatriates   It is likely that if there is a high presence of expatriates from the home country in the subsidiary, it will resemble the parent more than its local environment. The literature suggests that expatriates are often the carriers of parent country culture (see also Chapter 4), and this is supported by Rosenzweig and Nohria's findings. We have already seen that IKEA uses its expatriate start-up team to firmly establish the IKEA culture and practices, and only later to adapt to local conditions. Expatriates in Crédit Lyonnais are mainly used to develop managers' careers within the group operation, and in part to transfer technical expertise to the subsidiaries rather than to overtly communicate a specific organizational and business culture. To better understand this relationship, the nature of the international business (Chakravarthy and Perlmutter, 1985; Bartlett and Ghoshal, 1989) and the way that the parent uses expatriation should be taken into account.

Dependence on the parent   Subsidiaries that are more dependent on the parent for technical and managerial know-how will be more influenced by parent practices rather than by the practices of the subsidiary's local environment. The fact that Rosenzweig and Nohria's (1994) findings do not confirm such a relationship may indicate that the type of dependence on parent know-how should be taken into account. The dependence of IKEA's subsidiaries on the parent is related to the strength of the organizational and business culture and the dependence which this creates with the headquarters in Sweden. For Crédit Lyonnais, this type of dependency does not exist. Technical know-how may be required, but this can also be obtained from the local environment by recruiting experienced bankers from competitor banks. There may be a resource dependency in other areas, such as in capital and, to a certain extent, product development.

Communication with the parent   The more frequent the communication of subsidiary executives with members of the parent, the more likely the parent practices will influence the subsidiary's practices. This is supported by Rosenzweig and Nohria's findings. However, it is also likely to be associated with the presence of expatriates, particularly at top management levels in the subsidiaries, as is the case in IKEA. Financial reporting would be important in Crédit Lyonnais, as a major flow of information to the parent. Expatriates are likely to be present at all levels in management in the subsidiaries, and the resulting communication flows vary among subsidiaries as a result of this. The ability and willingness to establish communication flows for various purposes would also be important for sharing know-how, for example, as is suggested by Bartlett and Ghoshal's (1989) transnational model.

Nature of the business

Rosenzweig and Nohria (1994) simply distinguish between (following Porter) *global* and *multi-domestic* industries. In global industries with strong integration forces where demand is common across countries and competition is global rather than local, it is likely that subsidiaries will be less prone to follow local practices. Subsidiaries in multi-domestic industries are more likely to need to respond to local competition, and therefore are more likely to follow local practices. Their findings did not support such a relationship, and it may be that this classification does not sufficiently distinguish the types of international strategies pursued. Crédit Lyonnais is operating in a global industry where the main competitors are international rather than domestic, yet it provides autonomy and local responsiveness to its subsidiaries who are essentially operating in local markets. IKEA is involved in multi-domestic industries. It is unusual for furniture retailing to be an international concern, and IKEA's main competitors are domestic ones. Its main competitive advantage over them is its 'Swedishness'. So, there are contradictory pressures to conform to local requirements while maintaining a strong culture that permeates its internal people management policies as well as its business practices.

In Chapter 1, the main concern and implication for managers was how to adapt in an appropriate way to differences in cultural values between the parent organization and the subsidiary. By an examination of the various centripetal factors which are pressing hard for international integration (which may not be the same as taking an ethnocentric or parochial approach towards the management of subsidiaries), against those centrifugal factors which point towards local differentiation, it is possible to discuss an optimum stance for appropriately managing people in subsidiary operations. This should be achievable not only of charting a course through these two opposing forces, but also of drawing on the contributions that can be made from the parent and the different subsidiaries. This requires consideration of the strategic factors that should be addressed to provide the optimum balance between integration and differentiation, a consideration of cultural differences that exist among the different national operations (directly between parent and subsidiary, and among its various subsidiaries), and the relative contributions which can be made by people in the different national organizations to the global operation. Schuler, Dowling and De Cieri's (1993) integrated strategic framework captures some of the aspects, but provides little information on the optimization of appropriate people management policies and practices within these often contradictory forces. Some of these optimizing factors are captured in Figure 2.2.

Questions for managers

1 How could Crédit Lyonnais better manage the conflicts between local differentiation and global integration in its human resource management practices?

2 What HRM systems should Crédit Lyonnais put in place in order to better utilize its human resources across its international operations?

3 What can the management of Crédit Lyonnais learn from the experiences of the IKEA management in its internationalization process and strategy? What are the major differences and incompatibilities between the approaches of the two companies?

Figure 2.2
Strategic
optimizing
factors in
developing
appropriate
people
management
policies

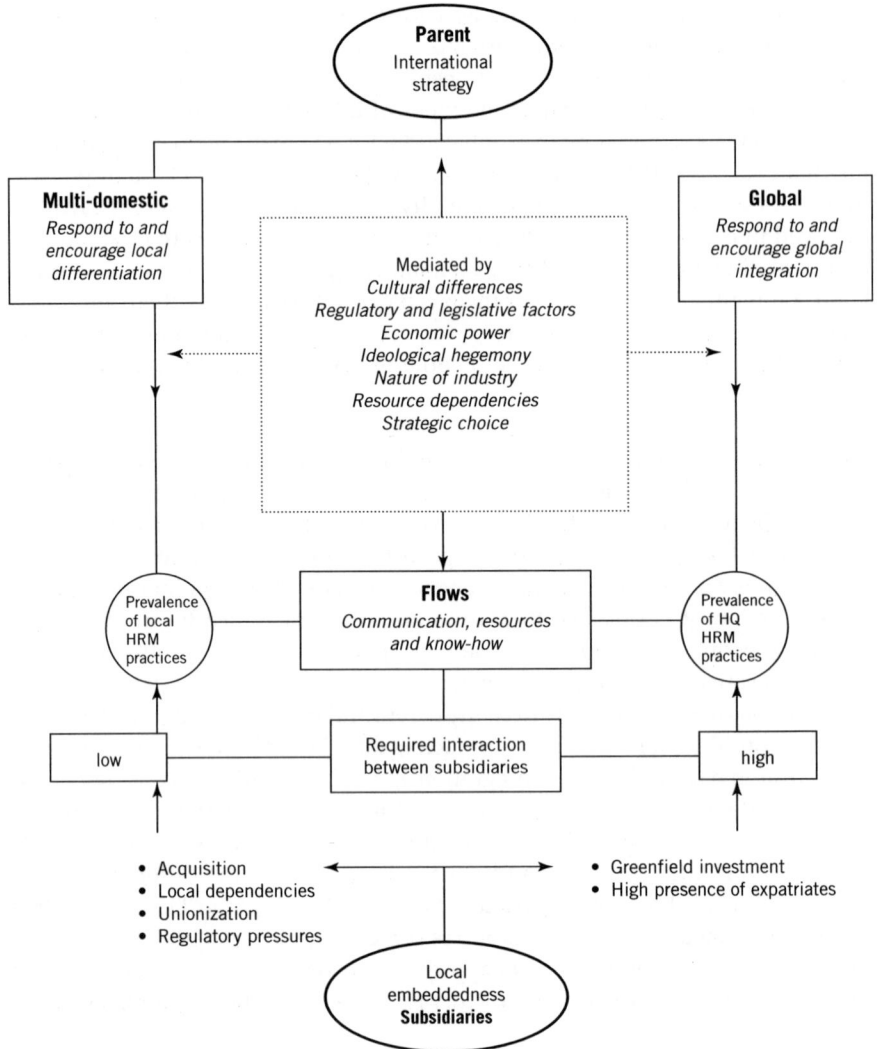

An agenda for research

Research has tended to focus on the integrating versus differentiating factors in headquarters–subsidiary operations, and has assumed that the multinational organization has been created and exists within a cultural vacuum: although some research, such as that of Rosenzweig and Nohria (1994), attempts to take as a mediating factor the cultural difference between headquarter country and subsidiary country. This should perhaps be made more central in constructing hypotheses about the transfer of knowledge across countries, and the impact on the nature of management. Included within such an analysis should be an awareness of the ability of the supranational in the economic power to impose forms of control on a local subsidiary or even a national industry. This, together with the ideological hegemony of management (normally Western) knowledge, and its effects on practices, particularly in the transitional economies of the former Soviet countries and the post-colonial countries of Africa, South Asia, Latin America and the Middle East, should be a more prominent focus of research. It is an area that is dealt with more specifically in Chapters 9 and 10. Other mediating aspects, which are included in Figure 2.2, have been more thoroughly investigated. These include regulatory and legislative influences, the nature of the industry, resource dependencies (which have been discussed in connection with Rosenzweig and Nohria's 1994 work) and strategic choice. The latter has been discussed particularly in connection with Perlmutter's (1969), and Bartlett and Ghoshal's (1989) work. Figure 2.2 is an attempt to pull the many strands of this chapter together, in order to propose possible relationships between factors that may be investigated in future research.

Among other things, Chapters 1 and 2 have looked at the internationalization process of a Swedish and a French organization. This takes as a starting point the positioning of these organizations in their own national cultural context. Little attempt is made in the management literature to suggest that the approaches of either French or Swedish companies are in any way universal, and that their management principles can be applied anywhere in the world. As a result of the ideological hegemony of American management thought as a product of post-war economic dominance (Boyacigiller and Adler, 1991), this is quite the reverse for US human resource principles (see also Introduction). Chapter 3 now focuses on this aspect, in connection with a major American consultancy organization.

Questions for researchers

1 What is the relationship between a company's internationalizing strategy, the culture of the home country, the culture of the host country, and the company's people management policies and practices in the host country?

2 How can an international company successfully manage the antithesis between the need for global integration and local differentiations? How do strategies and practices vary according to company, industry and country of origin?

Note

1. I am grateful to Virginie Arnaud of Crédit Lyonnais, France for this information.

The competent organization:
the American model

The competences approach to human resource management is now widely used in the Western world, and is a useful means of integrating policy both vertically and horizontally. Vertically, it links an organization's strategic objectives, operational objectives and task and behavioural requirements. It focuses on the needs of the operation which are linked with strategic objectives, and the types of tasks that have to be undertaken in order to achieve operational goals. Once the types of competence needed by people performing tasks (knowledge, skills, attitudes) are identified, the behaviour characteristics associated with these competences can be defined and identified in potential recruits to the organization. Horizontal integration can then be achieved by aligning selection, appraisal, reward and development criteria: it is logical to recruit, reward and develop people using the same competences throughout these processes. Hence the competences approach can be an effective way to ensure, throughout the organization, that people are recruited, developed and rewarded in line with the operational and strategic objectives of the organization.

This chapter is wide ranging as it looks at this integrating aspect of the competences approach and applies it in the identification of international management characteristics. Before doing this, the approach is positioned within its cultural context. The competences approach has arisen mainly in an American context, and has been exported to other Anglo-Saxon countries and many other Western countries and beyond. It is born of an individualistic, competitive, short-term culture with an instrumental perspective on the value of people in organizations. It accommodates individual job descriptions, results and rewards: an emphasis that may not be apparent in Japanese organizations for example. The weaknesses of this approach must be recognized in the international context.

This chapter has three main themes: the use of the competences approach; the nature of international management competences, with the focus mainly on cross-border operations in Europe; and the cultural context of the competences approach and its limitations. Its objective is to examine the relevance and applicability of this approach in other cultural settings (considering differentiation as discussed in Chapter 1) and its relevance in operationalizing international strategies across borders (integration, discussed in Chapter 2), not least through the recruitment of international staff. In order to examine this in the context of real culture and real management issues, the American firm Andersen Consulting, particularly in Europe, is considered, as an organization mediating an American management culture with other cultures in its international operations.

Andersen Consulting (Europe)

From its position as a leading US and international consultancy firm with a strong presence in the field of systems integration, a strong organizational culture with uniform methods and criteria for recruiting and developing specific competences, Andersen Consulting has had to move to a more diverse business integration platform comprising both generalist and specialist competences, and taking into consideration diversity in national marketplaces (Ackenhusen and Ghosal, 1992). The firm has had to grapple with the problems of differentiation and integration described in the last chapter. In order to best utilize a range of different types of competence it has had to draw on its expertise from around the world, perhaps acting like the 'transnational' ideal of Bartlett and Ghoshal (1989) discussed in the last chapter.

How can it best develop and integrate the range of competences required? What are the competences and capabilities required of new recruits, given the need to maintain its strong corporate culture and ways of doing things, while recognizing different levels of recruitment and moving away from recruitment from undergraduate university programmes? Are 'Andersen Androids' appropriate for an international firm operating in different cultural environments? Before attempting to answer these questions, it is necessary to look at the cultural context of the competences approach and the challenges of using this approach across cultures.

The American Model

Gannon and Associates (1994) use the metaphor of the American football game to explain American culture. This combines a high level of individualism and competitive specialization with 'huddling' and the ceremonial celebration of perfection. While American culture celebrates the high-achieving individual and denigrates failure, it also provides evidence of collegiality (what Schwartz, 1994, calls egalitarian commitment). Innovation and modification are constantly sought, yet values and ideals are slow to change. These values Gannon and Associates (1994) describe as equality of opportunity, independence, initiative and self-reliance. Competitive specialization can be taken to the extremes of emotional intensity and aggression (the United States has the highest rate of incarceration in the world with 426 per 100,000, compared with South Africa at 333, and Japan at 45). Extroversion is an associated feature of this, with an estimated 75 per cent of Americans being extrovert on the Myers-Briggs Type Indicator (the most widely used personality questionnaire in the United States). While American football rules seek to enhance competition on the field and the league, so does US legislation such as anti-trust laws. Technology, which is developed at a fantastic rate in the United States, plays a key role in competitive specialization (both on the field and in corporate life). The team in American football is divided into squads with which players identify more readily, as they do with the nuclear family rather than the extended family. Children are raised in the nuclear family to believe that they can achieve anything if they avail themselves of the opportunities offered.

At the same time 'huddling' or team play is important, but only when it is coming together (on a voluntary basis) to solve particular problems, and then going away again to compete on one's own initiative. Huddling is quite unlike the Japanese sense of community within the corporation. It is often seen as a necessity but not an obligation. Hence cooperation, rather than working as a loner, is sought. As a result of a short-term perspective and always in a hurry to get things done ('time is money') these associations can be superficial and short-lived. This is reflected in standardization of work processes (such as Taylorism) and the quick fix approach (the 'one-minute manager'). An emphasis on the 'bottom-line' and the achievement of results often leads to the standardized ranking of individuals and teams (students against their classmates, ranking of quarter-backs, and teams in the league). Judgements are standardized and objective, and this is often seen in corporate practices such as Management by Objectives and identification of competences of managers and key workers.

A form of solidarity is seen in the celebration of perfection. Ceremonies around the football match include celebration of the team and the country, and often include a religious input (more than half of Americans are estimated to be regular churchgoers). The historical perception of America as the utopia for people who were fleeing from persecution and subjection may be reflected in this. Nationalism is highly celebrated along with the belief that anything can be achieved by the individual within a country that is revered as the best in the world. This is a particular form of ethnocentrism, where other countries are looked down on or seen as benefiting from what is given (in the form of donations and investments, to management practices) by the United States (Boyacigiller and Adler, 1991, call this parochialism). Gannon and Associates (1994) assert that this is reinforced by constant depressing news of other countries as being volatile, violent and miserable, with little positive features highlighted by the media.

Most people in the United States work in the service sector, which accounts for 73 per cent of all civilian employees, one of the highest figures in the world, with only 24 per cent in the manufacturing and transportation sectors and less than 3 per cent in agriculture (Wheeler and McClendon, 1998). The American workplace is undergoing radical changes in response to greater domestic and global competition, including work systems innovations that are designed to increase productivity, reduce costs and improve quality. At the same time companies are downsizing and there is an increasing use of casual and part-time labour. New human resource practices are being implemented in work process design, employee stock ownership, outsourcing and contingent employment. However, Wheeler and McClendon (1998) typify this predominantly as a 'lean' production mode rather than a 'team' production model, where the former relies predominantly on top-down managerial and technical expertise, and the latter on decentralized decision making. This perhaps reinforces what we saw in Chapter 1, about IKEA's difficulties in operating more consensual approaches in an American setting, where management practices reflect a more top-down approach. This may not necessarily reflect a high power distance (the United States scores 40/104 and is ranked 38/53 on Hofstede, 1980, power distance index), but more an achievement orientation of American managers who wish to influence and take control of the operational performance on which they are judged.

Why American theories might not apply abroad

In 1980, Geert Hofstede wrote a now famous article entitled 'Motivation, leadership and organization: do American theories apply abroad?' Hofstede (1980b) points to the exportation of management theory from the United States to other countries that may be less individualistic, less achievement oriented, have a lower (or higher) power distance and have less tolerance of uncertainty. He points to the example of job enrichment that has been advocated by such proponents as Frederick Herzberg in the United States, which is aimed at restructuring individual jobs. The other approach at that time was the development of restructuring work into group work, forming semi-autonomous teams in such countries as Sweden and Norway, and exemplified by the experiments in Volvo. He points to the two fundamental differences in approaches. In America, the humanization of work takes the form of 'masculanization', allowing individual performance. In Sweden and Norway, which Hofstede terms more 'feminine', humanization of work is oriented towards more wholesome interpersonal relationship, and de-emphasizes inter-individual competition. This cultural orientation in the Swedish context was seen in the case of IKEA in Chapter 1.

In an example more salient to the current chapter Hofstede (1980b) examines the problems of introducing MBO (Management by Objectives) in other countries. Peter Drucker first advocated this as early as 1955, and it has been used extensively in American corporations to develop a results orientation focused on the ability of individuals to achieve pre-defined targets. Apart from this approach being based on a strong individualism with an emphasis on individual competences and results, Hofstede posits that MBO is grounded in the assumptions that subordinates are sufficiently independent from their superiors to negotiate objectives in a meaningful way (not too high power distance), that both are comfortable with taking the risk of not fulfilling objectives perhaps as a result of unforeseen circumstances (low uncertainty avoidance), and that individual performance is seen as important by both (high masculinity).

While MBO has been adapted to the German situation quite successfully (*Führung durch Zielvereinbarung* – management by joint goal setting) it has acquired a stress on team objectives. Hofstede argues that replacing the arbitrary authority of the boss with mutually agreed objectives fitted well with a lower power distance and higher uncertainty avoidance, while the lower individualism provided the team emphasis. In France the story was quite different. It was introduced in the 1960s and gained some currency as a way of democratizing organizations (instead of *Direction par Objectifs* – *DPO* it became referred to as *Direction Participative par Objectifs*). However, in the 1970s it soon fell into disrepute, as it went against the role authority within a high power distance culture. French managers found it difficult to devolve authority through the formulation of impersonal performance objectives. The concept of achievement–ascription (Trompenaars, 1993) might also be relevant here as MBO is connected with rewarding people by promotion and in the 1980s by performance-related reward systems. This is based on achievement in the job rather than ascription of status in an organization based on qualification and seniority.

Parochialism and universality

Following in a similar vein, Nakiye Boyacigiller and Nancy Adler (1991) describe the American approach to spreading management techniques to other cultures as parochialism which is based on ignorance of others' ways, rather than ethnocentrism which judges foreign ways as inferior. It simply assumes that what works well in the American culture will naturally work well anywhere in the world. The predominance of the United States in the world economy has supported and reinforced these assumptions, and has meant that most organizational theory was in fact 'made in the USA'. Some of the problems occur in this assumption of universality of organizational theory and management practice because of cultural differences between the originating culture (USA) and the recipient culture. Boyacigiller and Adler particularly point out the implications of:

- *Free will versus determinism*: theories and practices of training and development (and presumably other areas such as MBO, incentive schemes) assume that individuals are capable of changing and affecting the work environment, whereas many cultures, such as those in Africa and other emerging countries, are more deterministic, distrusting of authority and more accepting of fate or the will of God.

- *Individualism–collectivism*: Americans define themselves by their personal achievements and personal characteristics rather than their place and obligations within the group or collective. Hence corporate selection is based on practices that select strangers through an assessment of personal achievement rather than by hiring people you know such as relatives, whom you can trust and upon whom family pressure may be placed if they do not fit in.

- *High–low context*: The low context culture of the United States again emphasizes the impersonal nature of relations and communication in organizations and the contractual nature of employment relations. High context cultures put more faith in face-to-face personal agreement than written agreements and contracts. Little is explicitly coded, and expectations are more implicitly shared. Performance expectations may therefore be more implicit in Japanese organizations, whereas in American organizations these are spelt out in performance criteria and competences statements.

Management competences approach

The idea of management 'competences' is drawn from the basic assumptions of the skills approach in social psychology that suggests we can understand social action by looking at its component parts. One of the best illustrations of this is the skills model of the Oxford social psychologist Michael Argyle (1967) (Figure 3.1).

This is seen as a conscious process directed towards making changes in the environment. It requires some sort of motivation in order to drive the process, and specific attitudes (particularly towards intended goals) may influence the process and its outcome. It requires an ability to perceive the changes to be made, to understand how they can be achieved, and the ability to apply this understanding

Figure 3.1
Argyle's skills
model
(adapted from
Argyle, 1967)

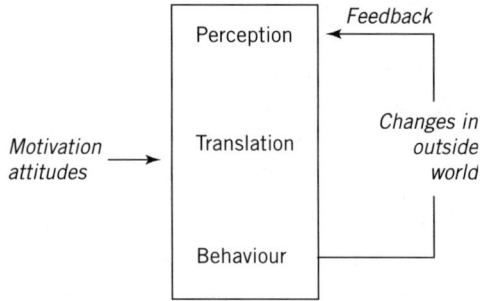

to the perceived situation and to formulate whatever action is required. We can monitor the actual changes made and compare them with our intentions. Through our ability to perceive what we are doing, we can then make suitable adjustments to our behaviour to try to ensure that the desired result is achieved. The factors involved in such a 'skilled performance' (in Argyle's, 1967, terms) are therefore:

- the motivation to perform (as well as the attitudes towards the performance and subject of the performance);
- knowledge and understanding of what is required;
- the ability (capability) to translate knowledge into specific behaviour;
- the performance itself which provides evidence that the above three factors are present.

The concept of 'skills' has a long pedigree. The latter-day equivalent of such an approach (which is largely based in behavioural and reductionist psychology) is the concept of 'management competences'. Thus Boyatzis (1982) sees competences as an effective mix of motives, traits, skills, aspects of one's self-image or social role, or the body of knowledge used by individuals. Constable (1988: 19) more specifically sees competence as 'the ability to use knowledge and skills effectively in the performance of a managerial role. All management skills must, therefore, be competences when performed effectively.' He points to a more tangible list of attributes such as the ability to make sound judgements, creativity, willingness to take risks, and a high energy level. He defines competence (Constable, 1988, following Boyatzis', 1982, definition of 'skills') as: 'the ability to demonstrate a system or sequence of behaviour as a function related to attaining a performance goal'. This is in fact very close to the concept of skills (or skilled performance) posited by Argyle (1967) above.

Boyatzis focuses on different types of competences by conceptualizing them in terms of 'types' and 'levels'. The former are associated with various aspects of behaviour and an individual's ability to demonstrate such behaviour. So, 'planning' competence is associated with 'setting goals', 'assessing risk' and developing a sequence of goal-related activities. 'Levels' of abstraction are seen by Boyatzis in terms of:

- the motive and trait level;
- the self image and social role level; and
- the skills level

At the motive and trait level 'planning' might be reflected in a desire to achieve certain goals; at the self-image and social level this might entail having a self-image of thinking ahead and being positive, and this would be projected in the manager's social role; and at the skills level the manager would perhaps develop a plan of action, assess risk and implement the plan through a series of behaviours. By using the 'type' and 'level' concept Boyatzis was able empirically to derive a number of competence clusters which included 'goal and action management', leadership, human resource management, 'directing subordinates', 'focus on other', and 'specialized knowledge'.

The identification of generic management competences that are applicable to good managers in any situation has become commonplace, and is used extensively to select and develop managers in American and other Anglo-Saxon organizations. A good example of this is the generic list of competences used by the American Management Association (Table 3.1).

Table 3.1 American Management Association Competence Model (adapted from Kubr and Abell, 1998)

Goal and action management cluster
Efficiency orientation: concern with doing something better
Proactivity: disposition towards taking action to accomplish something
Concern with impact: concern with the symbols and implements of power in order to have impact on others
Diagnostic use of concepts: use of a person's previously held concepts to explain and interpret situations

Directing subordinates cluster
Use of unilateral power: use of forms of influence to obtain compliance
Developing others: ability to provide performance feedback and other help needed to improve performance
Spontaneity: ability to express oneself freely and easily

Human resource management cluster
Accurate self-assessment: realistic and grounded view of oneself
Self-control: ability to inhibit personal needs in service of organizational goals
Stamina and adaptability: the energy to sustain long hours of work and the flexibility orientation to adapt to changes in life and the organizational environment
Perceptual objectivity: ability to be relatively objective rather than limited by excessive subjectivity or personal biases
Positive regard: ability to express a positive belief in others
Managing group process: ability to stimulate others to work effectively in a group setting
Use of socializing power: use of influence to build alliances, networks or coalitions

Leadership cluster
Self-confidence: ability consistently to display decisiveness or presence
Conceptualization: use of concepts *de novo* to identify a pattern in an assortment of information
Logical thought: a thought process in which a person orders events in a causal sequence
Use of oral presentation: ability to make effective oral presentations to others

The identification of competences required to do a particular job (such as finance manager in the motor industry, or indeed consultant in the firm of Andersen Consulting) has become central to the way American companies recruit, appraise, train, reward and promote managers. This is apparent at industry level in the UK Management Charter Initiative that charts managers' competences in terms of key purpose (organizational objective), key role (managing people, managing finance, etc.), units of competence, elements of competence, and performance criteria and range indicators. Hence a key purpose such as 'to achieve the organization's objectives and continuously improve its performance' will be traced down to the individual's behavioural level, and performance will be judged on prescribed criteria. This approach has filtered down to lower organizational levels in the UK where employees in different job functions may demonstrate competences in prescribed areas and gain a National Vocational Qualification at different levels. For example, competences in retailing prescribed at level 2 (LCCIEB, 1993) require that at foundation level retail operatives are able to:

1 provide a service to the customer

2 contribute to the maintenance of health and safety in the retail workplace

3 contribute to good housekeeping routines

4 maintain relationships in the retail workplace

5 contribute to the security of the retail workplace

6 handle stock

7 process the sale

8 contribute to the communications within the organization

9 deal with returned goods and complaints

10 display and merchandise stock.

The emphasis is on reducing competences to operational and behavioural elements, in order to produce a detailed description of what is required of the employee in performing a particular job. Employees are therefore fitted into roles or positions (by selection) that have been designed to meet operational objectives, which ultimately serve the purpose of meeting strategic organizational goals. With this set of descriptions, organizations are then able to evaluate an individual's ability to acquire these particular sets of attributes, and reward employees on the basis of their using them to meet operational objectives. Individuals can also be trained in these competences where they have a deficiency. Thus selection, appraisal, reward, promotion and training systems can be linked into human resource management systems aimed at the achievement of organizational goals.

The use of the competences model is seductive, and it has been widely applied, not simply in domestic operations but for the identification of competences required by international managers and other key employees.

European and international competences

Much discussion in the early 1990s with the advent of the European common market integration in 1992 revolved around the issue of what makes an effective Euromanager. Much of the language used has been taken from the competences model. As part of this debate the *Financial Times* held a conference in London on 'Creating a Euro-workforce in the '90s'. The human resource directors of Ford of Europe and American Express offered a view of their own operations in Europe.

Ford operates in 15 different European countries. It has, over the last 20 years, developed the policy that managers who have a national responsibility also have a European responsibility, so that the director of engineering in Germany is also the executive responsible for coordinating the engineering of engine and transmission systems in the European R&D locations. This principle is established down to middle management level. Thus managers have learned to work in a European environment, taking account of different legal requirements, customs and practice, as well as working with cross-cultural teams. There is also the practice of assigning managers to work in different foreign locations: it is normal to find a senior British manager working in Cologne or a German working in Valencia. Business is conducted in the local language, but English is the language of the company. With growing globalism and the need to see its European managers as part of the 'global village', these practices within Europe are likely to be extended to the world arena. All of this means that the job of the international manager in Ford will be characterized by:

- accelerating change;
- increasing technical complexity of decision making;
- a need to exert influence and leadership in a participative manner rather than through the traditional command structure;
- learning from experience, implementing continuous improvement, and the need to take a systems view of the business rather than a narrow specialist or functional view.

Successful international managers will therefore be measured by their ability to anticipate change and master complexity and paradox.

American Express sees that it has globally oriented products that should be capable of delivery locally, and so must be locally relevant. In order to meet the challenges of a new Europe, they do not want to create a bureaucratic structure that ossifies their management talent. Instead they have set the following goals for organizational development:

- Create a refreshed and common vision and values across Europe.
- Optimize the organization and its resources both locally and internationally.
- Ensure continued excellence in people management.
- Consistently develop management talent.
- Enhance the international team by recruiting the best people.
- Provide the best employee relations environment.

In their international managers they are looking for the following competences:

- leadership skills: an ability to create business vision, direction and values which motivate others;
- the intellect, flexibility, courage and imagination to recognize and respond to the rapid pace of change;

- the cultivation of a broad knowledge of the history, culture, law and languages of Europe, and the ability to set aside nationalism and its prejudices and stereotypes;

- willingness to be a team member who can work in multinational project groups and be prepared to move to different countries and cultures.

In order to obtain a more general view of cross-border competences Ashridge Management College undertook a survey of nearly 50 American, British and Japanese international companies to determine which characteristics of international management they most valued (Barnham and Oates, 1991). This resulted in the following list of broad competences in order of perceived importance:

- strategic awareness

- adaptability in new situations

- sensitivity to different cultures

- ability to work in international teams

- language skills

- understanding international marketing

- relationship skills

- international negotiating skills

- self-reliance

- high task-orientation

- open, non-judgmental personality

- understanding of international finance

- awareness of own culture

There are, however, three problems in the straightforward acceptance of the relevance of international competences in selecting, rewarding and developing key employees: differences in the ways managers and other key employees are regarded in different countries; the different degrees of internationalization of international companies; and problems inherent within the competences model itself, both methodological and cultural.

The cultural regard for managers and their competences

Within a global marketplace, international managers must by necessity be in competition, in multinational companies, with their counterparts in Europe, North America and Japan and other areas, for top international jobs. However, Adler (1991) remarks that what is a relevant management attribute for reaching the top in one country may not be seen as relevant in another. Drawing on the research of Derr and Laurent (Derr, 1986; Laurent, 1986; Derr and Laurent, 1987), national differences can be identified as follows:

North Americans: must be seen to have ambition and drive within companies that value entrepreneurs;

French: must be labelled as high potential, and be able to manage power relationships and to work within an organizational system which is seen as a hierarchy of levels of power, depending on their place within it;

Germans: believe in creativity as essential for success, within an organization that is viewed as a coordinated network comprising individuals who make decisions based on their professional expertise;

British: must create the right image and get noticed; see interpersonal skills as important within the organization which is viewed as a network of relationships where things are achieved by influencing others by negotiation and communication.

So while, for example, German companies may highly value technical expertise and creativity, French and British companies may see managers with these qualities as pure technicians. Similarly, French and British companies may view the qualities of entrepreneurship valued by the North Americans, as highly disruptive.

For a manager pursuing a career internationally, this may have consequences for the way his or her potential for development is seen by particular companies in specific home bases. For the multinational company developing its managers across a number of countries, this may also have implications for the way they select top management talent and how they develop management potential within and between the various countries within which they operate.

Different degrees of internationalization of companies

Perhaps one of the strengths of the competences approach is that if integrated properly across the human resource functions it should actually reflect the operating strategy of the organization. The reason why particular competences are required of managers should translate into the operating and strategic requirements of the organization. The different operating practices and international personnel policies of multinational companies will therefore reflect on the regard for international management competences and the need to select and develop them. Perlmutter's (for example in Chakravarthy and Perlmutter, 1985) identification of four different policies of multinational companies has already been discussed:

Ethnocentric: executives from the home country are developed for the key positions in all countries where the multinational operates; such is the case with many Japanese multinationals.

Polycentric: executives from the local countries within which the multinational operates are developed for key positions in their own country.

Regiocentric: executives within a particular region are developed for posts anywhere in that region, for example in the case of companies positioned within the European Community. Gillette is one example of this approach.

Geocentric: the best people anywhere in the world are developed for key posts anywhere in the world, as in the case of IBM (see also Hodgetts and Luthans, 1991).

The fact that multinationals have different policies regarding the development and deployment of key managers has implications in itself for the way 'international' managers are selected and developed. This point is worth looking at in more depth using the example of Shell International.

T. W. Liardet, the then head of management resourcing and development of Shell International (Financial Times Conference: Creating a Euro-workforce in the 90's, London, 1990), outlined the benefits seen by the company of an international management development system as follows:

- to enable a balance and breadth of global management understanding at senior levels of management;
- to enable the development of managers in depth as well as in breadth;
- to gain top management involvement by ensuring that managers know the global resources of the organization;
- to test high potential managers by throwing them in at the deep end;
- to encourage a drive for change by developing new ideas;
- to facilitate a cultural and functional interchange in order to encourage managers to take a fresh look at problems and issues;
- to stimulate individuals' career development by providing challenges and encouraging 'rebirth';
- to promote and effect the cohesion of the organization: the corporate glue.

International management development is therefore seen as a natural process for managers aiming for top management. The process of international development described by Liardet in Shell consists of four stages:

First stage within the operating company: initial training and testing takes place, together with the development of professional expertise. There is inter-functional posting within the immediate operating company, and managers are ranked in terms of their performance and potential in the local pool of junior managers.

Second stage within the region: the higher-ranked staff from the local pool progress to this stage where they are posted within the region to facilitate their broadening. Professional development training is provided, and testing for management ability. Ranking of performance and potential is then undertaken within this wider, regional pool.

Third stage across regions and in central office locations: only the highest-ranked staff from the regional pool go through to this stage, where postings are inter-regional and in central offices, and professional and general management development is undertaken at group level. Ranking of performance and potential is here undertaken at full international level. Only then do the most outstanding individuals go through to the fourth stage.

Fourth stage at group level: general group management.

From a survey of international management by a research group at Ashridge Management College in England, Barnham and Oates (1991) report on an approach to international management development taken by the Hong Kong and Shanghai Banking Corporation. The fundamental approach to international development within a management career is different to that seen in Shell.

Hong Kong and Shanghai Banking Corporation (HSBC) has a dual career structure for its managers. It recruits graduates who specifically choose a career within their own country (resident officers) or who choose an international career (international officers). Both categories of management recruits undergo the same six-month executive development programme, with a combination of technical and interpersonal skills and the opportunity to develop cultural sensitivity and synergy. Drawing recruits from all over the world on the same programme, with as many as ten different nationalities living and working together during this initial six months, often provides contacts that last a working lifetime.

The training programme is divided into four stages. The first is an orientation and team-building process over a two-day seminar designed to develop cultural awareness. This provides the basis for understanding how cultural background shapes individuals' values, attitudes and behaviour, and the way people from other cultures perceive them. The second stage is a ten-day outdoor development course designed to build team skills, cultural understanding and synergy in situations that require trust, participation and interpersonal skills. This is held in the Hong Kong New Territories. The next stage is a one-week course in interpersonal skills development. The fourth stage is an international assignment in order for recruits to gain experience in a branch as well as working in a different culture, reinforcing the learning undertaken in the first three stages. The main aim of this is to develop cultural awareness and sensitivity.

So the approach of HSBC is to expose management trainees at an early stage in their career to cross-culture differences, which will stand them in good stead for the remainder of their careers, whether they are to work internationally or domestically. This contrasts to the approach of Shell, which is to provide a wider geographical exposure for managers as they progress up the career ladder.

Different competences are valued and different approaches to developing management competences are applied in different organizations, depending to a large extent on their view of international management and how this fits in with their overall international strategy and positioning.

Problems inherent within the competences model

Davison (in an unpublished paper cited in Jackson, 1993c) argues that the idea of 'competences' of international managers may not be sufficient to gain an understanding of the requirements for managing across cultures. She suggests that what is needed is an ability to: deal with frustrations, isolation, failure; and to learn how to network, gain support and anticipate differences. She adds that such qualities as 'helicopter view' (a famous competence invented by Shell), intuition and cultural sensitivity may be difficult to directly teach and acquire. So, are the qualities needed of international managers un-trainable 'traits'? However, Davison adds, interpersonal skills can be learned at the level of managing intercultural teams no matter what personality traits one possesses. This, together

71

with an understanding of oneself as well as the other person's culture, is something that can be developed.

To take this further, the following related *methodological* problems seem to be inherent within the concept of 'management competences' (Jackson, 1993b):

Firstly, there is little coherent theory or theories underpinning the competences concept. Rather, it is (or they are) pragmatically and/or empirically based. The competences approach is based on the construction of typologies derived from empirical work with little theoretical justification or explication of an underlying framework or paradigm. Such projects as the Management Charter Initiative in the UK or the American Management Association Competences Model, and the use of the competences approach for assessment centres and training seem to reinforce this practical-pragmatic-empirical orientation. There is therefore very little reflection on the validity of the whole approach, and in particular this makes it susceptible to problems of cross-cultural transfers.

Secondly, generic competences typologies suffer from stating the obvious and/or from imposing an externally conceived structure on performance in specific organizations that may be inappropriate. Conversely, specific competences lists that are generated internally (or by external consultants) may suffer from 'reinventing the wheel'. In either case they may add little to our understanding of how managers perform well.

It is perhaps meaningless to say that to be an effective manager you need to be able to communicate, or you need to make decisions. This does not really tell us anything about what makes a good manager in a particular organizational setting. The 'skills language' approach of Hirsh and Bevan (1988) does a lot to dispel criticism of this nature, as it looks at the interpretation of 'communication' or 'decision making', for example, in each organization.

Thirdly, the concept of competences is based on reductionist principles, that is, it tries to analyse complex human action by taking it apart. The whole is ignored in favour of the parts. The intuitive is rejected in favour of dissection and analysis of the components.

This is a major criticism levelled against the social skills approach, which was introduced above (pp. 63–64) as a forerunner to the competences movement. Singleton, Spurgeon and Stammers (1979) point out that this approach follows the traditional systematic approach to analysis, that is, studying something by taking it apart. They point particularly to the difficulty in doing this with complex social phenomena that are interconnected in an intricate way. Another aspect of this, they say, is knowing where to stop in this reduction process: knowing when you have reached the basic unit of analysis. The overall problem, though, is that with social phenomena we are dealing with wholes (gestalts) and to take these apart leads to loss of meaning. Polanyi (1966) uses an analogy of a police photofit, where we can choose from thousands of pieces of physiognomy to build up a picture of 'a face', but it is still not quite right, some inexplicable quality is missing. Pye (1991) notes that this is the same as with management competences.

The 'component-parts assembly' approach to management training, for example, is based on the assumption that we can build up an effective manager by assembling the parts. There will still be something missing! Pye (1991) suggests that this something may be 'intuitive judgement', which has materialized in data collected from managers by Pye as expressions such as 'fairness', 'sparkle', imagination' and 'feel'. Although it could conceivably be argued that this 'intuitive' feel could be added to our list of competences, it is none the less difficult to define conceptually, behaviourally and by outcome.

Fourthly, there is a tendency to assume a (causal) link between a set of attributes, behaviours and management results, whilst little is done to actually establish this link. This may be because it is difficult or impossible to establish. However, it is also difficult to determine what the end result should be in this link. Pye (1991: 113) adds that with management competences the problem seems to be that 'effective managing is known only by its performance and is evaluated against prior performance'. This follows Lombardo and McCall (1982: 62) who point out that 'effectiveness is a function of who defines it'. Performance is essentially relative and a matter of 'policy' within an organization. This is perhaps more complex than simply an organization determining a formal policy of what constitutes management performance. Often there is no such clear-cut policy, there is often no reference to objective measures of results in performance appraisal documents. Even if there were clear and operational policies, these would still be open to interpretation by individual 'stakeholders' within an organizational unit. The perceptions of what constitutes good performance by a manager may be subject to a number of perceptions which may coincide or not (the use of 360-degree appraisal systems might overcome some of these problems, but in the cultural context of some country operations peer and subordinate assessment may be wholly inappropriate). These perceptions may be based on experience, a 'gut feel', and have no definite objective base. Similarly, these judgements may not be subject to 'dissection', may not be taken apart for analysis, and put back together via a training programme to create an effective manager. In particular the above discussion regarding different national perceptions of what a manager is may make transfer of competences from one culture to the other very difficult.

Finally, the competences approach is static, relating 'what is' rather than describing a process. This final point is related to a 'snapshot' methodology inherent in it. This is an important criticism when applying competences to management development and selection methods that are based on lists of competences that were collected historically. It is true that you can add to the list such 'competences' as 'adaptability', 'ability to manage change' and 'flexibility', to allow for the fact that managers are working in a changing environment, but to what extent is this moving away from the real task of trying to find out what performance characteristics are required in the future as well as now?

When the basis of the competences approach is examined, it reveals *problems in the cross-cultural transfer* of the approach itself. These relate specifically to the distinction made in the Introduction to this book between *instrumental* approaches to conceptualizing and managing people in organizations, and *humanistic* approaches. The competences approach is firmly rooted in the instrumental paradigm. The needs and objectives of the organization are paramount. Strategic objectives are translated into operational objectives. Operational competences are then identified which relate to the achievement of operational objectives. Characteristics of high performers are then identified as attributes, which can normally be assessed in some way. The presence of competences is identified in individuals in terms of requirements for a job which are defined by a detailed job description and specification of what is required of the individual in that job.

These may be specified as individual objectives and targets. If they achieve objectives individuals may be rewarded. Individuals are selected on the basis of ability to demonstrate that they have the required competences for the job (or at least if they do not have these in their entirety, that they can at least be trained to meet the requirements of the job). Hence these competences are used as the basis for recruitment, development, reward and promotion (often organizations do not coordinate their various human resource management functions so efficiently, but this is the ideal).

By contrasting the American model of management and organization to the Japanese, some of the issues may be drawn out. Olie (1990) provides an example of American managers of a Japanese banking subsidiary in the United States who had great difficulty managing with no clearly stated and measurable performance targets from their Japanese top management. The Japanese bankers were frustrated that they could not communicate their philosophy of banking, the meaning of the business to them, their responsibilities towards the local communities and relations with customers and employees, and with competitors and the role of the bank in the world at large. They felt that if the American managers could absorb all of this then they would understand. Then they could themselves define what their objectives should be in any situation, and they would never have to be given a target.

After Thurley and Widenius (1989), contrasts between the American and the Japanese models of management can be identified (Table 3.2).

Table 3.2 American and Japanese models of management (after Thurley and Widenius, 1989)

American	Japanese
Task performance	Job rotation
Job definition	Generalist roles
Individualism	Collectivism
Human relations	Employee protection
Rational management	Rationalism
Strategic management	Pragmatism
Specialist know-how	Work-group innovation

Hence, American management theory is firmly built on the tenets of scientific management (Thurley and Widenius, 1989), using a systematic approach to improving task performance. An individualist approach allows classical management theory to define roles in terms of specific jobs and responsibilities, where managers are individuals with their own interests and personalities. In order to serve organizational goals group norms are fostered through a human relations approach. Change management requires a planned approach to changing structures and cultures. Organizations should define the business strategies required to achieve market position and design structures to fit these needs.

Japanese management emphasizes equality as the basis for competition and cooperation (Thurley and Widenius, 1989), basing its practice on collective responsibility (all members feel responsible for the organization). Individuals do not own their jobs, as they may have to do anything, needing training to perform a variety of jobs. In this spirit, employees should be trusted to get on with their jobs and should have their potential stimulated. Employees should be protected by the organization as they are vulnerable, and life careers should be planned. There is a recognition that everything changes and management should be pragmatic, and flexible enough to adapt to the new circumstances. Finally, the work ethic is connected with the individual's interaction with the work group. It is through the work group that employees gain their identity and associate their activity with the *michi*, or 'the way'.

These contextual 'rules' and cultures have implications for individuals' motives and objectives, and for their management behaviour. It also influences the way we see that behaviour. For example, it is difficult to speak of individual management competences in the Japanese collectivist context. Thurley and Widenius (1989) therefore characterize these differences between Japanese and American management theory and practice as: work security versus individual freedom; organizational loyalty versus job competence; consultation and involvement versus management authority; and work group innovation versus specialist know-how.

Conclusions following this discussion should not reject the use of competences in management selection and development, as obviously there are practical uses in conceptualizing the aspects of management that can be selected and developed. There are limitations, both conceptually and methodologically, not least of all in the lack of a theoretical underpinning, which has implications for such problems as establishing cause–effect relationships between managers' capabilities and management results. Other aspects – which are often not dealt with explicitly when considering management competences, and are fundamental to a discussion of management performance – are the ways managers perform (by cultural rules and stylistic interpretations of these rules) and why managers perform (the structure and processes of their motivation to perform).

Within this context of the competences approach, which has implications for selection, appraisal, training and development, and reward systems, we now focus on the selection of managers in an international situation, in the context of the American firm, Andersen Consulting.

Implications for managers: selection of managers and key staff

Andersen Consulting (Ackenhusen and Ghosal, 1992) has traditionally recruited young graduates and trained them rigorously in a uniform training programme initially at their training school, and then periodically (spending some 10 per cent of revenue on training). This ensured that all recruits were instilled in the Andersen way of doing things. By moving from an IT base to business integration, a need arose to integrate expertise in operations, strategy, technology and organization (particularly the management of change). This meant they had a need for specialization as well as general competences across the four areas. To a certain extent they could bring in people from other offices in other countries, utilizing specific expertise in a transnational manner. But this often led to conflicts with national operations. Also there were differences in national markets: for example, the French market was more clearly differentiated between IT consulting and management consulting. The corporate IT function in French corporations was seen as having a lower status than in the UK. The UK market in IT was prepared to pay higher prices than in France. This all led to differences in recruitment in France. IT consultants were not drawn from the *grandes écoles* but the business integration consultants were. In Britain, where the two markets were not differentiated, consultants were drawn from the top business schools. This in itself, with a need to develop more specialization, was different to the classical Andersen recruitment of first-degree holders. Even more so with the need to recruit specialists in the area of change management, experienced individuals were brought in. In the UK Andersen broke with its tradition of growing organically, and acquired a small manufacturing consulting company to enhance its skills base in operations. Such specialists did not want to go through the traditional initial six-week training programme. At the same time the generalists who were recruited and trained in the traditional way felt that the specialists did not know how to do things in the Andersen way, causing some mistrust. The 'mid-west' culture discouraged gurus or luminaries, and individual aggrandizement was disparaged.

The need to utilize people with different specializations in different parts of the world also led to recruitment of people willing and able to participate in international work, and be deployed to specific projects anywhere in the world.

The competences required to meet these various needs therefore became complex: generalists (Andersen traditionalist) versus specialists (not steeped in the Andersen way), national market (e.g. France) versus national market (e.g. UK), specialists national versus specialists transnational. Later, differential recruitment became more formalized, so that recruits entering Systems Integration were still young university graduates, and were put through the same rigorous six-week training programme at Andersen Consulting's 151-acre campus in St Charles, Illinois. Recruits to the Strategic Services division were obtained from the business schools, with an MBA and often with prior work or consultancy experience. Often, at a more senior level, consultants were recruited from competitor firms (Nanda and Yoshino, 1995). These different recruits were also more sharply differentiated by the different compensation levels in favour of strategic services consultants that Nanda and Yoshino report. Although sharing common human resource management philosophy and practices across the country practices, there was a growing awareness of country differences in decision and consultancy practices, if not competences. Increasingly Andersen Consultants have been organized on a matrix basis, with core competences in specific areas (strategy, change management, technology, process) being used across geographical and functional lines of business (Turpin and Hennessey 1999).

From the discussion in this chapter it should be apparent that the competences model, which is rooted in an instrumental paradigm of human resource management, is a useful tool for identifying the nature of 'human capital' required to fulfil the objectives of the organization. This suffers problems when an organization goes international. Firstly, those competences that were adequate in the domestic context may no longer be adequate. From a discussion of the requirements of managers in the European Union at the beginning of the 1990s, it can be seen that different types of requirement involving cultural fluency across borders become necessary. Being able to identify individuals who can meet the requirements to work across cultures may be problematic, as Andersen Consulting found out: this disrupted domestic operations and somewhat confounded the idea of a transnational organization. In addition, not only must international competences be identified, but different competences in different countries may be required, as the work of Derr and Laurent (Derr, 1986; Laurent, 1986; Derr and Laurent, 1987) pointed out, and as the experience of Andersen's operations in France identified. If we follow through the logic of their research findings, the antitheses between selecting and developing generalists versus specialists may alter from country to country, where key employees in Germany may be recruited for their specialist technical skills, and in Britain for their general managerial skills.

Within the logic of an instrumental paradigm, the competences approach may be problematic, as we noted above. The 'photofit' approach to selection/ development may miss out vital components (a person's integrity for example is difficult to measure), especially when working across cultures, as Davison has pointed out. The cause–effect problem may also be an issue, and establishing predictive validity for even sophisticated selection processes such as assessment centres can be problematic.

When companies venture outside an individualistic/achievement culture, emphasis on reward based on the use of competences (e.g. in the case of MBO in France cited by Hofstede, 1980b), and indeed the importance of systematically breaking down job functions into required competences, may no longer be relevant. This may have become an art form in Britain (e.g. the Management Charter Initiative) but is largely absent from the thinking of such companies as IKEA. The competences approach seems symptomatic of the American emphasis on the bottom-line and the achievement of results leading to the standardized ranking of individuals (Gannon and Associates, 1994) of the quick fix approach (e.g. The 'one-minute manager' of Kenneth Blanchard, [e.g. Blanchard and Johnson, 2000]) and of the excellence movement (e.g. Peters and Waterman, 1982).

When companies venture outside cultures that place an emphasis on instrumental views of people in organizations, the concept of individual competences seems illogical. If the logic is to ensure best fit of individuals to particular job roles, what happens when the roles are fluid and fit around the development needs of individuals and team, such as in Japanese management (e.g. Whitehill, 1991)? Different approaches may therefore be necessary when operating in countries that may have a more humanistic view of people in organizations, as may be the case in Africa, Asia and Latin America.

Questions for managers

1 How can Andersen Consulting develop and integrate the range of competences it requires for its international operations?

2 What are the competences and capabilities required of new recruits to Andersen Consulting, given the need to maintain its strong corporate culture and ways of doing things?

3 How relevant is the competences approach for Andersen Consulting working outside Anglo-Saxon cultures?

4 What are the alternatives to the competences approach?

An agenda for research

Simplistically, it would be easy to say that the future research agenda in the area of competences would be to investigate more fully differences in management competences among different cultures. The work of Derr (1986), Laurent (1986) and Derr and Laurent (1987) points in this direction in identifying those characteristics of managers that companies from different countries favour. Perhaps a more challenging research agenda is to investigate the uses, misuses, and absence of this approach in different countries. So far there has been little systematic research on this, despite there being many comparative studies on human resource management practices in different countries. Although Nordhaug (1998) firmly places the conceptual foundation of the competences approach in human-capital theory, he does little to break out of this paradigm in suggesting a classificatory framework for research, other than to address the shortcomings of task-specific competences by introducing firm-specific competences to allow for more adaptability and flexibility, and to cope with the issue of changing needs and redundant competences. This provides a notion of organizational competences. Although this may be moving over to a macro-view, and have similarities to the more holistic approach discernible in Japanese management systems, it may still be missing the point. The relationship among cultural values (e.g. individualism–collectivism, masculinity–femininity, universalism–particularism), cognitive systems (e.g. instrumental–humanistic perceptions of human value) and relationship between job and employee as manifested in selection and development practices needs to be investigated. Hence, it may be proposed that:

- in cultures that are individualistic (propensity to reward individual performance: Hofstede, 1980b), masculine (propensity to emphasize performance and results: Hofstede, 1980b), and universalistic (propensity to employ strangers based on a pre-defined set of rules: Trompenaars, 1993) it is more likely that managers will perceive individuals in an instrumental way (as a means to the ends of organization: Jackson, 1999), and therefore develop systematic means of fitting the individual to the job (competences approach);

- in cultures that are collectivistic (propensity to value group performance, and reward conformance to the group: Hofstede, 1980b), feminine (propensity to emphasize nurturing and social values: Hofstede, 1980b), and particularistic (propensity to employ people from in-group such as family, who are known and upon whom group pressure can be exerted: Trompenaars, 1993), it is more likely that managers will perceive individuals in a humanistic way (as having a value in their own right and as group members: Jackson, 1999), and therefore develop ways of fitting the job around the individual as part of a group, and developing them within it.

Perhaps more interesting (and more challenging) is to investigate the tensions created by the antithesis of the two approaches when they come together through, for example, Western acquisitions in emerging countries. We have already seen the tensions created in two relatively culturally close countries (Sweden and USA), where IKEA did not systematically identify competences, and performance related to this. Research on these issues will enhance the ability of managers working across cultures to manage people in other cultures more effectively, or at least to understand to what extent the competences approach may be useful, needing to be adapted or modified, or needing to be rethought altogether.

Questions for researchers

1 What is the relationship between national culture and the use of the competences approach?

2 What different concepts and approaches are used in countries with dissimilar cultures?

3 How prevalent is the competences approach, and what is its perceived relevance in different countries?

4 How do management competences required for managers by companies vary across different countries?

The missionary organization: the Dutch model

chapter four

The Dutch model: the missionary spirit

The Netherlands is better known for its exploits outside its borders than within them. In historical times it was recognized for its foreign policies: Europe's leading trading nation (with England as its chief commercial rival), a navy four times the size of that of England in 1650, and its growth as a major colonial power, particularly after the decline of Spanish and Portuguese competition after 1588. The Dutch East India Company was founded in 1602, and from this grew a rich and worldwide commercial empire. In the same year the world's first stock exchange was established in Amsterdam. With the spread of Dutch commercial influence in the world it is not surprising that Dutch missionary work followed hard on its heels. Not only was the Dutch Reformed Church active in this respect, but the person chosen to head the newly formed London Missionary Society's first mission in South Africa in 1794, and one of this country's eminent missionaries, was a Dutchman, Johannes van der Kemp (Mostert, 1992). It is perhaps no accident that one of the most prominent international cross-cultural academics, Geert Hofstede, is Dutch; one of the best known international cross-cultural consultants, Fons Trompenaars, is Dutch (and also French), and that the missionary spirit is also alive and well in one of the world's renowned international organizations, Royal Dutch/Shell. Not only has the Netherlands been a major force in going out into the world, it has also developed a receptive attitude to immigration and a tolerance of difference in a society composed of different strands in such areas as religion, race and lifestyles.

The Netherlands is largely ignored in the comparative literature on management and human resources. Garrison and Verveen's (1994) study is an exception. Although one of the smallest European countries, it has considerable economic strength built on its industrial achievements as well as its position as a major trading nation (reported to be ranked sixth in the world in the 1992 World Competitive Report). It has strong social legislation and labour law. Some companies operating in the Netherlands have seen this as uncompetitive and have shifted some operations to other countries, again reinforcing a trend towards internationalization.

Hofstede's (1980a) cultural dimensions depict the Netherlands as medium to low in uncertainty avoidance, high in individualism and fairly low in power distance. Perhaps what distinguishes the culture and groups it with the Scandinavian cultures is its high femininity: its unassuming, low-profile organizational culture.

The objective of this chapter is to examine expatriation in the context of the strategic positioning of international enterprises and the careers of international personnel. It is difficult to say that Shell is a typical Dutch company, but it may be possible to propose that its rationale and *modus operandi* are within the Dutch missionary spirit. This international company provides the real context for exploring the many aspects and issues of expatriation.

An American company in the Netherlands

One of the few case studies to depict the problems of an American company operating in the Netherlands is the company called 'Manners Europe' (DiStefano, 1992), a 'do-it-yourself' retail company that found discrepancies between the achievement and production orientation in the United States and the Netherlands. This was reflected in the operation of an MBO system tied to compensation. Apart from the incremental tax system operating in Netherlands, which the Americans felt went against incentivizing people, there was a perception that the Dutch had a different view of compensation. This view was articulated as an assumption that everyone gives 100 per cent of his or her effort all the time. Therefore they should be paid 100 per cent as a normal exchange, and not given a bonus. The company also had sales staff refuse commission arrangements to work for less on a non-incentive basis.

DiStefano (1992) also tells of an incident with two accountants in the company, one in his late teens who produced five times the work of the other: an older man in his late twenties with family responsibilities. When the Dutch chief accountant and director of administration recommended a greater increase for the older person in the salary review, the American director of finance refused to give it, as the older man was considered a poor performer and refused to work overtime (DiStefano notes a general problem in obtaining employees' commitment to work overtime when it was necessary: the Dutch staff seemed to be putting their family and social lives first). The older accountant questioned the raise that was given to the younger person who was considered a high performer, saying he did not need the raise, as he was single. The American management concluded that the principles the Dutch were applying – that education, age, marital status and financial need should have more of an influence on salary level – contradicted the American principle that people should be rewarded after demonstrating their accomplishments.

These examples seem to reflect a higher ascription versus achievement orientation in Trompenaars' (1993) terms when comparing Dutch management culture with American culture. American management culture (see Chapter 3) stresses status and reward based on achievement. A more ascriptive culture will base reward and status on who you are and where you come from, your educational diplomas, and seniority in the organization (see also the Japanese model in Chapter 5). These examples may also reflect a higher level of femininity in Hofstede's terms for the Dutch personnel, for whom work does not have such a high centrality as it does for their American counterparts, for whom family and outside-the-work situation is important, and high achievement is not such a priority. Different cultures respond differently to the relationship (and often contradiction) between the world of work and the world outside work, as was discussed in the Introduction. Some cultures blend the two, yet in different ways: American culture in terms of a contractual relationship with high priority given to achievement in work, in respect not just of monetary reward, but also of status within society (Chapter 3); Japanese culture in terms of capturing the wider collectivist societal culture in corporate obligatory relationships, again making work central, but blending it more completely with life outside work. The Dutch approach may be similar to the Swedish discussed in Chapter 1, which ensures that a lower position is given to the world of work, and where shows of high achievement are frowned upon; in a way, this forms a protection (overtly, in good social security arrangements) against work life encroaching too heavily on the 'real' world of social and family life.

Yet there does not seem to be a contradiction between a more 'feminine' (Hofstede, 1980a) attitude towards the world of work, and a highly enterprising and successful (in both economic and social terms as was seen above) society, and one which seems to have worked actively to encourage the missionary spirit, and enterprise outside its borders.

Royal Dutch/Shell

Shell is an unusual company. Whether or not it is a typical 'Dutch' company is difficult to say. This is because it is both Dutch and British, and possibly just a bit American. It is a product of an alliance between the Royal Dutch Petroleum Company of the Netherlands and Shell Transport and Trading Company of Britain formed in 1907. The two parent companies have retained their legal identities, so that shareholders do not have shares in 'Shell' but in either one or the other of the companies. These two listed companies own the stock of three group holding companies in a ratio of 60 per cent by the Dutch and 40 per cent by the British. The holding companies are Shell Petroleum Company Ltd (UK), Shell Petroleum NV (The Netherlands) and Shell Petroleum Inc. (USA). The group holding companies own controlling shares in about 270 operating companies in 130 countries, and interests in another 1,500 companies worldwide (Hendry, 2000).

Shell forms one of the world's largest multinational companies, with over 100,000 staff and a total asset value of $110,068 million. Its two central offices are in London and The Hague (Mahieu, 2001). Its traditional operating structure has been a functional/regional matrix devised by McKinsey in the 1950s. This was replaced by a simpler functional structure in 1996, which was intended to focus more on core activities and to speed up decision making. Throughout the 1990s the operating companies enjoyed much autonomy, with the head office providing long-range strategy and career management functions (Hendry, 2000).

Mahieu (2001) argues that the business environment in which Shell has always operated has shaped the approach to developing managers. It has been characterized by a growing demand for energy that has fuelled economic growth. Business ventures in this industry are long term oriented. They favour capital-intensive, large-scale undertakings, which are global in scope. High-calibre professional people at ground level manage them. Hence a global outlook, a long-term orientation and a notion of a career-long employment and development of expatriates and local staff have become the main characteristics of Shell's approach.

Shell has always taken people in from university, and 'grown their own timber' by providing technical, professional and management development opportunities. This has involved moving people through the organization every few years, and providing them with assignments of increasing complexity and scope to test their general management and leadership capacities. This basic philosophy still exists, but Shell also recruits more senior people directly into the company. At all levels, it is understood that people are moved to a new position and new challenge after a few years, to create a 'flux culture' and conditions under which people are expected to grow (Mahieu, 2001).

The first two assignments for people joining from university would be designed to provide a grounding and develop a professional competence in a particular functional discipline. This would then be expanded across cultural boundaries for high potential people. Shell has maintained an expatriate staff of some 5,000–6,000. This has offered a great many learning opportunities for the staff involved, as well as transferring knowledge across the group. Following the foundation of professional expertise, this would be supplemented by cross-functional experience to broaden perspectives, with a view to reaching a person's ultimate potential by the age of 50.

Throughout the organization Shell has used a set of common criteria for job evaluation and grading, and to identify the strengths and weaknesses of people. This was encapsulated in a common set of broad competences: 'helicopter', 'power of analysis', 'imagination', 'sense of reality', and 'leadership effectiveness'. 'Helicopter' is a now-famous Shell competence that was introduced into the company by Professor van Lennep of the University of Utrecht and incorporated into an appraisal framework by a Shell executive, M. Muller. It was described as 'the ability to look at problems from a high vantage point and shape the work accordingly on the basis of a personal vision as well as the urge and the ability to place facts and problems within the broader context, by immediately detecting relevant relationships with systems of wider scope' (reported by Mahieu, 2001). Staff appraisal was based on these broad competences, forming an estimate of a person's potential. This was expressed as a job level that they were expected to reach towards the end of their career. Yet there was flexibility that allowed the ordering of the importance of these different broad competences to differ between countries. So, 'reality' was valued highest in the Netherlands, 'imagination' in France, 'leadership' in Germany, and 'helicopter' in Britain (see Trompenaars, 1993: 175).

Decisions about the allocation of assignments were taken by assessing a person's potential and development needs, in relation to the needs of the organization. Competences needed to fulfil an assignment were assessed in relation to the people available. Promotion guidelines were used to determine how long someone should stay in their current job, and when it was time to move on. Analysis was used to predict people's development and movement over time (supply) and compare this with the number of jobs at different levels that would become available (demand). This was used to inform recruitment and resourcing decisions.

This approach based on the use of potential, promotion guidelines and supply and demand analysis worked well for Shell, a company which was able to focus on the long term, where the demand for talent was based on a fairly stable situation, and which had a relatively closed system of staffing, employing people directly from university and growing them internally until they reached their ultimate potential. However, towards the mid-1990s circumstances and thinking were beginning to change.

Why expatriation? A strategic perspective

Here, the various issues of expatriation are reviewed, in order to look more closely at the problems and perspectives that they raise. The analogy of the missionary has been used because quite often, like the missionary, the expatriate goes abroad in order to fulfil the needs of the parent organization to introduce methods of working, new technology or marketing methods, and sometimes to propagate corporate culture (the way we do things around here), as was seen in IKEA and to an extent also in Shell. Like the missionary, the expatriate is preaching a message. When this message is taken directly from the home country and implanted in the host country, management techniques and methods may result which are inappropriate to the host culture. The problems of this occurring, and why it might occur have been discussed already in Chapters 1 (the multicultural model) and 3 (the American model). Like the message of the missionary, this may well address a problem of the human condition (e.g. in the corporate world, the need for higher productivity) and may be sought avidly, but its subsequent adoption may be inappropriate. Adapting principles to the local conditions may be one way of doing things, as with Shell's broad competences, but the cultural values on which principles are based may be quite different, as in the case of Manners Europe.

The reasons for expatriation

Expatriation can be looked at as a way of fulfilling the strategic requirements of the organization; as part of the career planning process of the company; and as meeting the needs of individuals in their career aspiration.

Fulfilling the strategic needs of the organization These strategic considerations were examined in Chapter 2, by reference to Perlmutter's and others' models of international strategy. Hence, within ethnocentric organizations expatriates from the parent company manage subsidiaries. This may be regarded as the highest level of missionary work (taking the message to the subsidiary) and often occurs at the early stages in the development of international organization, although IKEA displays many features of this. It is often a good place to be from the perspective of an individual who wishes to pursue an expatriate career: but only within the home company and not the host country. In the polycentric organizations locals manage subsidiaries. Hence there are few expatriate assignments. Although this may help to facilitate political integration and acceptability of the company in the host country, it provides a low control for the home company and is a poor environment in which to build an expatriate career. Crédit Lyonnais, discussed in Chapter 2, exhibits many features of this approach. A regiocentric organization provides good opportunities for expatriate careers within a specific region such as Europe and like the geocentric organization is staffed without regard to the expatriates' nationalities. Shell may well be a good example of a geocentric approach.

Being part of the career planning process of the company Career planning is important to both manager and key employee and to the organization for which they work, for the following reasons (Jackson, 1993c):

- *Employee loyalty*: if an organization has a good career programme, then good and ambitious employees can be retained.

- *Avoiding future shock*: an organization should be prepared for the future; there is a need for both individuals and the organization as a whole to 'learn to learn'. This is all part of a good career programme.

- *Performance motivation*: knowing the context of your job is a good motivator. Even though the current job may be uninteresting to you in its own right, a planned career puts it into perspective.

- *Integrating objectives*: a good career programme should integrate the needs and objectives of the organization in its future development, with the needs and aspirations of individuals. Often if the two sets of objectives do not meet, then the individual may leave for another organization which better matches his or her aspirations, or if the organization retains large numbers of individuals working at variance with the organization's objectives, this may have a negative effect on organizational performance.

Meeting individuals' career aspirations Not only do managers as individuals have a responsibility for their own career development, they also have a key role to play in the organization in respect of other people's careers. Managers and key employees (undoubtedly in an individualist, but not necessarily in a collectivist culture: see discussion below) therefore should:

- include career development within the performance appraisal and review process: to develop people a manager needs to unify the person's career path, their current job, performance appraisal and the feedback they provide;

- facilitate job experience and training to fulfil an individual's career plan: this encourages motivation as well as developing the individual and the organization for the future.

Yet although expatriation may be a factor of the strategic arrangements of internationalization and career planning within the organization, much of the literature suggests that expatriation is not straightforward.

Is expatriation problematic?

Hiltrop and Janssens (1990) assert that the demand for expatriates is increasing as a result of a rapid growth of multinational companies and international joint ventures, and as expatriates meet the needs of the parent company to implement corporate strategy or supply a skill or knowledge which is not available locally. However, expatriates are expensive to employ as the cost of additional allowances and redeployment increases the base salary by 25–100 per cent. In addition, expatriate assignments present expatriates and their families with a number of difficulties and challenges. The causes of these problems of transfer anxiety, culture shock, social dislocation, adaptation, and feelings of abandonment often may be traced to a combination of cultural, political, economic and legal differences.

Hiltrop and Janssens also assert that failure rates are high. This is a typical claim within the literature, and this particular work can perhaps be used as an example. They point to a study of Swedish expatriates numbering 639 in 26 different countries. This showed that 25 per cent returned home before the end of the assignment, giving cultural adaptation problems as the highest reason, sometimes manifested in traumatic reactions such as insomnia. They also suggest that US studies have shown even higher failure rates, with 50 per cent not completing assignments in 'developed' countries and up to 70 per cent not completing in 'developing' countries. This of course adds to the expense of expatriation, as premature repatriation is costly both to the company and to the expatriate. This is mainly as a result of the wastage of relocation and training expenses already paid (at the time of writing some US$55,000–100,000 per expatriate). The psychological costs of failure, as well as possible cost to career progression, may also be substantial to the expatriate.

Harzing (1995), another Dutch academic, challenges this widely accepted wisdom. She states that there is no empirical foundation for the existence of high failure rates when measured as premature re-entry. This is a persistent myth which seems to be founded on a massive misquotation in the literature of three articles, only one of which shows empirical evidence of expatriate failure rates, and this evidence shows them to be rather low (Tung, 1981). She also posits that rather than premature re-entry being a measure of failure, it may be that that those who stay on in their assignments and perform inadequately are more damaging to their organization. At the personal level, failure might be more pronounced for the expatriate returning home after a seemly successful assignment, but having much larger problems readjusting to the home organization and the home culture.

Hiltrop and Janssens' (1990) article refers to Desatnick and Bennett (1978) who, although stating those high figures for American expatriates, do not substantiate them in any way, and do not give their source. Hiltrop and Janssens refer to a Swedish study by Torbiörn (1982), which does appear to be a legitimate study, but is only one study referring only to Swedish expatriates, and is not widely quoted in the literature. Harzing's (1995) view is that these references do not provide the grounds for assuming a high failure rate. Indeed, Tung's (1981) study indicates that American expatriate recall rates are higher than European and Japanese rates: 76 per cent of the American multinationals had recall rates above 10; but only 3 per cent of European firms and 14 per cent of Japanese multinationals. In fact, Harzing remarks, very few companies in Tung's study had recall rates of more than 20 per cent.

To this Harzing (1995) adds that over the years companies should have learned from their mistakes and should now have recall rates considerably lower than this. In the absence of any substantial empirical research on this, Brewster's study of 25 Western European companies in 1988 showed that 72 per cent had failure rates of less than 5 per cent (cited in Brewster, 1991). Hamill's (1989) study of seven British firms indicated expatriate failure at less than 5 per cent, and Scullion's (1991) survey of 40 British and five Irish companies found only 10 per cent had failure rates above 5 per cent. This is an area that needs far more empirical investigation.

Choosing expatriates

In order to make sure that expatriates' assignments are as successful as possible, companies need a means of selecting people who are likely to succeed. There is evidence that at least Anglo-Saxon companies rely heavily on the competences approach (see also Chapter 3) to select people, although as in the case of Shell, selection may be from a pool of previously identified 'high-flyers'. Phatak (1992) lists nine skills that (presumably American) companies look for when selecting their international managers:

- *technical ability*: the ability to do the job is of course a prerequisite;
- *managerial skills*: those skills which are associated with being an effective manager are important;
- *cultural empathy*: sensitivity to other cultures and a non-judgmental understanding of other cultures is probably essential;
- *adaptability and flexibility*: this includes the ability to integrate with other people and other cultures and different types of business operations; being adaptable to change; having the ability to solve problems within different frameworks; sensitivity to differences in different cultural situations; and flexibility to manage a continuous operation despite gaps in information and assistance;
- *diplomatic skills*: an ability to deal with others, negotiate and to represent the parent company on foreign assignment; this may even involve interaction with politicians and government officials in some developing countries;
- *language aptitude*: the ability to learn a language quickly is a useful attribute;
- *personal motives*: a positive reason for wanting to take on foreign assignments;
- *emotional stability and maturity*: this involves having the staying power and emotional maturity to maintain equilibrium in a foreign environment as well as being non-judgmental in relationships with others;
- *adaptability of family*: this factor is crucial to the success of a foreign assignment, because if the family get homesick or they simply are unhappy in the foreign environment, this may lead to low performance and other problems for the international manager.

Similar factors are outlined by Dowling and Schuler (1990) as follows:

- *Job factors*:
  - technical ability
  - managerial skills

- administrative abilities
- knowledge of host country and headquarters operations

- *Relational dimensions*:
  - tolerance of ambiguity
  - behaviour flexibility
  - being non-judgmental
  - cultural empathy and low ethnocentrism
  - interpersonal skills

- *Motivation*:
  - belief in the mission
  - congruence with career plan
  - interest in overseas experience
  - interest in the specific host country
  - willingness to learn new attitudes and behaviour patterns

- *Family situation*:
  - spouse willing to live abroad
  - adaptive and supportive spouse
  - stable marriage

- *Language skills*:
  - knowledge of host country language
  - understanding of non-verbal communication

Yet Deller (1997) decries the overuse and over-quoting of lists such as this. Often their construction is based on impressionistic criteria. The extent to which these selection criteria can be generalized to other cultures is much under-researched and is normally not considered in otherwise perfectly competent critiques and studies such as Deller's. The extent to which East Asian, South Asian or African companies, for example, use these or different sets of criteria in selecting expatriate staff, and the alternative approaches used other than a competences-based one, still need to be investigated.

Acculturation

Once selected, the level of acculturation in the foreign assignment may well determine the level of success of expatriates. Mendenhall and Oddou (1985) point to four dimensions that relate to successful expatriate acculturation: self-oriented dimension, other-oriented dimension, perceptual dimension and cultural toughness dimension.

Self-oriented dimension This relates to those activities that serve to strengthen self-esteem, self-confidence and mental hygiene. The dimension contains three sub-factors:

- reinforcement substitution: replacing activities which bring pleasure and happiness in the home culture with similar but different activities in the host culture (e.g. art, sport, cuisine, music), that is, learning to enjoy a parallel activity in the host culture;

- stress reduction: managing stress through adaptation and creating 'stability zones' (e.g. through meditation, writing a diary, pastimes, religion) which can be retreated to, in order to develop a rhythm of engagement with the host culture and withdrawal from it;

- technical competence: being able to accomplish the objectives of the assignment by employing technical abilities for the job.

Others-oriented dimension This relates to activities and attributes which enhance the expatriate's ability to interact effectively with host nationals. This dimension contains two sub-factors:

- relationship development: the ability to develop long-lasting friendships (e.g. mentor relatonships);

- willingness to communicate: including the willingness to use the host language (rather than fluency in the language), and involving observation, listening, experimentation and risk taking, and active participation.

Perceptual dimension This relates to the ability to understand why foreigners behave the way they do. It involves being non-judgmental and non-evaluative. While not reflected in classic competences, it may be possible to provide training to develop people's awareness.

Cultural toughness dimension This is based on the assumption that some cultures are more difficult to adapt to as they are more different than other cultures from one's own.

Tung (1981) proposes a selection-decision process that includes variables in the nature of the assignment of task or relationship emphasis, and in the difference or similarity between the host culture and the home culture. Hence, if the two cultures are highly diverse, and there is an emphasis on relationship variables (for example a customer focused job), then a highly rigorous orientation process will be necessary. If the two cultures are quite similar, and the emphasis is on task variables (for example a highly technical job), then a less rigorous orientation process is sufficient.

Although there may be a case for cultural-specific training, addressing the dimensions identified by Mendenhall and Oddou (1985), and the variables of Tung (1981) may be part of a cultural-general approach to development that equips managers and key staff to be flexible across cultures. Alternatively, this process may be seen as simply part of the management learning and development process where expatriation is not seen as an add-on, but as an integral part of developing effective managers, as seems to be the case in Shell (Mahieu, 2001) but not necessarily in a company like Crédit Lyonnais (see Chapter 2).

Why expatriation? The career perspective

International career planning is relevant not only to the organization, but also to the individual. Stewart (1986) describes career-planning strategies as akin to drawing road maps:

- career goals: the starting point is deciding where you want to go;

- career path planning: secondly, you have to decide how you want to get there, as there are alternative routes;

- training and job experience: you need to acquire the skills and knowledge to get where you want to go, and for when you get there;

- ongoing assessment: at any one time you need to know how far you have come, how far to go, and what else you will need to get there.

Of course, people adopt different strategies and career patterns based on a number of assumptions, some of which are derived from their cultural background. We can outline three different possibilities:

- *Chance*: you may rely on pure chance to provide the right job at the right time. The degree to which events are left to chance or fate may vary from one culture to another, for example between 'developed' and 'developing' countries (Jaeger and Kanungo, 1990).

- *The company will take care of your career*: In this type of strategy you rely on the organization to provide the right opportunities. This can work in a paternalistic company. For example, a belief that the company will provide may be implicit in a Japanese company. To use this strategy in a Western paternalistic company, perhaps you need to be able to 'sell yourself' within the company, to make sure that you are noticed!

- *Self-designed*: This is considered the ideal in the more individualistic cultures of North America and Western Europe. Following this type of strategy, you are more likely to be motivated and a high performer. You will have a clear idea of your personal goals, skills and motivation. You will also know how to prepare for the next step in your career and will be able to balance the personal costs and benefits involved.

Specific studies relate to why expatriates choose or do not choose international assignments. Adler (1991) surveyed 1,129 MBA students in business schools in the United States, Canada and Europe in order to determine reasons why they would accept international assignments, and why they would not (Table 4.1)

However, the career choices that a person makes may be influenced by cultural factors.

Table 4.1 Reasons for choosing international assignments (Adler, 1991)

Reasons for accepting international assignment	Reasons for not accepting international assignment
The cross-cultural experiences, seeing other cultures, learning new languages (52.2 per cent)	Location unsuitable 'uncivilized', dangerous or hostile, politically unstable (58.5 per cent)
A more interesting job with more responsibilities, more status or autonomy (40.2 per cent)	Unsatisfactory job, boring, high risk of failure, isolation from home company (34.6 per cent)
Higher salary (27.7 per cent)	Problems with family or spouse such as dual career, spouse unwilling to move
Career advancement (20.7 per cent)	(33.4 per cent)
Good location, climate, politically stable, good social life (15.9 per cent)	Inadequate salary package (22.9 per cent)
	Unwilling to make new life abroad, and to learn new languages or adapt to culture
A more satisfying life, with more freedom, fun, excitement, more variety and higher quality life (10.9 per cent))	(19.4 per cent)
	Unwilling to disrupt home country life (13.8 per cent)
Good situation for spouse or family (3.5 per cent)	Contract too long (5.8 per cent)
Short-term assignment (2.6 per cent)	

Cultural factors in international career choice

A number of cultural factors influence both the type of career strategy adopted, and the type of career pursued. Hofstede's (1980a) dimensions of national cultural values, power distance, individualism/collectivism, masculinity/femininity and uncertainty avoidance, were outlined in Chapter 1. Hofstede (1991) addresses specifically the implications of masculinity/femininity and of uncertainty avoidance on career choice, and assumptions can be made about the possible implications of the other dimensions.

Uncertainty avoidance

The main correlated factors of the uncertainty avoidance construct in Hofstede's research in IBM in over 50 different countries were as follows:

• job stress

• adherence to organizational rules

• a preference for a long-term career in the organization

It would seem that the higher a national culture is on the uncertainty avoidance index, the more people wish to reduce uncertainty in their life by maintaining a long-term career in the same company. It is more likely that more employees will wish to stay with one company throughout their careers in such high uncertainty avoidance countries as Greece, Portugal, Belgium, Japan and France than in low uncertainty avoidance countries such as Canada, the USA, India, Great Britain, Ireland or Denmark. Certainly for France, this coincides with what Barsoux and Lawrence (1990: 61) find with respect to management careers:

> The notion of career strategy seems fairly weak in France. The managers [we] interviewed tended to be vague about what they hoped to achieve by what age. No doubt this has something to do with a certain reticence to 'count one's chickens' or to appear overtly ambitious . . . The few who did reveal specific goals and timescales had to be prompted to do so. It could be posited that this toned-down view of careerism is related to the rather predictable nature of career progression – and the fact that one's education holds sway over all other possible variables.

It seems that once on the company career ladder (which is largely determined by your higher education qualification: perhaps a function of power distance, which we will discuss later), the strategy of letting your company take care of your career is a fairly typical one.

Collectivism/individualism

The concept of performance appraisal and career planning outlined above may be anathema in a highly collectivist society. Hofstede (1991: 66) comments:

> In a collectivist society discussing a person's performance openly with him or her is likely to clash head-on with the society's harmony norms and may be felt by the subordinate as an unacceptable loss of face.

It is not likely, therefore, that career planning can be discussed openly in terms of the employee's strengths and weaknesses. Certainly, bad news such as news of an employee's poor performance would be communicated via an intermediary or through the indirect method of withdrawing a routine favour in such collectivist societies as China, Malaysia, Thailand or Japan.

The 'work goals' shown in Table 4.2 were identified in Hofstede's analysis of collectivism/individual.

Table 4.2 Work goals in collectivist and individualistic societies (Hofstede, 1991)

Individualism	Collectivism
Having time to spend on personal life	Having training opportunities
Having the freedom to develop your own approach to your job	Having good physical working conditions
Having challenging work to do, to obtain personal sense of achievement	Fully using skills and abilities in the job

On the individualism side are inherently individual values of personal life and freedom, and on the collectivism side are things that the organization does for employees such as providing suitable conditions and opportunities. This must not only influence the types of career 'choice' available to individuals from opposites sides of this dimension, but also influence attitudes towards career planning and career mobility.

Another aspect of a collectivist culture which has a bearing on career choice is the fact that employers do not employ individuals, but members of an 'in-group'. It may be that employees who are not members of the in-group will not have a career in a company. People are expected to act according to the interests of their in-group, and this logically assumes that out-groups exist which do not show allegiance to your in-group, and therefore are not to be trusted as loyal employees.

In an individualistic society such as the USA or UK, the employment contract is seen in commercial terms where it is possible in the interests of the individual's career or finances to break off a relationship with one employer and go to another. However, in a collectivist society such as Japan an employment relationship often involves family connections, and is characterized by mutual obligation of protection by the employer and loyalty by the employee. A 'career' is not then regarded in the same way in these two types of cultures.

Power distance

It has already been mentioned, in connection with high uncertainty avoidance, that in France your career is often taken care of if you have the necessary academic qualifications. It may be assumed that education distinguishes rank in many French companies as an indicator of power distance. France is a high power distance society according to Hofstede's (1991) research. However, education is only one factor in the way in which power is distributed in such cultures. According to Barsoux and Lawrence (1990) this factor is important in France. The money your family has, your family background, class and caste may all distinguish different hierarchical levels in both organizations and the society as a whole.

Not having access to the career ladder may be a hindrance (and indeed a factor in not having a concept of career in the first place) to anyone's career in any society. In a high power distance society we are more likely to find those with easy access to a career because they have the necessary prerequisites, and others who have no hope of pursuing a career as they do not have the prerequisites.

Masculinity/femininity

As a cultural value there are four main ways in which this dimension influences careers and career planning:

- the regard for females as part of the workforce;
- the attitudes to different jobs as being either masculine or feminine;

- the centrality of work to a person's life;
- the attitudes to achievement and competition.

Essentially, in a society high on Hofstede's (1991) masculinity index, men are supposed to be tough and women tender. Another aspect in the difference between a masculine society and a feminine society is the difference between assertiveness and modesty. Also, as Hofstede (1991: 80) points out, what is considered 'feminine' and what is considered 'masculine' differ considerably between cultures:

> Women dominate as doctors in the (former) Soviet Union, as dentists in Belgium, as shopkeepers in parts of West Africa. Men dominate as typists in Pakistan and form a sizeable share of nurses in the Netherlands. Female managers are virtually nonexistent in Japan but frequent in the Philippines and Thailand.

The implications for careers are, firstly, that in some societies women may not be seen as part of the workforce, or if they are they may occupy the lowest-level jobs, or certain jobs that are usually ascribed to women, such as nursing. This also varies in industries: for example heavy engineering is not usually seen as an industry for females in the UK. Banks, despite employing a majority of females in the UK have a small minority in middle to senior management positions. Women tend to prosper more in the UK in such occupations as local government and some branches of the civil service, but still tend not to reach the senior management positions in large proportions.

Secondly, and following from the above point, certain jobs may be viewed as 'feminine' and some as 'masculine'. In IBM, Hofstede (1991) identified six occupational groups from most 'masculine' to most 'feminine'. These were: salesmen, professionals such as engineers and scientists, skilled technicians, managers, unskilled and semi-skilled workers, and office workers (the latter being the most feminine). This generally goes from the more competitive and achievement-oriented occupations, to the less competitive and less achievement-oriented jobs.

Women and expatriation

Within Hofstede's (1980a) framework, the level of femininity–masculinity within the home culture, compared with that in the host culture, could be expected to influence the number of women in the expatriate management workforce. For example, Adler (1986–87) posits two models containing underlying assumptions about gender differences, which may be assumed to differ between countries. The first is an 'equity model' that sees male and female as having equal contributions to make, and therefore treatment in the workplace should be based on equity. The contrasting view is that of the 'complementary contribution model'. This assumes that there are differences between men and women, and that their different contributions should be recognized and valued. This may well parallel masculine and feminine national cultures respectively. Adler points out that these are not complementary models. Looked at from the perspective of the equity model, seeing females as different and complementary to men may be construed as placing them in an inferior role. Similarly from the perspective of the complementary contributions model, not seeing women's unique contribution negates their identity as women. We may expect greater numbers of women managers from equity model/feminine countries. However, with approximately 40 per cent of managers in the United States, estimated to be women and 27 per cent in the United Kingdom, the estimated number of female expatriates from these two countries is 3–5 per cent of the total (quoted in Harris, 1995: although she does not indicate her source).

Hodgetts and Luthans (1991) relate a case of a female assistant manager working in a large international hotel chain in a Western country. She is keen to progress, and has asked for an overseas assignment. This is a normal way of progressing up the career ladder. By taking an expatriate appointment, promotion is often gained more quickly. Particularly in destinations that are regarded as more remote and not so popular, the expatriate can increase his or her chances of promotion by doing a good job. This woman has asked for an assistant manager's position in the company's hotel in Cairo. The head of international operations is somewhat concerned. He feels that this is not the right appointment for her, and it would be a difficult environment for her to work in. None of the company's hotels in the Arab world have had female managers. This would be a mistake not just for her career, but for the company as well. He offered to provide her with an alternative assignment where she would have a better chance of succeeding. However, she was adamant. She had looked into this carefully and she was sure she could make a success of it.

Harris (1995) identifies a number of factors that may influence the low representation of women in expatriate assignments, as follows.

Organizational factors

Expatriates are often drawn from an identified pool of high potential individuals within the organization, aged from about their late twenties to early thirties, following the development, maturation and experience of the domestic operation. This is likely to militate against the selection of women because of the presence of the 'glass ceiling', and also because often technical competence as opposed to relational skills is still valued for expatriates. An additional organizational factor may be the perceived strategic function of expatriation in the transfer of socialized knowledge and organizational cultures as a form of control on subsidiaries. This often requires access to the informal organizational network, often denied to women, and frequent movement of the 'socialized' expatriate to new assignments with consequent domestic disruption, all of which may disadvantage the female expatriate.

Socio-cultural factors: host country barrier

Host countries may be seen as being prejudiced against female managers. In fact Adler's (1987) finding of the success of women expatriates in South East Asian countries contradicts this assumption. She contends that often women are seen as foreigners who happen to be women, not as women who happen to be foreigners, and are not subject to the same limitations. Hence often women expatriates will not have the same restrictions that host-country women would experience. Harris (1995) after Moran (1985) postulates that the concern of companies to send women abroad because they will not be accepted in the local culture often stems from the male managers in the home country blaming other cultures for their own prejudice.

Socio-cultural factors: dual career issues

There has been discussion in the literature on the problems of spousal adjustment to expatriate problems. In particular this has focused on the dual-career couple. The traditional profile has been the married man with his family. These problems may well be magnified if the expatriate is a woman, with the man facing an additional hurdle of being the secondary breadwinner or a homemaker. The woman, as expatriate's spouse, may make this transition easier as a result of socio-cultural norms.

As yet there has been little extensive research on these issues, which may make it difficult for the international operations manager in the hotel case above to make an informed decision regarding the appropriateness of the expatriate assignment in Egypt for the female assistant manager. Certainly the company has assumed difficulties without having experienced any. Adler's (1993) conclusion, from her Pacific Rim studies, about some of the advantages for female expatriate managers may also have a bearing on such a decision. She states that women often have more visibility, as foreign clients are more curious and anxious to meet them; they have better interpersonal skills and often find it easier to talk to local men than male expatriates do; and they have novelty value, with foreign clients assuming they must be the best, to have been sent by their companies in the first place.

Other cultural factors in international career choice

Apart from the cultural factors discussed above which may impact on career choice, including those aspects connected with the different treatment of gender differences, the following ought to be considered. They were examined by Jaeger (see Jaeger and Kanungo, 1990; Jaeger, 1990) in connection with differences between 'developed' and 'developing' countries.

Long-term/short-term focus

Management in many 'developing' countries tends to have a short-term time and activity orientation that is not conducive to planning. Career planning in many developing countries (for both the organization in planning its resources, and for the individual in planning his or her future) would be inhibited by this short-term time orientation. It would also be limited by a lack of belief in people's ability

97

to substantially change and the creative potential of individuals. Connected (Western) management techniques that would also be limited are strategic planning and Management by Objectives, which have implications for career planning in the West but may be inappropriate in developing countries.

External/internal explanations of causality and control of outcomes

Such writers as Rotter (1966) have undertaken research on individual differences in 'locus of control', whereby some individuals are more likely to attribute external causes to outcomes which are beyond their control, and others are more likely to attribute internal causes which they control. Hence you may attribute your lack of career progression to your inability (internal causes) or to patronage and unfair promotion practices in the company (external causes). Jaeger and Kanungo (1990) notice a tendency in developing countries to attribute external causes to events in people's lives. As the above example shows, this 'locus of control' is not particularly conducive to personal career planning.

In sum, we may expect to see an emphasis on career planning where competition and assertiveness is stressed, and where work is central to a person's life (masculinity); where there is a stress on individual attainment (individualism); where there is access to prerequisites of attaining promotion and position (a function of power distance); and where there is a degree of tolerance for uncertainty (low uncertainty avoidance). Career planning is also more likely to occur where there is a longer-term time orientation, and where events are more likely to be attributed to internal rather than external causes. Needless to say, we find these factors more prominently in the Anglo-Saxon countries where personal career planning is seen as part of the development of managers. One additional cultural factor, which does turn out to be more complex than it would immediately appear, is work centrality.

Work centrality

Hofstede (1991) also distinguishes masculine and feminine societies by the degree to which work is central to people's lives and the degree to which assertiveness and competition is stressed (usually for men). These are broad generalizations across a national culture, and we would also expect to see considerable differences between occupational groups and sub-cultures in the same country. This may have implications for the centrality of career planning to one's life.

Other cross-cultural work undertaken on this is that of the Meaning of Working International Research Team (MOW, 1987) that looked at the centrality of work to people's lives in eight different countries. Subjects were asked how important working was for them in relation to other life roles (leisure, community life, religion and family). Work centrality seems to be a concomitant of the importance of career planning. However, when this is taken with the different national cultural dimensions (Hofstede, 1991) discussed above this does not seem to be the case, as the eight countries, from high to low work centrality are as follows: Japan, Yugoslavia, Israel, the USA, Belgium, Netherlands, West Germany and the UK.

So, in the previous discussion on cultural dimensions we would assume that in Japan personal career planning is largely unimportant and in Britain largely important. However, the results from the MOW (1987) team indicate otherwise. It may be that on an individual basis, personal career planning is more or less appropriate depending on those factors that motivate the individual. At the same time, we should be mindful of more general national cultural factors, which may mean that career planning is more or less appropriate generally. This has tremendous implications for human resource specialists working across cultures in multinational organizations: the extent to which careers can be guided or planned by the company in line with human resource planning will vary according to the nature of the culture of a country of operation.

Implications for managers

The environmental and industry forces that shaped the way that Shell approached expatriation, as part of long-term management development and human resource planning, are changing. By systematically identifying potential, using promotion guidelines and supply and demand analysis of staff, Shell was able to operate effectively in a business environment which focused on the long-term, where the demand for talent was more or less predictable and stable, and which operated within a closed labour environment with staff joining from university expected to realize their potential within the one organization (Mahieu, 2001).

A number of major changes were initiated in Shell in 1995 in response to perceived changes in the business environment involving liberalization, globalization and technology and the effective management of a highly skilled, globally deployed workforce, where often people work in virtual teams around the clock, where organizational boundaries are becoming blurred with people working in a variety of different organizational units, sometimes in joint ventures, and on variable types of contracts on payroll or as contractors. Shell developed 'global scenarios' to try to anticipate the different consequences of these changes and forces over the next 20 years. Structural aspects were also addressed, including the efficiencies of the two central offices, and the matrix structure and role of the national organizations was challenged. This had consequences for management development as part of a general drive for more transparency in the company, more emphasis on immediate success and performance rather than on long-term potential; this was a response to the need for staff to have more control over their own careers and more limited mobility, constantly requiring new skills, a less central approach to identifying talent and development, and the use of intranet technology to do things differently (Mahieu, 2001). This has led to open resourcing, new criteria upon which to assess and develop people, a new performance management system, and a new approach to management learning.

Open resourcing   This was introduced in 1997. The hiring line manager posts all vacancies, and people are free to apply if they are nearly at the end of their current assignment. The HR function may help in formulating the requirements for the position and application processing. The hiring line manager conducts the selection process often approaching the applicant's current line manager for references, selecting, providing feedback to unsuccessful candidates, and negotiating terms with the successful one. This generally allows for a wider choice for the parties involved. It is conducted in an open environment so that if there is an 'internal' candidate, this has to be declared. Personal development centres are available for counselling and learning about career strengths and weaknesses, and some placement processes are still needed, for example to place new recruits and returning expatriates or to deal with potential redundancy situations.

New assessment criteria The three new criteria of 'capacity', 'achievement' and 'relationships' were introduced in 1996 in order to put more emphasis on performance and relationship skills. Although the 'potential' concept was reintroduced there was a need to reduce the self-fulfilling prophecy nature of this which often made it an end in itself. Potential is now seen more as an estimate rather than a fixed category, and can change on the basis of current performance. There are no guarantees.

Performance management This has shifted to reflect individual performance contracts, personal development plans, and variable pay with merit and bonus payments based on individual performance and business performance.

Management learning This also has changed to reflect a need for more flexibility. Rather than fixed and formalized training programmes related to the job grade of individuals, learning is more openly accessed by those who can benefit. Local experiences are shared globally through the use of technology.

Yet Mahieu (2001) describes Shell as still having a 'flux' culture where people move jobs after three or four years. There is still a commitment to 'grow their own people' and still succession planning for the top 200 position. The talent pool and skills development is not simply left to internal market mechanisms. There is a talent review process in each part of the business. This identifies skills gaps. Development plans take place at both the individual and the company level.

Within a company such as Shell there seems little evidence to suggest the high failure rates assumed so readily in the literature. Rather than simply going out as missionaries to spread the message or the corporate culture, or to transfer skills or technologies to subsidiaries or affiliates, the concept is that international assignments are part of the culture of the company, and part of the continuous development of the individual. Failure rates may be higher in companies that see international assignments as a one-off. In this case training and orientation is also provided as a one-off for the individual going abroad. This may be effective or ineffective. Selecting and developing people with a broader, flexible perspective, who fit into an international 'flux' may be the answer for some organizations. However, this is dependent on the type of internationalization strategy the organization has (see Chapter 2).

The implications for managers therefore seem to be:

- Expatriate policy should be in line with the strategic intent of the organization.
- Drawing from a 'pool' of potentially international assignees who are seen as

high flyers, and as part of a more general management development process, may be more effective and prevent failure, but may go against the selection of women unless there is a deliberate policy to include women within the pool.

- Continuous cultural-general training as part of a management development process which encourages flexibility across cultures may be more effective than culture-specific training on a one-off basis.

- When expatriates are drawn from different countries, career expectations may be different as well as expectations of the way careers should be managed. The level of 'intervention' required by the company may therefore be different across different cultures.

- Adequate research and risk taking regarding women in 'difficult' cultures should be undertaken. Evidence should be produced if the 'risks' are seen as too high.

Questions for managers

1 In view of the changing context within which Shell operates, how is it possible to reconcile the need to be flexible and maintain an open market system for selecting expatriate managers for specific posts within the company, and the need to manage the careers of individuals and human resource planning to ensure an adequate supply of talent at any one time?

2 How can companies like Shell ensure that managers and key personnel are adequately prepared for international assignments?

3 In view of the experiences of Shell outlined above, is there really a problem with expatriate failure? How can this best be safeguarded against? How might this differ between companies such as Shell and Crédit Lyonnais, which have different international strategies?

An agenda for research

There is little evidence in the literature of a cohesive and overarching conceptual base or theoretical model within which the various aspects of expatriation may be understood from a cross-cultural perspective, and which includes both corporate and individual perspectives. This chapter by no means represents a comprehensive discussion of the many aspects of expatriation. It started by using the metaphor of the missionary organization, and Royal Dutch/Shell appears to be a well known example of an international organization integrating its expatriate policies into its general drive to develop cadres of managers who are flexible enough to operate anywhere in the world, and indeed who may be drawn from anywhere in the world. This may not necessarily be because it is a partly Dutch organization. However, it may be proposed that certain forces have acted upon the Netherlands to make this country more receptive to differences within its national boundaries, and to have been outward facing in its commercial activities over the centuries. It should also be noted that the Netherlands is not the only

101

country to produce such expatriate organizations. A limitation on the metaphor of missionary is that the international logic of Shell is such that it is not attempting to deliver a message to different parts of the world, as in the case of IKEA's missionary management teams setting up operations in different countries and attempting to transmit a strong corporate identity.

The case, together with a consideration of some of the literature in this area, has suggested a number of issues that not only require some research attention, but also need to be integrated into a broad theoretical framework.

Figure 4.1 attempts to map out some of the key variables that may influence the outcome of a successful expatriate assignment from the initial personal inputs of a particular desire for an international career, along with capabilities which may influence eventual personal success; and the corporate inputs of the strategies of internationalization and international operations that were discussed in Chapter 2. Those personal propensities and abilities will act on a person's willingness, as well as his or her own perceived suitability, to submit to a selection process of a particular nature. This might be to a longer-term commitment to an international 'pool' of high-flyers, or simply a one-off job. These decisions, especially the degree to which a person may want to submit to a company's intent to manage his or her career, may in part have cultural antecedents. On the company's part, the nature of selection will be dependent on the international strategy. This is closely bound up with the level of integration of expatriation in the organization's operating strategy, as reflected in the nature of expatriation as a one-off assignment, part of a management development process that may partly be *ad hoc*, but where an overseas assignment is seen as part of developing general management capabilities (this was seen in Crédit Lyonnais in Chapter 2), or an integral part of building a pool of high-flyers who can undertake assignments anywhere in the world (as seems to be the case in Shell). However, the business environment may act on this, so that in Shell the unpredictability of the environment has resulted in an open market for many international assignments. The country of origin (as well as the nature of the industry) may influence both selection criteria and the level of intervention deemed appropriate in a manager's career. This will feed into the selection process, as well as the level of integration of expatriation in the operating strategy of a company.

Once selected, and as a result of the corporate factors just discussed, the nature of integration into the management development process of expatriation may be continuous and progressive, it may be *ad hoc* (for example, a decision is made as to whether a particular person would benefit in his or her development by three years in a foreign assignment), or a foreign assignment may simply be a one-off decision which may have more to do with immediate corporate needs rather than management development. Decisions by the individual to submit to these different processes, and to make career decisions at any stage may be influenced by cultural factors; and decisions of this nature will be affected by the corporate factors discussed above (which may include cultural factors).

The nature of the management development process will reflect these factors so that assignments seen as a progressive facet of development will require a more continuous process of training and development. Such aspects of flexibility, 'helicopter' and more general capabilities in working internationally will be encouraged and supported. Training is unlikely to be specific to a particular country. An *ad hoc* view of international assignments as part of management

Personal factors and objectives
– desire for international career
– interpersonal capabilities
– technical capabilities

International strategy
– ethnocentric
– polycentric
– regio/geocentric

Level of integration of expatriation within organization's strategy
– one-off assignment
– part of management development process
– building a pool as part of HR planning

Nature of selection
– process (one-off/pool)
– criteria

Business environmental
– stability
– unpredictability

Country of origin of expatriate
Expectations that may have cultural antecedents
– manage own career
– company manages careers

Country of origin of company
Criteria used for selecting expatriates who may have cultural antecedents

Level of intervention in career development and planning

Nature of integration into management development process
– continuous
– *ad hoc*
– one off

Nature of cross-cultural training
– culture-specific
– culture-general

Culmination of individual variables

**Level of acculturation/flexibility
Level of technical capability**
– Nature of assignment (task/relationship)
– Cultural difference (between host and home)

Culmination of corporate variables

Success of expatriate assignment
– for parent organization
      – success of assignment
      – for career/HR planning and development
– for subsidiary/affiliate
      – success of the assignment
      – transferring/developing capacity
– for expatriate
      – success in assignment
      – developing skills
      – career development

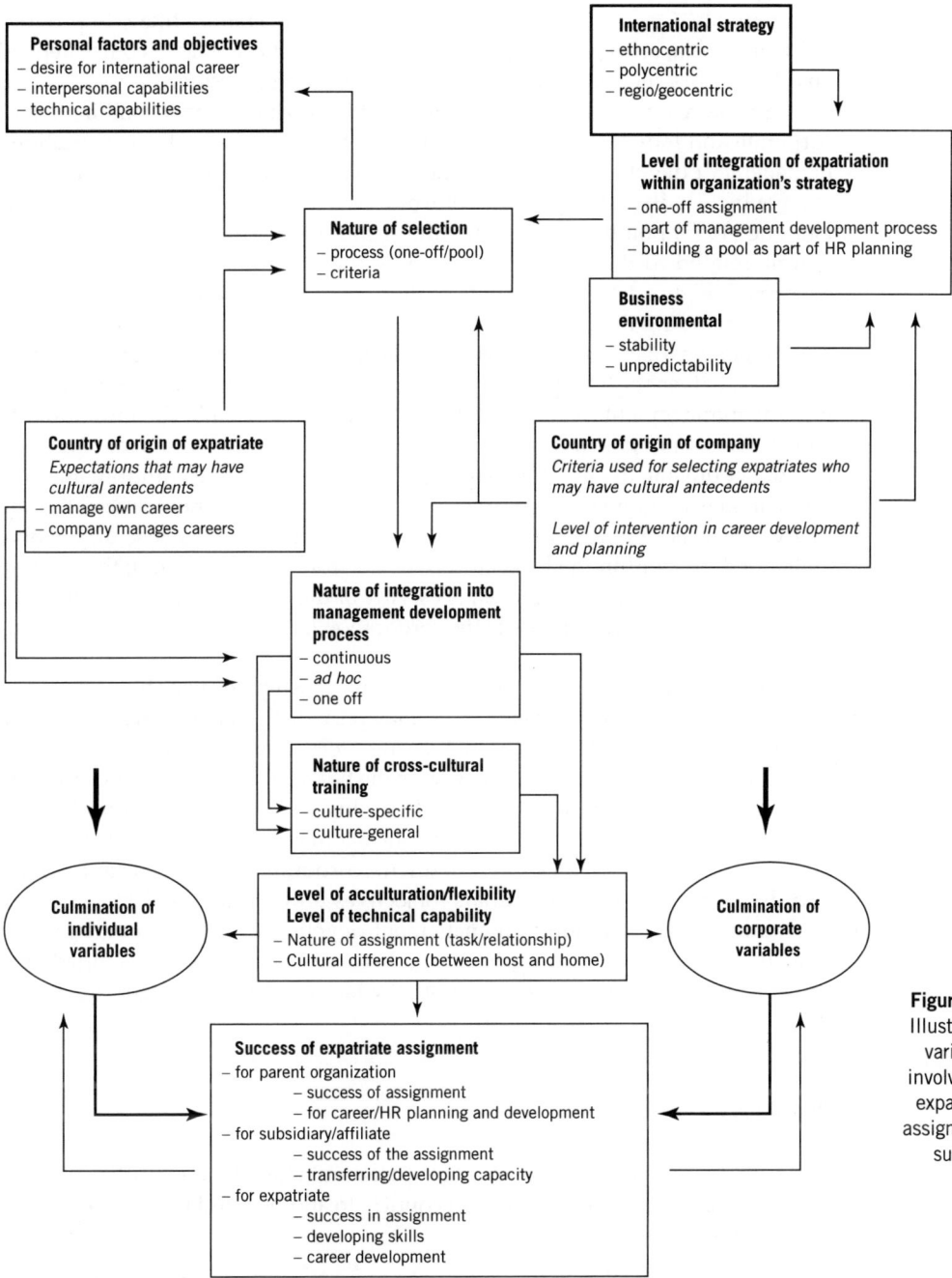

Figure 4.1
Illustrative variables involved in expatriate assignment success

development is more likely to produce culture-specific training, whereas this will be the norm for one-off assignments.

It is unlikely that one-off, culture-specific training will yield the high degree of acculturation that may be needed in assignments with high relationship requirements. Ongoing development within a 'pool' is more likely to produce individuals who are highly adaptive across cultures. This would of course depend on other factors such as the effectiveness of selection processes.

So, success in an expatriate assignment is dependent on a combination of corporate and individual variables, as well as the dynamics of the expatriation/management development process described in Figure 4.1. Defining a lack of success by alluding to expatriate return rates is a narrow gauge of success, as Harzing (1995) points out. Any definition should be broad enough to include criteria related to the parent organization, the subsidiary and the individual concerned. Figure 4.1 outlines some of those possible criteria. Success, or lack of success, including the longer-term outcomes for the corporation in pursuing its current policies of expatriation, will be fed back into the process shown in Figure 4.1. These will enable companies such as Shell to modify the levels of integration into the management development process, and will enable the individual to enhance his or her position in the company, or make career choices that may take him or her outside the present company. These could involve withdrawing from international assignments (and/or the management development process), going 'native' (that is, staying in the country of the assignment because of personal embeddedness within the local culture or environment), or exiting the existing company to pursue other career choices. Any of these choices may impact on the medium to longer-term success to the corporation (for example losing individuals from the 'pool').

All these assertions (taken from the relationships of variables posited in Figure 4.1 and discussed in this chapter) may provide the bases of hypotheses that could be tested in further research. It seems clear that taking a view that there are high levels of expatriate failure across the board, which can be addressed by particular types of training that provide for higher levels of acculturation and therefore success, is an altogether simplistic one. The multiplicity of connections between the many variables connected with corporate strategy, cultural origins and difference criteria, individuals' objectives and culture, and the extent of integration of expatriation in management development, should all be investigated. This will enable a more comprehensive theory to be developed, and provide more solid evidence on the basis of which corporate managers may make decisions.

Questions for researchers

1 Are there high failure rates among expatriates? How do these differ from one home country to another, one host country to another, and from one company to another?

2 Is there a relationship between country of origin of the expatriate and success or failure in an assignment (e.g. are Dutch managers more successful expatriates than British or Japanese managers)? How does the difference in culture between host and home culture affect this?

3 What is the relationship between the way expatriates are prepared for an assignment and success in an assignment? Are there differences in this between culture-general training and culture-specific training? (This question could be extended to include any or all of the variables identified in Figure 4.1.)

The motivating organization: the Japanese model

Job satisfaction in organizations in Japan is reported to be low (de Boer, 1978) yet productivity is often reported to be high (Chen, 1995). Job satisfaction is a measure of motivation, but it is only one part of it. Motivation generally is a key factor in productivity, organizational effectiveness, as well as in the well-being of people. The way people are motivated is an aspect of the way organizations, in different parts of the world, manage the disjuncture between life at work, and life outside work (see Introduction). Incentive schemes based on pay are often developed in individualistic cultures, where the relationship with employees is seen as instrumental and contractual. This may be based on an achievement motive perspective (McClelland, 1987). More sophisticated HRM systems in many Western countries emphasize a wider spectrum of incentives based on the design of jobs, levels of involvement and participation, promotion opportunities, working conditions, as well as pay. MBO-type systems can be introduced to reinforce the achievement motive. These aim managers and key employees towards discrete, individually achievable targets. Based on high achievement of the individual in the immediate job, and related to pay levels, this type of incentive may not be appropriate in hierarchical or high power distance cultures (Hofstede, 1980b) and in collectivist cultures (see Chapter 1).

Although there is some evidence of the introduction of pay incentive schemes in countries that are assumed to have a collectivist culture (in China for example: Jackson and Bak, 1998), in Japan a more inclusive concept of motivation is employed which is based on instilling commitment to the organization, and by the organization. This may provide at least one explanation of why work satisfaction is low, while general commitment to the company and productivity are high.

The objective of this chapter is to examine the motivation of personnel from the more holistic approach of developing overall commitment, and to do this through a specific cultural lens: that of Japanese corporations. Looking at Chiba International in its overseas operations, and Sumitomo Metal Industries operating in Japan provides the context of real cultures and management issues. The relevance and transferability to the West is explored, in order to see what the lessons are for global management generally.

Corporate commitment

Etzioni (1975) has classified employee commitment, or involvement in the organization, into four different levels:

- *Moral involvement*: positive and intense orientation, with an internalization of organizational goals and values;

- *Calculative involvement*: based on exchange where the organization is seen as a means to an end. Employees will work spontaneously and cooperatively if this is seen as benefiting them directly, but will leave if a more lucrative opportunity occurs outside;

- *Compliant involvement*: some identification with the organization, but behaviour is based on compliance. The organizational values are espoused but not owned;

- *Alienative involvement*: a negative set of attitudes that reject the organizational values. Membership continues because of lack of alternatives. Effort is minimal.

Instrumentalism has already been discussed as a regard for individuals as a means to an end in an organization. Relations are contractual, with no feeling of mutual obligation. Humanism indicates a regard for people as an end in themselves. Whether or not this end is that of the individual as an entity, or the collective as an entity that comprises the individual, might be further defined by the level of collectivism or individualism within a society. It is these cultural aspects that may influence the nature and levels of employee/corporate commitment, as well as specific organizational and management factors. For example, Smith et al.'s (1996) study suggests that Japan and Korea are both high on a measure of 'loyal involvement' (contrasted with 'utilitarian involvement': see Chapter 1 for a discussion). This correlates positively with Hofstede's (1980a) dimension of collectivism, and suggests a moral involvement with the organization as distinct from a contractual involvement. Bae and Chung (1997) have shown Korean organizations to be different from those of Japan in the lower level of solidarity shown towards co-workers. Although Korean employees expect a higher level of commitment from their companies towards them, the corporation shows a lower level of solidarity to workers than either its Japanese or its American counterpart. Chen (1995) depicts Korean people management as being less consultative that that of Japanese firms, with a lower loyalty downwards, yet with loyalty expected upwards, and as representing a more authoritarian system than that of Japan. Korea has been more influenced by American management systems (as well as Japanese ones) than Japan. Chen notes that Korean workers put a stronger emphasis on extrinsic rather than intrinsic factors of motivation. Some organizations have MBO systems and focus on wages and conditions.

The greater mutual commitment found in Japanese organizations may represent a 'capturing' of the wider societal values of collectivism and humanism. It may be that Japanese organizations have been more successful at doing this than organizations in other collectivist cultures. The metaphor of the 'motivating' organization may therefore be appropriate in describing this more holistic approach to motivation. This chapter explores its facets (see Figure 5.1), and looks at the extent to which such approaches may be successfully exported to other countries. It does this within the wider framework of organizational motivational systems that are schematized in Figure 5.1.

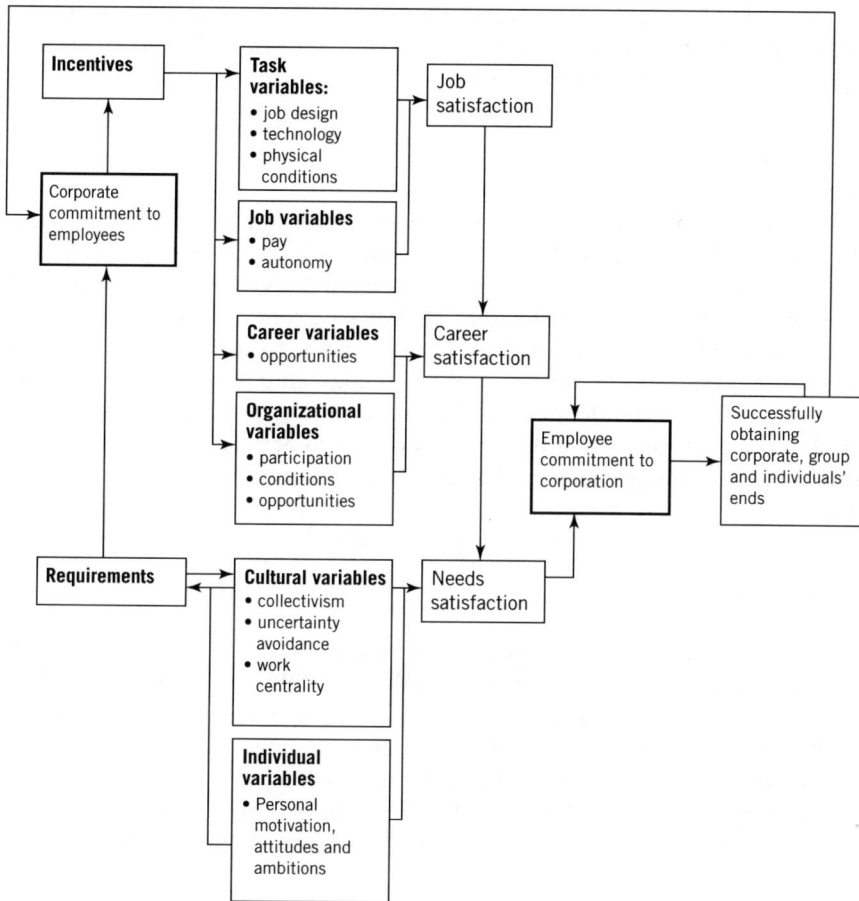

Figure 5.1
Relationship
between incentives,
needs and
commitment

Task, job, career and organizational incentives

A major factor in any consideration of employee commitment and motivation is the reward or compensation package that the employee receives. Money, for example, is more or less important to people in different circumstances. In any event people work for a living: the extent to which people work to live or live to work was a question investigated by the Meaning of Working International Research Team (MOW, 1987); most people would not go to work if they were not paid in some form. This is one of Herzberg's (Herzberg et al., 1959) 'hygiene' factors and a prerequisite for someone to do the job. The way these 'rewards' are allocated and distributed may also be a factor in the level of commitment and motivation, but so might the way income, and other aspects such as the nature of the profession, are seen as status factors in a society.

Incentives focus on the external factors of motivation, rather than the internal needs or drives of individuals. This is the area over which the manager has more influence when motivating subordinates: making sure the incentives match the needs. To a large extent much of the work in this area in the Western world has focused on the satisfaction of needs within the framework of Maslow

(1954) and Herzberg (1966) (for example Alderfer, 1972). Aspects of this that have been of concern in organizations (Jackson, 1993c) include task, job, career and organizational variables (see Figure 5.1).

Task variables

These include job design and working conditions, including available technology. The way a job is designed influences the amount of intrinsic motivation, that is, the satisfaction of doing a job well or the enjoyment derived from the job, as well as the amount of autonomy within that job. Working conditions normally satisfy more basic needs for comfort and well-being, and are a prerequisite to higher order needs satisfaction. The levels of technology employed may be a factor in employees' physical safety and well-being when performing a particular set of tasks, as well as providing the ability for them to perform a task effectively. Inadequate technology may result in low motivation in the task, and low job satisfaction.

Job variables

These may include pay and degree of autonomy. Pay is usually regarded as high in the list of extrinsic incentives of a job, and is probably more complicated than merely satisfying Maslow's lower order needs. Money is also part of a symbolic system within Western society, representing a person's 'worth'. Money may therefore be bound up with higher order needs such as self-actualization. With the nature of pay as part of the reward package, the levels of autonomy desired may vary among different cultural groups. This will be discussed below.

Career variables

These mainly involve promotion opportunities and providing extrinsic rewards, and satisfy a range of needs within Maslow's hierarchy including increases in pay, and self-fulfilment.

Organizational variables

These involve different levels of opportunity to progress in the organization as well as general physical and 'climate' conditions. Participation in decision making may be a key factor closely connected to the way jobs are designed and to the management style of the manager and the structural communication arrangements of an organization. This may also influence the amount of intrinsic reward derived from a job.

Needs satisfaction and culture

Incentives are therefore bound up with needs or desires (requirements that people have in their jobs: Figure 5.1). If individuals do not have a need to participate in decision making within an organization, this cannot very well be used as an incentive. The extent to which tasks and job variables meet the needs and desires of employees determines the level of job satisfaction. This may be a narrow view of satisfaction and motivation. The extent to which career incentives enable people to rise above immediate job satisfaction was discussed in Chapter 4. Job satisfaction is really a subset of overall motivation. A person can undertake a job that is not intrinsically satisfying, but may be motivated to do well in that job to gain promotion. In a way, 'satisfaction' depicts a state of equilibrium in the sense that it is neither a pulling or pushing force for moving a person to do something: it merely means that they are content with what they are doing, and that they do not want to alter or change the job or themselves. A consequence of this may be high performance. The relationship between the various motivating factors that contribute towards employee commitment is complex. Employee commitment itself transcends performance in a particular job (which is not necessarily a direct outcome of commitment).

Yet career satisfaction (as well as job satisfaction) is dependent on factors which relate to cultural values as well as individual attributes (Table 5.1). Different factors are more likely to influence what Kelly, Whatley and Worthley (1991) call life goals (generalized measures of work motivation) depending on the national and regional culture. For example, it is possible to distinguish broadly between East Asian and Western cultures in this respect.

Table 5.1 Cultural differences indicating motivational factors (after Harris and Moran, 1987)

| | Motivators | |
East Asian		Western
Equity		Wealth
Group		Individual
Saving		Consumption
Extended family relations		Nuclear and mobile family
Highly disciplined/motivated workforce		Decline in work ethic and hierarchy
Protocol, rank and status		Informality and personal competence
Avoid conflict		Conflict to be managed

Although this is a fairly broad classification, it may be that factors such as those described here result in different motivational influences in job satisfaction as well as commitment. Hui (1990) describes a discrepancy model of job satisfaction (Figure 5.2).

The degree of dissatisfaction with work derives from a perceived discrepancy between actual outcomes of the job and the jobholder's expectations. Where there are insufficient resources to get the job done well, such as in technologically backward or impoverished countries, there may be low job satisfaction. Conversely, where workers' expectations are very high and the outcomes are not the desired and expected high results, job satisfaction may be low. De Boer (1978) gives India and the Philippines as examples of the former, with Japan and France as examples of the latter.

A person's expectations of a job are also influenced by personal goals and the cultural values in which he or she has been socialized. This is where cultural factors make a difference to motivation at work, and several studies have shown

Figure 5.2 Hui's
(1990)
discrepancy
model of job
satisfaction

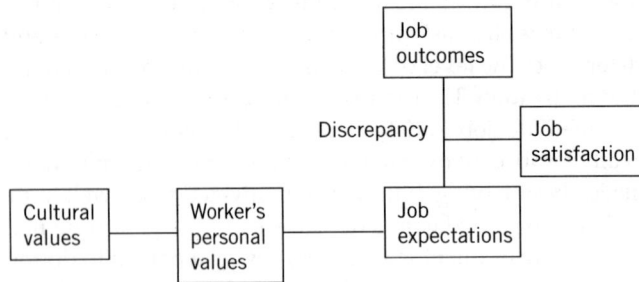

that individuals from different cultural backgrounds have different attitudes towards their work. Hui (1990) reports studies which found that French Canadians are more satisfied in their work than English Canadians; in a study of over 10 countries (de Boer, 1978) Sweden had the highest number of people who were satisfied with their job (63 per cent), then the United Kingdom (54 per cent), Brazil (53 per cent) and Switzerland (50 per cent), with Japan having the smallest proportion of satisfied workers (20 per cent). Other researchers have drawn the same conclusions about Japanese workers, with a possible explanation that they are strongly committed and motivated, but job outcomes do not conform to expectations and thus do not lead to job satisfaction.

Figure 5.1 shows the level of satisfaction as a function of the satisfaction of needs, based on individual and cultural variables that may impact on a person's requirements for the task being performed, the job being filled, and the career being pursued. Corporations also have requirements, and these may influence, or even dictate, the types of incentives which are provided. The corporation will provide incentives for individual high performance, loyalty, long-term commitment or whatever is seen as fulfilling the objectives of the organization. The wider cultural environment within which the corporation operates in turn influences this. It was suggested above, for example, that companies in some types of collectivist culture, such as Japan, are more likely to focus on longer-term commitment, whereas companies in individualistic cultures such as in the Anglo-Saxon countries may focus on shorter-term objectives based on individual task-directed performance. When corporations operate in other countries, they may try to adapt these HRM systems accordingly, or they may simply import them in their entirety.

These aspects are now investigated through the 'Japanese model' of the motivating organization.

The Japanese model and Matsushita

Japanese management, and what the West can learn from it, has been popular since Pascale and Athos published *The Art of Japanese Management* in 1981. (Coincidentally two other classics of this genre were published at this time: William Ouchi's *Theory Z: How American Business Can Meet the Japanese Challenge* in the same year and Kenichi Ohmae's *The Mind of the Strategist* in 1982.) Pascale and Athos tell the story of Matsushita. Konosuke Matsushita started off as an apprentice in a cycle shop in 1918, then founded his business in the consumer electrics industry and it went on to become one of the 50 largest corporations in the world. He based his initial strategy on developing his own distribution system, dealing directly with retailers. This was in direct contrast with Japanese practices. Matsushita has been built on developing market share and passing on the cost savings from high volume production to consumers in lower prices. The company does not introduce new products but improves on the quality and price structure of imitations of original products. Extensive R&D is invested in this purpose. Its assumptions are that profits are tied to growth, and that long-term investment in growth will eventually pay off in profits.

Matsushita introduced decentralization into his domestic organization to retain its entrepreneurial character. With each product, independent progress could be clearly measured, managers would be self-sufficient and close to consumers, small divisions would be flexible, and divisional management would gain the required training for general management positions. Together with this decentralization, the founder sought to alleviate the problems that this brought: decreasing control, low inter-divisional cooperation, and reduced strength to cope with threats to a whole product group. He did this by centralizing accounting, by introducing a central 'bank' for divisional profits, and by centralizing the personnel and training functions.

The entrepreneurial spirit that was nurtured within the organization was tempered by a rigorous planning system that comprised five-year, two-year and six-month plans. The latter consisted of very detailed operating plans that were reviewed on a monthly basis. Performance was measured on the basis of attaining objectives set out in the six-month plans, and rewards were given accordingly. Aberrations and failures to achieve objectives had to be explained.

The publicly expressed management aim was to 'develop extraordinary qualities in ordinary men'. Top management took a 'hands on' approach with Matsushita talking with his divisional heads every day, and spending time on the shop floor. Local managers were expected to take initiatives and solve problems where they arose. The prevailing management style was tough-minded and pragmatic, encouraging competition and conflict. Disagreements were solved on an impersonal basis with facts provided and 'acceptance time' built into the process of conflict resolution, to allow time to think about the problem in a different way.

As with many Japanese companies, emphasis was placed on training. Professional staff started in the company with six months of selling, and also spent time on the production line. Promotion was accompanied by training for the new job. Five per cent of employees were rotated to different divisions to encourage integration. There were lifelong employment policies to maintain shared values that were also promoted through the training process. The company encouraged employee suggestions, with monetary rewards. The number of suggestions was used as a measure of divisional morale.

The skills of Matsushita himself were revealed in terms of innovation, efficiency and managing people, and in his ability to put together and manage an organization that balanced and reinforced all aspects and components working together. His policy was to step back and to let others develop in this mould in order to continue with a dynamic and strong organization that would be capable of adaptation to the environment, and growth.

The main integrating force in all this is what has been termed superordinate goals or the shared values which are instilled largely through training, and which are stated in the following business principles:

1 Recognize responsibilities as industrialists.

2 Foster progress.

3 Promote the general welfare of society.

4 Promote further development of world culture.

This is reflected in the employee creed: progress and development can only be achieved by the combined effort and cooperation of everyone in the company. This should be kept continuously in mind in devoting efforts to the ongoing improvement of the company.

The seven spiritual values further elaborate the philosophy:

1 National service through industry

2 Fairness

3 Harmony and cooperation

4 Struggle for betterment

5 Courtesy and humility

6 Adjustment and assimilation

7 Gratitude.

The extent to which people management practices can be successfully used outside of Japan will be investigated later. Chen (1995) refers to the main aspects of Japanese management style as perceived by the West. These include its main features: group consensus in decision making, career job security, pay and promotion dependent on seniority, and in-house unions encompassing all employees.

Chen believes that the Western admiration of Japanese management stems from the higher productivity obtained by Japanese corporations and the devotion of employees to the company. Certainly Japanese employees put in longer hours than their counterparts in Western countries, have lower absenteeism rates, and fewer industrial disputes. Employees also participate heavily in productivity improvement suggestion systems and quality circles. Yet Chen (1995) tells of the criticism of Japanese management within Japan (after Hazama, 1993) and warns against transposing a system, which was born out of Japanese culture, to other types of cultures. Reading (1992) also is uncomplimentary towards the Japanese way. He states:

> The quality of life in Japan remains depressingly poor. Most Japanese are overworked, overcrowded and ill-housed, coerced to conform to group norms by employers, bureaucrats and *yakusa* gangsters. . . . Most workers are paid serfs, chained to their employers. When young Japanese leave school or university and choose a job, they do so for life. The brightest may even be kidnapped by potential second-rate employers, and held captive until all better jobs have been filled. . . . Although the danger of losing one's job is slight, companies have

absolute power to decide where their employees work and what they do. . . . Individual prosperity depends on collective success, to which all must contribute. The suicide rate is high and death from overwork, *karoshi*, is commonplace.

Given the different perceptions of reality, it may be possible to provide a balanced view of Japanese management. The main features seem to be:

- *Managerial autonomy and long-term planning*: Japanese managers have to worry less about the often parasitic interests of the shareholders (shares are paid on par value not on earnings, and board members are all senior executives of the company, not outsiders); companies can greatly influence ownership of the company (companies select shareholders who are often banks and other institutions, rather than shareholders selecting companies), and managers do not have to serve the passive interests of workers with little stake in the company (Japanese employees are often tied to the company for lifetime employment and managers are less subject to the short-term contingencies of the labour market, and of meeting union demands for competitive pay). Managers are therefore not pressured to meet short-term earnings require- ments and can take a longer view, both financially and in relation to employee long-term plans.

- *Corporate rigidity and hierarchy*: Japanese companies tend to be rigidly organized and very hierarchical. Under the level of chairman and then president, each department constitutes an autonomous power base, with the department head having the same authority as the president of a small company (Chen, 1995). The functions of these senior level managers are mainly theme establishment, strategic development, internal loyalty promotion and high level external relations. It is mainly the section managers below them who are the main instigators of new projects.

- *Participatory decision making*: The *ringi* system of decision making is well documented (Chen, 1995). *Nemawashi* is a practice used by management to informally and initially sound out employees' ideas on a proposed course of action, and *ringi seido* is a formal procedure of management by group consensus. This normally is initiated in one section, and forwarded to all relevant sections at the same level, then to section managers, department managers and president. In both cases the idea is to obtain consensus, involvement and participation in decision making. The final decision is taken at the top, and the process can be lengthy. Chen (1995) remarks that too many unnecessary people can get involved in the process, and too many meetings are often held to discuss unnecessary questions (the Japanese Management Association estimates that Japanese managers spend about 40 per cent of their time in meetings). The final decision is often affected by the relation- ship between the participants. Further, management can be very autocratic, with the *ringi* system being merely a confirmation process. Quality circles are an import that were conceived by Deming and Juran in the United States and adapted and refined by Japanese enterprises, and then reimported back into the United States and other Western countries and regarded as a key feature of Japanese success. They emphasize group working and bottom-up management, making recommendations upwards concerning product or service quality and operations, and which mirrors the *ringi* system (Gill and Wong, 1998).

Japanese people management and Sumitomo Metal Industries

Sumitomo Metal Industries (SMI) was established in 1897. Today it is one of the leading companies in the Japanese steel industry, although it has also diversified into construction engineering, plant engineering, systems engineering, electronics, advanced materials and biomedicines. It has a one trillion yen turnover, of which 80 per cent comes from steel. Tsuda (1996) describes the extensive programme of human resource development within the context of changes that are affecting the steel industry.

Japanese views on work are changing. Along with the conventional workers' attitude that diligence is an important contribution to their own company, more people are attaching importance to 'mental and physical affluence'. There has also been a reduction in the workforce in manufacturing industries. The upshot of this is that young people do not show as much interest in manufacturing as they did in the past. This has been exacerbated by the internationalization of the workforce and employment of foreign blue-collar workers. The working environment has changed with the introduction of microelectronics and computers, which have changed modes of operation. Managers have had to comply with social demand for a reduction in working hours and an improvement in working conditions, eliminating the three 'Ks': *kiken* (dangerous), *kitsui* (hard) and *kitanai* (filthy). All this has been coupled with pressures for improved productivity.

There has also been an increase in the number of ageing employees in the workforce, coupled with a reduction in new hires during the global oil crisis of 1978–81. Hence, towards the mid-1990s there were low numbers of employees in their late 20s and early 30s, and high numbers in their 40s and early 50s. With a reduction in the total number on the production lines, this has interfered with the smooth transition of tasks from skilled technicians to their successors, and has affected the maintenance of high levels of technical performance.

Within Sumitomo there was therefore a requirement to meet the needs to develop an adaptable and efficient workforce. Tsuda (1996: 537), the executive vice-president of SMI, writes:

> SMI seeks to become a 'technoheart company', meaning a 'company based on superior technologies' that are always ready to cope with the changing requirements of the future. Such a 'technology-based company' requires the acquisition and fostering of excellent human resources to augment the competitiveness of such resources. 'To value humanity' is tantamount to having workers carry out the work most suitable to their careers while also achieving high quality performance. The education and training necessary for this purpose should be carried out not only by the workers themselves, but also as part of advanced programmes organized by the company and utilizing improved education facilities.

As a result, under the guidance of its philosophy of 'valuing humanity and technology' the company has undertaken long-term, continuous and extensive educational and development programmes, from top managers down to blue-collar workers. It had already established, in 1952, an Apprentice School to provide in-company education and training for junior high school graduates of three years in 'moral education and practical affairs'. For each grade it has about 40 apprentices who may eventually become 'central figures on the production line'. Other programmes that are long established are for new employees and others under foreman level, and take 13–17 months to complete. The company has also established a junior college offering a two-year programme on industrial technologies on a full-time basis.

Management development programmes are aimed at making the best use of the corporate organization of what Tsuda refers to as the '4Cs' abilities: coordination, communication, creation and culture-orientation.

Training programmes are also directed at the ageing workers, to increase their abilities to perform broader duties. They too are expected to 'improve morale, revitalizing older workers, and to meet the demand for a reduction of working hours through multiplied skills and restructured duties' (Tsuda, 1996: 540).

Human resource practices in Japan may be characterized as follows:

Lifetime employment

Gill and Wong (1998) point out that this means remaining on the payroll but not necessarily remaining in the same job or same plant for the duration of one's working life, and after Beardwell (1994) they term this lifetime commitment rather than employment. As such it is a guiding principle not a guarantee, applying only to large industrial organizations, and to only about 30 per cent of employees or 'salarymen'. Its aim is to encourage stability, commitment and a sense of belonging to the corporation. Although there may be an element of obligation and even a sense of being tied into the company, or even a creation of dependency and suppression of individual creativity, it does allow the long-term development of employees and succession planning which benefits the company and employees. It is seen as a means of fostering employee commitment, and Western organizations such as banks, local government and civil service organizations, as well as specific companies such as IBM, ICI, Unilever and Michelin, have also used this approach (Gill and Wong, 1998, after Kendell, 1984). It does prevent companies responding rapidly to economic downturns, and the 1990s have seen an erosion of this policy (Chen, 1995), a trend that those and other Western organizations mentioned above went through in the 1980s. To a certain extent this is seen in the case of SMI where there is, partly because of economic and social circumstances, a desire to retain older workers and develop them to become more flexible.

Seniority-based pay and promotion

Employees have largely been recruited from school leavers or university graduates, rather than experienced workers trained by other companies. They are

117

started at a lower level of pay. Their induction programme and training is designed to encourage them to conform, as well as developing skills. The tremendous amount of resources that SMI has put into education at a very early age (from junior high school, and including 'moral' education) is indicative of this. Pay increases year by year, and this is assumed to correlate with the employee's development of skills (Kuwahara, 1998). So regular pay increases and career advancement are provided on the basis of age and length of service to the company. Again, this encourages employees to remain with the organization in order to benefit from this system. Yet there is an erosion of this system, with ability and performance being used as additional criteria for increases in pay and promotion, and Nissan, Fujitsu and Honda have introduced performance-related pay (Gill and Wong, 1998).

While the seniority system is still culturally entrenched, it has been going through changes, with younger outstanding managers looking for alternative career opportunities by trading job security for career opportunities (Chen, 1995). It should also be noted that pay structures in Japanese firms have lower differentials than are found in many Western companies, and are more egalitarian in concept. Employees therefore share more equally in the fortunes of the company including its ups and downs. Bonuses are paid semi-annually, amounting to about one-third of total pay. This provides a flexibility that is contingent on the performance of the company. In times of economic downturn, casual or non-salarymen are the first to go, followed by bonus payments, followed by negotiations for a cut in basic pay, and this only after announcing cuts in executive pay. It is these pay components, plus other benefits such as family allowances, housing assistance and separation pay, which contribute to the sense of belonging and community (Chen, 1995).

In-house trade unions

Unions based on the enterprise and comprising all employees in the company regardless of job or occupation have been the dominant form of trade union and reflect the principles of loyalty, the corporate family and obedience. They are involved in wage bargaining and resolving workplace problems, but are generally not confrontational (Gill and Wong, 1998). A leading position within the union offers prospects for a good career in management (Chen, 1995). This factor, linked with lifetime employment and the seniority system, means that employees who have been recruited relatively young, and have been through the union and then management ranks, may eventually become board members. The interests of the corporate family are therefore provided for through this process (Kuwahara, 1998 terms this a 'quasi employee-managed' organization, because although not directly managed by all employees, directors are mainly those who have been promoted up through the organization, and recommended by the president, who has himself been through this process).

Ishida's (1986) model of the Japanese system of human resource management reflects these principles and provides a more systematic appreciation of the connections between the various factors involved (Figure 5.3). Strategies to internalize the labour market are based on the environmental factors of relative stability including an ageing workforce (as was seem in SMI) as well as technological innovation. The society is fairly homogeneous and collectivistic, with high levels of internationalization, and the values of an affluent society. Ideology is based on the emphasis on people. ('Human resources' seems to be used as a generic term here in line with other Japanese authors writing for Western readers, such as Tsuda, 1996, rather than in the specific way it has been used in the present text: that is based on ideological or value-laden concepts and a view of human beings as means to an end. The term 'humanity' used by SMI might be a better descriptor in Ishida's model, and reflects the accompanying terms 'community orientation', 'groupism' and 'egalitarianism'.)

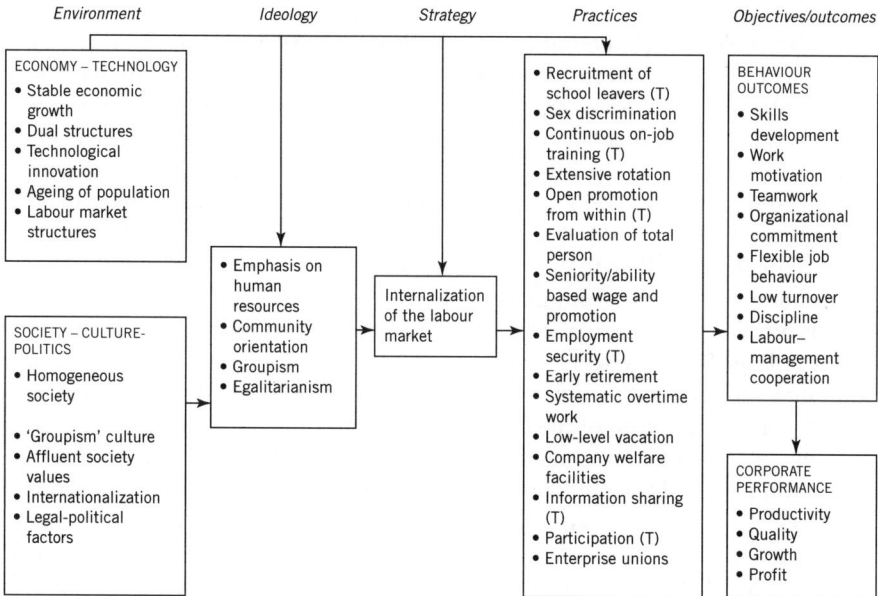

Environment	Ideology	Strategy	Practices	Objectives/outcomes
ECONOMY – TECHNOLOGY • Stable economic growth • Dual structures • Technological innovation • Ageing of population • Labour market structures **SOCIETY – CULTURE- POLITICS** • Homogeneous society • 'Groupism' culture • Affluent society values • Internationalization • Legal-political factors	• Emphasis on human resources • Community orientation • Groupism • Egalitarianism	Internalization of the labour market	• Recruitment of school leavers (T) • Sex discrimination • Continuous on-job training (T) • Extensive rotation • Open promotion from within (T) • Evaluation of total person • Seniority/ability based wage and promotion • Employment security (T) • Early retirement • Systematic overtime work • Low-level vacation • Company welfare facilities • Information sharing (T) • Participation (T) • Enterprise unions	**BEHAVIOUR OUTCOMES** • Skills development • Work motivation • Teamwork • Organizational commitment • Flexible job behaviour • Low turnover • Discipline • Labour– management cooperation **CORPORATE PERFORMANCE** • Productivity • Quality • Growth • Profit

Figure 5.3 Ishida's (1986) model of the Japanese system of human resource management

Note: those practices with a (T) suffix are transferable to Japanese overseas subsidiaries, and have been added by the current author.

The internal market is created by developing loyalty to the one organization from an early age, continuous on-job training, job rotation, promotion from within, seniority-based pay, employment security, and extensive welfare facilities. These are seen in Ishida's model under 'practices'. The outcome which Ishida describes, including high levels of 'work motivation', is high productivity and other measures of corporate performance.

The current author has also indicated on the model, from Ishida's (1986) study (Figure 5.3), those work practices that may be transferable across cultures to other countries that Japanese firms operate in.

Do Japanese people management techniques work outside Japan? Chiba International

Chiba International is based in California, and is a subsidiary of Chiba Electronics Company of Japan. It makes high precision electronic parts for customized integrated circuits used in the computers in military hardware. It began by acquiring a loss-making manufacturing plant from an American competitor in San Jose, putting in a team of Japanese headed by a Canadian-born executive who had been reared in Japan, and turning it around in the space of two years (Pucik and Hatvany, 1998). Now all the lower level workers are American, and 14 out of 24 top executives and 65 out of 70 salesmen are American.

The management philosophy is to aim for the material and spiritual fulfil-ment of all employees, to serve mankind, to satisfy customers' needs, to obtain a just profit, to be a united family, and to expect employee commitment to meet the company's needs.

Practices include many meetings and outside company activities. This includes a morning meeting before work starts. All workers stand in a line denoted by metal dots in the courtyard. Speeches are made by managers on different aspects such as safety or on personnel, sales or production matters. Speeches on sports events and motivational aspects follow, with group exercise for one minute. The company song had not been introduced at the time of writing (Pucik and Hatvany, 1998), and this is how the Japanese management liked to introduce things: very slowly, in order to gain acceptance. The sales force is paid a straight salary rather than on a commission basis. There are expectations of dedication and loyalty from managers but no guarantee they will become chief executive, because of the presence of Japanese top executives, and an apparent glass ceiling. There are some problems of American–Japanese interaction that in part may result from the high expectation of dedication, and the effects on family life, and partly because of the cliquish behaviour of Japanese managers getting together after work and conversing in Japanese. The business is run on the basis of careful financial tracking, open communication and a no-layoff commitment. A corollary of this is the expectation of job flexibility, with workers having broad job categories. There is a close appraisal system and performance monitoring, with pay rises based on merit. The development of quality and developing the expertise of their own people has led to success and acceptance in the community.

Ishida (1986) conducted an investigation into the question 'do Japanese people management work techniques work outside Japan?' through small-scale questionnaire surveys and intensive interviews with Japanese subsidiaries in South East Asia (Singapore, Malaysia, Thailand and Hong Kong), the United States and the former West Germany, and concluded that Japanese managers (mainly subsidiary chief executives) abroad regard the following as the main features of Japanese human resource management:

- community orientation,
- groupism,
- class egalitarianism,
- employment security,
- seniority-based promotion and salary systems,
- information sharing and employee participation,
- flexible job behaviour, and
- low turnover

They do not regard egalitarianism in ability and informality in organizational structure as factors unique to Japan. Factors that are transferable to overseas subsidiaries seem to be: community orientation; class egalitarianism; job security; and worker participation.

Certainly these aspects seem to be present in people management practices in Chiba International. Factors that are difficult to transfer seem to be: group-oriented behaviour; commitment to the organization; low turnover; flexible job behaviour; and wage and promotion seniority systems (which they would have no intention of trying to implement).

Subsidiaries are more likely to take positive steps to 'Japanize' themselves in South East Asia than in Germany or the United States. German conditions are more compatible with employee participation, although these are not as advanced as the Japanese. To a certain extent Chiba had managed to introduce some of these elements into their Californian plant. Job flexibility was expected, as was commitment to the organization, although the glass ceiling for managers may have militated against this. They also seem to have introduced a salary system based on an annual appraisal rather than on a commission base. This may be seen as going half way towards a system that is more based on the uptake of skills, performance and some aspects of length of service. A modified Japanese style of human resource management is used in various parts of the world (Ishida, 1986).

In addition, specific practices that are listed in Ishida's model of Japanese human resource management systems are also regarded by him as being transferable, as a result of his study.

A study undertaken by the Japanese External Trade Organization (JETRO, 1992, and quoted in Yoneyama, 1994) indicated the extent to which people and other management practices were transferred to Japanese wholly owned subsidiaries in Europe (Table 5.2). This partially confirms Ishida's findings.

Table 5.2 Percentage of Japanese wholly owned subsidiaries in Europe in which the management practice is implemented (from JETRO, 1992)

Evening events	79.3
Open office	71.8
On-the-job training	69.9
Common cafeteria	68.4
Work uniforms	56.9
Quality circles	39.1
Daily general meeting	36.2
Bonus	33.3
In-house union	15.5
Lifetime employment	14.9
Just in time	10.9
Morning physical exercise	5.2
Promotion by seniority	4.6

Yoneyama focuses on some of the constraints that impede transfer to European countries. These are described as follows:

• *Recruiting young graduates.* This is preferred in Japan as young graduates can be integrated more easily into the corporate community and trained in-house if they have not worked for another corporation. This is considered as a long-term investment. Yet in Europe the links between Japanese companies and European universities are not strong; many subsidiaries are too small to generate a regular recruitment round; it is not necessary to adopt lifetime employment and European employees tend to be mobile between companies; and the system of promotion by seniority does not work very well.

- *In-house training.* This is highly developed in Japan and people are considered as a key success factor, with lifetime employment justifying the long-term investment in training. Yet mobility of employees is much higher in Europe, and Japanese subsidiaries are reluctant to invest in the training of European staff who may seek other positions outside once they are trained.

- *Job rotation.* This is used extensively in Japan in order for employees to get to know a variety of jobs, and to build a network of relations that help people succeed in managerial positions. Yet in Europe qualifications are often specialized, with employees preferring to develop this specialization and not to go against the normal entry and promotion route.

- *Promotion by seniority.* Salary bands have low differentials in Japan at the beginning of the career, and promotion by seniority reflects a step-by-step approach, and a group orientation. European countries either provide promotion prospects through a hierarchy of diplomas, or on the basis of individual performance in the job.

- *Lifetime employment.* It may be that European employees do not want lifetime employment in a Japanese company, if it means accepting all the other aspects that go with it, such as promotion by seniority, and the longer time frames for training.

- *In-house unions.* It is difficult to go against trade union traditions in the host country, and normally Japanese subsidiaries adapt to local conditions in this respect.

Japanese methods and principles of people management all focus on gaining mutual commitment of people and the corporation. The corporation is seen as a family that looks after its own (that is, in-group members: see for example Hui, 1990). Individual achievement motivation (McClelland, 1987) may not be an appropriate drive to encourage and reward. Motivation should be seen within the whole context of mutual loyalty and commitment. Yet Japanese organizations may have to do some adapting in the Western context in order to operate effectively. The way performance is both conceived and rewarded may therefore differ from culture to culture. Whilst individual performance is often rewarded in Western organizations by performance-related rewards, payment by seniority in Japanese organizations is valued as a way of rewarding commitment to the corporation. This may be far more important than rewarding short-term objective-related performance that does not produce any long-term commitment and sacrifice for the company.

Implications for managers: reward systems across cultures

It is therefore relevant to deal with the problem of how staff, operating in different cultural environments, should be rewarded. A perspective on the function of reward systems (Greene, 1995) is that they should:

- fit the organizational context in which they operate, such as the organizational mission, culture, environment, strategy and structure;
- identify the behaviour and results which are needed and define the rules which govern how individuals and groups behave;
- provide rewards which are equitable, competitive, timely and in an appropriate form;
- be understood and accepted by employees as consistent with their values and priorities and be regarded as equitable and competitive.

Although Greene (1995) ties reward systems directly into performance, he contends that such systems should be sensitive to cultural differences, and notes that it is difficult to explain performance-contingent reward strategies to those who prefer income continuity. He suggests that the impact of reward systems delivered to a culturally diverse workforce can be informed by such value systems as those suggested by Hofstede (1980a), Kluckholm and Strodtbeck (1961), Schein (1985) and Trompenaars (1993). From this it is possible to extend Greene's observation and to speculate that the appropriateness and impact of reward systems will be contingent on such cultural values as:

- *Universalism–particularism*: the extent to which rules concerning the allocation of salary and benefits are universally applied;
- *Individualism–collectivism*: the extent to which rewards are distributed on the basis of individual performance;
- *Locus of control*: the extent to which employees feel they have sufficient control of their environment in order to benefit from performance-related pay;
- *Ascription–achievement status*: the extent to which it is appropriate to reward ascribed status or achievement in the job;
- *Masculinity–femininity*: the extent to which it is appropriate to reward high task achievement in the job; the extent to which basic and overtime pay is structured; the extent to which commitment is rewarded (work-centrality as a subset of masculinity);
- *Power distance*: the extent to which reward is based on hierarchical position rather than task performance, and the level of pay differentials between hierarchical levels;
- *Uncertainty avoidance*: the extent to which pay systems should reflect a need for pay consistency.
- *Short-term, long-term orientation*: time scales of pay systems, particularly those based on achievement of performance objectives.

Schuler and Rogovsky (1998) investigated the relationship between such values and reward systems across national cultures. Taking their data on reward systems from three major international surveys (IBM-Towers Perrin, Price Waterhouse-Cranfield, and International Social Survey Programme) they proposed that:

- *Reward systems based on status* (seniority-based and skills-based) would be more prevalent in countries with higher levels of uncertainty avoidance. This proposition was supported by their findings.

- *Reward systems based on individual performance* (pay-for-performance, individual performance and pay using an individual bonus or commission) would be more prevalent in countries with higher levels of individualism and less prevalent where there are higher levels of uncertainty avoidance. The results supported a link with individualism, but mostly did not support the link with uncertainty avoidance.

- *Social benefits and programmes* (flexible benefit plans, workplace childcare programmes, career-break schemes and maternity leave programmes) will be less prevalent in countries with higher levels of masculinity (cultures with high femininity and that value quality of life and caring for people are more likely to be concerned with employees' personal and social needs and life outside work); and be more prevalent in countries with high levels of uncertainty avoidance with an emphasis on predictability and security in career planning and workday scheduling. The results indicate a relationship between masculinity and a lower use of flexible benefits, workplace childcare, career-break and maternity leave. The link with uncertainty avoidance is not well supported.

- *Employee ownership plans* (employee share options or stock ownership plans) are likely to be more prevalent in countries with low power distance (reflecting an egalitarian attitude towards ownership), and in those with higher levels of individualism (where a calculative involvement of employees, through contractual and financial relations with the company, will provide a bigger incentive to perform), and in those with lower levels of uncertainty avoidance (as employees and organizations may be more willing to share risk). The results support this, indicating that employee ownership plans are more likely to be found in countries with high individualism, lower uncertainty avoidance and lower power distance.

Motivational systems across cultures

Reward systems may only be part of the whole picture. Motivation should perhaps be regarded as an integral part of total commitment of the corporation to the employee and the employee to the corporation (where the corporation is seen as an extension of the people within it, rather than as a mechanism to obtain executive goals of a specific set of stakeholders: see also the Introduction of this book). Perhaps Japanese organizations have been more successful than other collectivist societies in capturing the wider societal collectivism within the corporate. This may be connected with the perception of people as part of the collective with mutual responsibilities.

Many aspects of Japanese management have been written about within Western texts since Pascale and Athos (1981) and principles have been borrowed, adapted and even recirculated to Japanese companies. Yet is it possible to make Japanese approaches work in other cultural settings? It may have been that adaptations of these techniques in the situation described in Chiba were successful in an American context because of the levels of collegiality discussed in Chapter 3, and the celebration of perfection proposed by Gannon and Associates (1994). There are problems of creating an 'internal market' within many Western settings which may militate against developing higher levels of commitment. But these levels of commitment that might be achieved in Western contexts of high unemployment may yet be forms of calculative or even compliant involvement (Etzioni, 1975) where employees are simply afraid of losing their jobs. The mindset of instrumentalism may be the biggest barrier to adopting approaches that are based on a mindset that is more in line with the humanistic one proposed in the Introduction. A reappraisal of the concept of 'human resource management' and its ideological and values foundation is really necessary. A management that learns from cross-cultural experience by understanding fundamental differences in knowledge sets, based on different value approaches, is required. This aspect is incorporated in the next chapter, which focuses on the learning organization.

Questions for managers

1 Which aspects of those policies implemented by Chiba in California could be successfully implemented in your country and area?

2 How does the concept of 'valuing humanity' in the people management policies of Sumitomo differ from the concepts of human resource management as practised in your organization, or an organization with which you are familiar?

3 How could your organization, or one with which you are familiar in your country, obtain the type of total commitment obtained in companies like Sumitomo and Matsushita?

An agenda for research

The conceptual framework in Figure 5.1 attempts to integrate the various elements of motivation into a more complete concept of motivation, drawing on the commitment approach of the Japanese model. The relations between these elements should be more fully investigated in future research. This is particularly the case with the relationship between commitment and aspects such as job satisfaction. Hence Japanese managers may score low on job satisfaction (de Boer, 1978), but still be committed to obtaining high levels of productivity. The cultural aspects of this as antecedent variables in the construction of 'locus of human value' (see Introduction) should also be incorporated into this investigation. For example, are corporations more successful in a collectivist society where managers and employees share the same humanistic locus of human value, and employ practices that reflect this? The way organizational management responds to the potential antitheses between the world inside work organizations and that outside may be crucial in obtaining high levels of commitment.

The study by Schuler and Rogovsky (1998) went some way in establishing a connection between cultural values and reward systems. As noted above, their results suggested a connection between status-based reward systems and high uncertainty avoidance, individual performance based systems and individualism; systems incorporating extensive social benefits and femininity, and employee ownership plans with individualism, low uncertainty avoidance and low power distance. However, it did not establish connections between these different types of reward systems and other incentives (task, job, career and organizational variables in Figure 5.1) and their relationship with job, career and needs (based on cultural and individual variables) satisfaction (Figure 5.1), and the connection with corporate commitment. In other words, did these types of incentive work, and how was this success measured? Success could be measured in terms of individual performance, group results or commitment to the organization, for example. The connections indicated in Figure 5.1 should therefore be used as the basis for further study of these issues, with researchers asking some of the following questions:

Questions for researchers

1 What are the key cultural variables that influence the success of motivational systems within organizations?

2 What are the connections between incentives provided by corporations and the cultural requirements of people working within them?

3 How do measures of success of motivational systems vary among different countries' cultural contexts?

4 How should the success of Japanese people management policies and techniques be assessed in different countries' cultural context?

The learning organization: the British model

chapter six

The British model

The concept of the learning organization is an outgrowth of Anglo-Saxon management culture. Not all learning organizations are British, and not all British organizations are learning organizations. This chapter argues that the concept of action learning, which was developed in Britain, spearheaded the development of the concept of learning as an experiential activity that takes place as part of the management process, rather than for example in the classroom. This led to the idea of the learning organization. Pucik (1988) makes the point that Japanese organizations have often more successfully leveraged their learning capabilities in Japanese–Western strategic alliance to create an asymmetrical distribution of benefits in their favour through acquisition of new knowledge from the partner and within the cooperative venture. Lessem (1989) discusses the developmental nature of Japanese corporations. Yet the way that Japanese corporations view people in organizations (see Introduction and Chapter 5) may be fundamentally different to the way that people are perceived as human resources, and more latterly as 'intellectual capital' or 'knowledge resources' (e.g. see Snowden, 1999) in Western, and predominantly Anglo-Saxon organizations. The approach towards development and learning may therefore be fundamentally different between the British and Japanese models, with the former using a concept of developing valuable human resources, the latter employing a philosophy of 'valuing humanity' (Tsuda, 1996: 537). It may be that these two traditions are moving closer together in contemporary theories of knowledge management, and that systems approaches employed previously in theories of the learning organization (e.g. Argyris, 1992) are being broken down (e.g. Snowden, 1999; Nonaka et al., 2000).

The objective of this chapter is to trace the development of the concept of the learning organization (and onto knowledge management) through its inception in Britain, its various crossings of the Atlantic and back again, and more recently its joining with concepts emanating from Japan. Its transferability, in concept and practice across cultures, is investigated. Training and development in organizations is discussed as part of a total model. To place this in the context of real cultures and real management issues, British Petroleum and its offshore operations are focused upon.

British management culture

Britain is low on Hofstede's (1980a) measure of power distance (lower than the United States and close to the Scandinavian countries), very high on individualism (with the other Anglo-Saxon countries), high on masculinity (higher than the other Anglo-Saxon countries), and very low on uncertainty avoidance (slightly lower than the other Anglo-Saxon countries). Britain is also short term oriented along with the other Anglo-Saxon countries on Hofstede's measure of long-term orientation (1991). Schwartz (1994) did not include the UK in his study, but that of Smith, Dugan and Trompenaars (1996) clusters the UK with the other Anglo-Saxon countries in being high on egalitarian commitment (low on conservatism) and midway between utilitarian involvement and loyal involvement.

From the literature that seeks to describe the British general and management culture (Gannon and Associates, 1994; Tayeb, 1993; Dubin, 1970) the main features may be summarized as follows.

- a valuing of personal and psychological privacy;
- denigration of emotional outbursts; being reserved;
- friendliness and sincerity;
- orderliness, patience and seeing a task through;
- well defined status and roles (class distinctions);
- little mobility and a preference not to make changes for the sake of change;
- making the best of things and playing the game right, not necessarily to win, but to see fair play;
- love of humour, often as a device to lighten the occasion;
- politeness and modesty, as well as indirectness;
- regard for pragmatism and common sense in the work situation rather than precise rules, but a strong sense of order and tradition means rules that are spelt out will be obeyed;
- an element of formality in the workplace between different levels;
- preference for well defined job functions;
- the view that meetings are important and managers expected to be good communicators;
- individualism, which is reflected in non-conformity rather than competitiveness, but needing group consensus in order to make a stand;
- work is motivating when seen to be useful to self and others striving towards a common goal;
- social control based on persuasion and appeal to sense of guilt in transgressing social norms.

British Petroleum

BP may be the archetypal British company. It was born out of the colonial period in 1901 when the wealthy Englishman William Knox D'Arcy obtained a concession from the Shah of Persia to explore for and exploit its oil resources. When oil was eventually discovered, the Anglo-Persian Oil Company came into being in 1909. The company that was to become BP sought British government help in 1914 to avoid falling under the domination of Royal Dutch/Shell. The sum of £2 million began the majority shareholding of the government in BP that would last until 1987, when this was reduced to a tiny residual holding. After a number of acquisitions, including Standard Oil in the United States in 1987, it merged with the American giant Amoco in 1998 to form the company it is today, employing 97,000 people with revenues of $120 billion (British Petroleum, 2001).

In 1990, John Donegan, group management development and training manager, described BP as a 'learning organization' (Donegan, 1990). For the company this meant:

- Recognition that organizations must adapt to a future of constant change.

- Acceptance of the key role of people in this process of adaptation.

- Facilitation of the learning and personal development of all people in the organization through a truly empowering culture.

- The use of combined energy, creativity and commitment generated among employees by this developmental climate to fuel an ongoing process of organizational transformation (Donegan, 1990: 302).

From a perspective of 'management of scarce human resources in the 1990s and beyond' (1990: 303), he states that BP appreciates that the key to competitive advantage lies not just in the professional quality of the staff, which its competitors have as well, but in having staff who are prepared to go the 'extra mile' through a feeling of responsibility and empowerment, and releasing personal creativity and motivation to complement professional expertise. Not least this involves developing the capability to respond to the challenges of change. The approach taken is one of 'individual self development', where managers and staff are not passive in the process, and where suitable values and styles of openness and trust are developed to facilitate this type of learning. Development is directed at all, not just those with potential, and reflects a 'people friendly climate'. Part of this involves staff appraisal and feedback, with team performance as the benchmark, rather than individuals. It also involves developing a 'counselling culture': developing 'all' equally, including women, yet recognizing differences. This approach should be given, not least to reflect the needs arising out of the general demographic downturn and an increased demand for qualified professionals and managers.

Further, Donegan (1990: 307) says, 'the BP experience has been that to become a learning organization one must first become, for managers, an "unlearning organization". After all, forgetting the inappropriate mythology of the past and learning the new realities is what culture change is all about.' He then goes on to describe a competences approach (see Chapter 3) to management

129

development, by identifying what qualities the company requires for the future (in line with current debates in the late 1980s/early 1990s). The process also involves fast-tracking of managers, and the development of global managers to meet future challenges of globalization.

Cassells (1999) takes up the story in the upstream business of BP of the North Sea and Atlantic oil fields. He focuses on the strategic learning capabilities of BP at the end of the 1990s, when there was a realization that some types of learning can lead to rigidity. A need was perceived to overhaul the approach to organizational learning to prevent it becoming a core rigidity rather than a core competence. Emphasis was placed on a strategic concern, with institutionalizing an appropriate learning style, on the importance of pace of learning, on structuring learning capabilities for competitive advantage, and on recognizing the implications of collaborative approaches to learning through alliances to provide returns. The emphasis on learning as a competitive advantage was based on a view that because organizational learning arises from complex interactions among terms and individuals, the resulting knowledge and expertise is less likely to be imitated.

Much emphasis in exploration activities was previously placed on learning by detailing areas of uncertainty and writing highly competent reports which added to uncertainty reduction but led to long delays in the oil field development and production activities. This was replaced by an approach that recognized the limitations of uncertainty reduction, and emphasized the identification of key factors that ensured success or failure of a project. Possible outcomes could then be identified and contingency strategies put in place. The emphasis was therefore on action learning as a means of assessing uncertainty. This approach shortened the time between discovery of an oil field and its exploitation. Through the creation of task-oriented teams information, knowledge and learning flowed more quickly. The approach to identifying possible key problems and contingencies also led to the identification of available skills and opened up opportunities of allying with other organizations to enhance learning.

Action learning and the experiential approach

Training has for many years been regarded as important in British companies, and often central to human resource management in addressing performance issues and managing change. For example Keep (1989: 111) wrote in a UK volume on current issues and new perspectives in human resource management: 'training and development should be regarded as central to anything that can sensibly be termed HRM . . . the adoption by companies of a strategic approach towards the training and development of their workforce represents a vital component of any worthwhile or meaningful form of HRM (or HRD)'. However, its perceived importance has not always been reflected in the expenditure on training by British companies. This was partially why the above quotation was penned in the first place. A number of international comparisons made in the 1980s, such as the Institute of Manpower Studies (NEDO/MSC, 1984) *Competence and Competition* study, revealed that Britain was lagging behind other European countries in expenditure on training (there is currently a lack of meaningful international comparative data on training expenditure: Ross et al., 1998). For example, this position contrasts with the legal requirement of French companies to spend a percentage of payroll on training, with South Africa more recently following this lead.

Yet Britain is the home of 'learning' theories, although such theories have been picked up and developed by American theorists and consultants, and have been exported to many parts of the world.

An approach to both individual and organizational learning, based on this concept of learning by doing, which has been widely adopted in British and international companies is that of 'action learning'. This was originally developed in the UK in 1960s by Reg Revans (for example, Revans, 1965) who then began to set up educational programmes in Belgium, India and Egypt, based on these principles.

He sees learning as inextricably bound up with the process of management, arguing that everyone in the organization should be engaged in learning. This presupposes the availability of information in the organization sufficient to enable learning to take place throughout the organization. He also sees the scientific method as providing the model for effective learning. Revans (1965) suggests that there are four forces bearing on management decision making:

- the need for economy of time and management effort;

- the analytical approach of the scientist, available to the manager, whilst not forgetting intuition which is the first weapon of management;

- the ability to understand and contain variability and risk by the use of statistical methods;

- a greater understanding, through the social sciences, of human beings as a determinant of success in the enterprise.

The first two aspects were seen as crucial in the upstream work of BP. Revans goes on to develop this into a specific methodology of management learning that he calls 'system beta', with five phases:

- survey: the first phase of observation;

- hypothesis: theory development and conjecture;

- experiment: testing in practice;

- audit: the comparing of actual and desired results;

- review: relating the specific result with the overall context.

Revans also describes a 'system gamma' that is the personal predisposition of the individual manager, his or her mental set or subjective consciousness. This has an influence on the way problems are approached and tackled. A further system, 'system alpha', describes the relationship between the impersonal situation and the personal value system of the individual manager, illustrated in such questions as 'what values are guiding my actions?', 'what is preventing the fulfilment of those values?' and, 'how can I unblock these barriers?'

It was on these basic principles that action learning was established: on the premise that knowledge can only be the outcome of action. But the understanding

131

of 'self' goes hand in hand with external impact, so that you cannot change the external world without changing your own internal development. This internal development, and understanding of the relationship between self and external work-related issues, is facilitated by a small group (a 'set' of four or five learners), coming together regularly to support and help one another and mediated by a facilitator. Activity is directed through individual projects within the participants' organizations.

This learning process combines the methodology of the scientific and analytical with the commitment of the self, and the need to examine motives and beliefs under the scrutiny of the group process. Essentially it is an experiential approach to learning that has been extensively used within UK organizations, and the concepts have been exported to other Anglo-Saxon countries, notably the United States. It is also reflected in many of the 'knowledge management' approaches later developed, such as that of Nonaka in Japan (e.g. Nonaka et al., 2000), and discussed later in this chapter.

The American David Kolb (1976, 1984) developed the concept of experiential learning as a process or cycle comprising four stages, which also mirror Revans' system beta, as follows:

- concrete experiences; followed by

- observation and reflection; leading to

- formation of abstract concepts and generalizations; leading to

- testing of the implications of concepts for future action, which then leads to new concrete experiences.

Kolb sees this as the way learning happens, as it is governed largely by the pursuit of goals that are appropriate to our own needs. Thus we seek experiences that are related to these goals, we interpret the experiences in the light of these goals, and form concepts that are relevant to our needs and goals. When goals are not clear, learning tends to be erratic. As a result of personal preferences and inclinations, individuals tend to emphasize a particular aspect of the learning cycle. Kolb uses the examples of the mathematician who emphasizes abstract conceptualization, the poet who values concrete experience, the manager who is concerned with application of concepts, and the lover of nature who develops observational skills. The development of such preferences may provide both strengths and weaknesses.

This approach to experiential learning, and the concept of learner preferences and their identification in order to make learning more effective, was reimported to the UK through the work of Honey and Mumford (1982). Both Kolb's and Honey and Mumford's work entail the use of questionnaires to elicit the balance between learning styles that individual learners have. Corporate trainers in the UK have used the Honey and Mumford instrument extensively.

Transferability across cultures

In the cross-cultural context, Hughes-Weiner (1986) qualifies the learning process described by Kolb:

- *Concrete experience*: people from different cultures are likely to have different backgrounds and different experiences. Their readiness, for example, for class-room learning therefore may be quite different.

- *Reflective observation*: as a result of different behaviour patterns, socialization and institutional and work experiences, individuals from different cultures may make different assumptions about what they see and understand through their experiences. People from different societies are likely to acquire different bodies of knowledge.

- *Abstract conceptualization*: because people from different cultures have different cognitive frameworks, this may lead them to focus on irrelevant information or misinterpretations in a particular situation, thus drawing wrong conclusions and theories in a different cultural situation from their own.

- *Active experimentation*: behaviour differences between cultures may lead to misinterpretations and misattributions of the meanings of such behaviour outside their own cultures, leading to confusion and frustration.

No empirical verification of these assumptions was offered by Hughes-Weiner. Indeed when Allinson and Hayes (1988; Hayes and Allinson, 1988) undertook a cross-cultural study using the Honey and Mumford instrument they identified cross-cultural differences between British, Indian and East African managers in two broad learning styles: an 'analysis' orientation and an 'action' orientation. This provides an inadequate working explanation of learning differences as it gives insufficient detail to assist management trainers who are working across national cultures. Trainers must develop a capability to adapt and deliver quality training and management development by taking into account the differences in management learning between cultures. It is perhaps unfortunate for this requirement that the experiential model largely reflects approaches to management educational and training accepted in the Anglo-Saxon world which are based heavily on the concept of the independent learner, the instructor as facilitator and the value of interactive and experiential methods of education. The concept of 'learning' in the Anglo-Saxon sense is also very difficult to translate into other European languages. Often the norm is that 'instruction' is teacher based, rather than the more interactive and egalitarian 'client' or learner-based approaches that view the 'learner' as self-directional and the teacher or trainer as a facilitator and resource.

Work undertaken by Triandis, Brislin and Hui (1988) seems to challenge prevalent Anglo-American approaches to training on the basis of cross-cultural differences between 'collectivism' and the 'individualism' of Western cultures. Similarly, such training approaches are questioned by empirical findings in an Australian–Asian empirical study (Niles, 1995) which suggest differences in motivation for learning based on McClelland's (1987) concept of 'Achievement Motive', where social approval is important for Asian students and achievement important for Australian students. Sawadogo (1995) also calls into question the relevance of Western training concepts in sub-Saharan Africa, such as that of the independent learner, the teacher as facilitator and the role of feedback, suggesting that Western training methods are largely inappropriate.

133

In order to partly overcome the problems of simply transposing the experiential model onto other cultures, Jackson (1995, 1996) reformulated the Kolb model along the lines suggested by Hughes-Weiner (1986) and tested this empirically across different cultures. He proposes four learning modalities as follows:

- *Receptivity*: learners are predominantly receptive to practical stimuli or theoretical stimuli for learning depending on their cultural backgrounds and their experiences in national educational systems. This could involve either on-the-job learning or off-job theoretical study.

- *Perception*: learners are more intuitive about sorting and judging information, or are rational in a step-by-step approach in judging the quality of information that is the basis for making decisions. This represents the difference between being responsive to new and untried ideas in a holistic way, and being responsive to facts and details and proven approaches. This again reflects experience within their national culture.

- *Cognitive*: learners are more subjective in the way they make decisions and solve problems based on personal judgements, or base their decision making more on logic and scientific approaches. This represents a distinction between a preference for scientific approaches and subjects that provide definite answers, and a preference for more judgmental or subjective approaches of the humanities, and can be influenced by national or cultural differences.

- *Control* (labelled 'behaviour' in previous work): learners prefer to rely on their own initiative, or on the direction of an instructor. This has implications for the level of control required or expected from the learner. This is likely to reflect prior educational experience in national systems which reflect either a controlled instructor-led approach, or a more facilitative learner-initiative approach.

Results from surveying management 'learners' (both management students and managers) across the UK, France, Germany, Poland, Taiwan and Lithuania are as follows:

Receptivity modality In the *practical-theoretical* dimension the main difference exists between the Polish and French groups, with the Polish management learners having an overriding preference for practical educational stimuli, whilst the French have a comparatively theoretical preference. This is particularly the case where the Polish learners have a preference for practical class activity, learning by doing, learning from simulations in the class, but with a strong preference to learn alone. The learners from Taiwan are the most socially oriented, expressing a preference for learning with others. The Lithuanian learners are somewhat different to the Polish on this dimension, in that they have a comparatively greater preference for learning from reading text, but prefer to explore how to do things rather than looking at underlying concepts. The British too are social learners with a preference for practical activity and learning by doing. The learners from Taiwan also express these preferences. The French are the most theoretical in comparative terms, but still express a preference for learning by doing, and overall prefer to learn alone. The German learners express a preference for learning by doing and learning from simulations in the classroom, but are generally less practical than the learners from Taiwan and Poland.

Perceptual modality Again, on the *intuitive-rational* dimension, the Polish learners account for the major differences. They express an overriding preference for dealing with information and ideas in a rational way, except that they favour ingenuity over practicality. The other national groups seem to favour an intuitive approach, and this is expressed most strongly in a preference for designing plans and structures as opposed to precisely implementing detailed plans. Here the British learners express this preference most strongly. Both Lithuanian learners and those from Taiwan express a preference more strongly for practicality over ingenuity.

Cognitive modality The Poles and Lithuanians show the greatest preference for decision making through logical processes, with the learners from France, Britain and Taiwan being the most subjective in their approaches to making decisions. However, the Poles show a preference for making decisions on the basis of what seems right, which appears to contradict a logical approach. The German learners also show a preference for a logical approach rather than dealing with beliefs, feelings or what seems right.

Behaviour modality The learners from Poland and Taiwan show the greatest preference for an instructor-directed approach, with the Germans and Lithuanians the least so. Of the Western Europeans, the French have the least preference for self-initiated learning, with the Germans and then British preferring a self-initiated approach. The German sample, of all the national groups, believe most that they should question a teacher's proficiency if need be. The Polish indicate that they are the least likely to do this. The Lithuanians believe strongly that teachers should be regarded as equals, with the learners from France and Taiwan believing more that teachers should be treated as superiors.

It is evident from this study that British management 'learners' favour practical and social learning activities, are intuitive, subjective and favour taking the initiative in their learning. This may be an ideal cultural basis on which to build concepts of a total learning organization.

The organizational learning concept

It is mainly such Anglo-Saxon approaches to experiential learning that have given rise to the cultural product of the concept of organizational learning. Organizational learning may be regarded as experiential learning at the corporate level. Although organizations as entities cannot learn (only individuals as corporate agents can learn) conditions in the organization can be created in order to facilitate this learning. Hence Argyris' (1992) single- and double-loop learning

Figure 6.1
Argyris' single-
and double-
loop learning

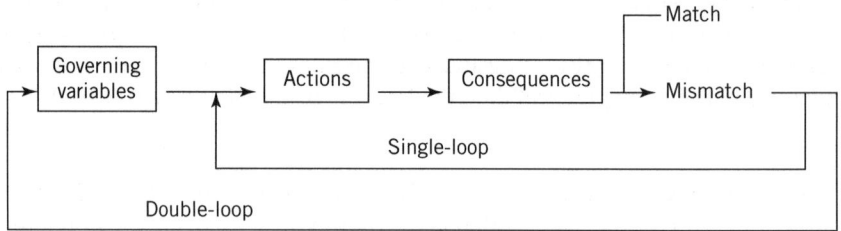

represent a cyclical process where actions (single-loop) or governing variables (double-loop) are adapted or changed (Figure 6.1).

Single-loop learning takes place when mismatches between the outcomes that are intended and those that actually occur are corrected by simply changing the actions that were initiated in the preceding cycle. Double-loop learning occurs when these mismatches are corrected by examining and altering governing variables and then actions. Such governing variables are sets of beliefs and values that can be seen to drive and guide people's action as agents for the organization. Learning occurs only when the solution to a new problem is actually implemented. Hence simply discovering problems and inventing solutions while necessary for learning are not sufficient for organizational learning to take place. It could be said that the four stages of Kolb's learning cycle, or the five phases of Revans' 'system beta' should be completed before learning takes place, and that this is comparable to Argyris' model. This model is also comparable to an open systems model that explains how organizations as systems receive feedback from their environment from consequences of their outputs. Kolb, Rubin and Osland (1991) elaborate such an open systems model, and this is an example of organizational theory which has been much criticized by people such as Silverman (1970) over the last 30 years. This is because of the reification of organizations as entities separate from the people who comprise them, the perceived rationalistic cause–end relationship, and an instrumentalism based on 'executive goals'. As was seen above, Kolb suggests that individual learning is governed by people's needs and goals. People seek experiences that are related to their goals; they interpret them in relation to these goals and test the implications that are relevant to their needs. Organizations, however, pursue goals that are related to such aspects as short-term profit, long-term survival or the achievement of social goals as in the case of public institutions (Bovin, 1998). Such goals can more accurately be referred to as executive goals rather than organizational goals (Silverman, 1970).

Peter Senge (1990), who has had much influence in developing and propagating worldwide the concept of the learning organization, proposes five 'component technologies' that contribute towards developing learning organizations:

- *Systems thinking*. This is essentially an ability to see above the isolated parts of the system, and to see how it all fits together.

- *Personal mastery*. This involves continually clarifying and deepening personal vision, to focus on energies, and developing patience in order to see reality objectively and to provide a commitment to develop mastery.

- *Mental models*. This involves an ability to understand and change shared mental models which pervade the organization and prevent change.

- *Building shared vision*. This is more than publishing a mission statement; it is developing an ability to unearth shared vision and foster commitment rather than compliance.

- *Team learning*. This begins with the capacity of members of a team to suspend judgement and start to think together and to recognize the patterns of interaction within a team that militate against learning. Senge (1990) contends that teams are fundamental learning units in an organization.

Bovin (1998) suggests that the learning organization as a concept is a means of addressing the requirement for the future organization in the changing international environment. This may also explain the differences between the concept of training and development as an organizational sub-system, and an organization (presumably as an entity) to learn. He contends that the classic business process (presumably predominantly in Anglo-Saxon organizations) in the 1970s and 1980s was that: (a) a mission was formulated; (b) strategy was developed to achieve overriding business goals; (c) detailed objectives were set to ensure the achievement of strategic goals; (d) in order to achieve these objectives the necessary structures and processes were established; (e) job structures and job descriptions were then formulated to fill the organizational structure; (f) people were acquired who had the appropriate competences to fill the jobs as specified; (g) people were developed to fit the organization.

'Advanced' organizations (according to Bovin, 1998) are now realizing that this model is inappropriate because of changing demographics, as the gross number of people and specialist skills available are decreasing. Hence 'human assets' must be more 'efficiently utilized'. At the same time competition for those competent people is increasing. Managers have to change their style to reflect more employee involvement, personal creativity and must move from positional power to team leadership based on empowerment (although this seems a huge leap in logic, and certainly does not reflect cultural differences in people's perception of leadership and power relations in organizations). Bovin also adds that because of more international competition, internal business investment is even more closely scrutinized and higher levels of return on investment are needed. Therefore there is a need to maximize on the currently available human potential, and for a more efficient control on the investment in people development. Hence Bovin's suggested business process of the future seeks to recognize that people have different abilities, tending to do what they are best at, and doing this more successfully as part of a team (Figure 6.2).

A learning organization is 'an organization which facilitates the learning of all its members and continuously transforms itself' (Pedler et al., 1989 quoted in Bovin 1998: 363). Rather than the essence of the learning organization being training, this implies individual and organizational self-development, with an emphasis on the two aspects of learning by individuals and learning by the organization (see Mumford, 1988). The former can be achieved by moving people around into new experiences and expanding responsibilities, but also by carefully monitoring performance (Bovin, 1998). The latter, the organization, learns by discovering and correcting deficiencies in its actions (Bovin, 1998, but also see

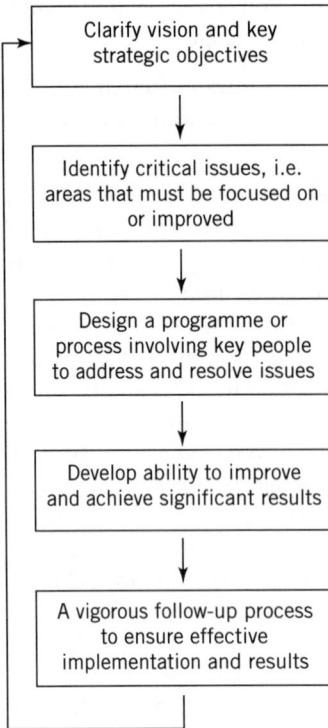

Note: Feedback loop inserted by current author.

Argyris', 1992, single-loop learning). It corrects actions by receiving information from its internal environment (e.g., new product information, results from corporate climate surveys, suggestions at meetings and financial reports) and external environment (e.g. customer complaints, opening of new markets, new technology, actions of competitors and changing fashions and consumer taste). This learning may be revealed in policy statements, but quite often is stored in managers' 'mental maps' (cf. Senge, 1990), which guide their decisions. According to Edmondson and Moingeon (1996), definitions in the literature of what organizational learning is have included: encoding and modifying routines, acquiring knowledge which is useful to the organization, increasing the organizational capacity to take productive action, interpretation and sense making, developing knowledge about action–outcome relationships and detection and correction of error. There tends either to be a focus on how organizations as social systems learn, adapt and change, or how the individuals within organizations develop, adapt and update their cognitive models. Presumably the former perspective is one of the primacy of organizations as systems (systems theory) where individuals act as the agents of the organization, and the latter perspective is one which sees the organization as facilitating (or hindering) the development of individuals. Yet even this last perspective indicates that the reason for this is the pursuit of organizational goals (an instrumental perspective) rather than the organization valuing and focusing upon the development of its people as an end in itself (a humanistic perspective).

For the main characteristics of a learning organization Bovin (1998) provides a view from some of the main contributors to the British literature on the debate: Pedler, Boydell and Burgoyne (1989). A learning organization:

- has a climate in which individuals are encouraged to learn and to develop their full potential, and people perform beyond their competence by taking initiative and using and developing their intelligence and being themselves in their job;

- extends the learning culture to include customers, suppliers and other significant stakeholders where possible by such means as buyer–supplier workshops in total quality programmes and customers invited to in-organizational training;

- makes human resource development strategy central to business policy in order that the process of individual and organizational learning becomes a major business activity;

- provides a continuous process of organizational transformation designed to harness the products of individual learning in order to make fundamental changes in assumptions, goals, norms and operating procedures (Argyris', 1992, double-loop learning) on the basis of internal drive to self-direction, not simply reacting to external pressures.

Training and development within a total model

Learning organizations are based on assumptions that favour teamwork, active participation of people in decision making and increased empowerment of people (Bovin, 1998). The whole tendency of training and development within this type of concept is away from a central training function that prescribes training and towards responsibility of line managers. Senge (1990) refers to 'leaders' having a role shift away from charismatic decision making and towards being designers, teachers and stewards who design overall ideas of purpose, vision and core value, as teachers assist their subordinates to understand the workings of the organization including causes of problems, and as stewards build bridges between people's needs and aspirations and the achievement of the goals of the organization and therefore attempt to diminish the possible contradictions between individuals' needs and the interests of the organization.

Training is used to ensure readiness for change and maximize the specific competences of individuals in relation to the needs of the organization. Training needs, within this model, should be determined by the individual in consultation with peers and based on the needs of the organizational unit (Bovin, 1998). The place of the training function should be at the centre of the strategic management process in order that it may facilitate change by translating the values and direction of the organization into a strategic human resource strategy (Donegan, 1990). The trainer would therefore be seen as a consultant within the organization and an agent of change.

From learning to knowledge: from Britain to Japan

In Chapter 3, the problem of the competences approach in identifying the 'whole' person, in an analogy with the police 'photofit', was discussed. It may be possible to identify explicit attributes of knowledge, skills and abilities that are required to successfully perform the tasks of a job, and to train people to develop or enhance these sets of competences. It is very difficult however, to identify and develop more tacit, implicit or intuitive aspects that make up the whole person. This has been discussed in connection with developing ethical managers (Brady, 1990; Jackson, 1993a). It may be possible to develop the 'knowing that' aspects at the conceptual level, such as rules embodied in codes of conduct and laws, and the consequences of action in cost-benefit or policy analysis. However, the 'knowing how' aspects such as compassion, goodwill and empathy are difficult to encompass in training courses. Similarly, in connection with measuring and developing management performance, Jackson (1991) discusses the differences between the 'conceptual' aspects of management performance, and the 'intuitive' aspects. He also argues that because of the nature of different organizational cultures, intuitive management may be more favoured in some organizations and businesses over conceptual management, and vice versa. He found that the rationalistic approach to management training favoured in a parent high street (retail) bank in the UK was contrary to the intuitive way that managers operated and performed highly in its consumer credit subsidiary (Jackson, 1993b). He conceptualized the management development process in the bank as a whole as a desire to move managers and teams from a situation of 'incongruence' where there was poor communication, incongruent individuals, a weak team culture and lack of identification with the team, and a lack of sharing of objectives, to a situation of 'congruence' where there is good communication, congruent individuals, and a strong culture, identity and sharing of objectives within the team. The management training process that had been developed in the parent bank was conceptualized as being aimed at getting managers from incongruent to congruent through a two-week course built on rational principles of management, delivered in a classroom, and requiring managers to stand back and 'think' about the processes and principles. The chief executive required the whole of the banking group to adopt this programme, and the HRM executive in the consumer credit company was concerned.

The dilemma that they were confronted with is captured in Figure 6.3. There was a concern that if the management training programme were successful, this would have a negative effect on the work of the credit company, whose managers and staff had traditionally worked 'by the seat of their pants' in an intuitive way. They were highly sales and results oriented. They valued experience and 'instinct', and there was a danger that the training would slow reactions down if people had to rationalize each step and stage of their tasks. Figure 6.3 also relates back to Boisot's (1987) concept of the nature of information in an organization.

Boisot (1987) represents the two dimensions of uncodified–codified, or the level to which information is structured, and undiffused–diffused or the amount of sharing of information as a 'cultural space' within the organization. Hence technical proprietary knowledge is highly codified and heavily guarded, and therefore undiffused. As in the case of BP above, this information is subject to copying because it is highly coded. Although BP was careful about sharing this

Figure 6.3
Information
handling styles
and management
training (adapted
from Jackson,
1993b)

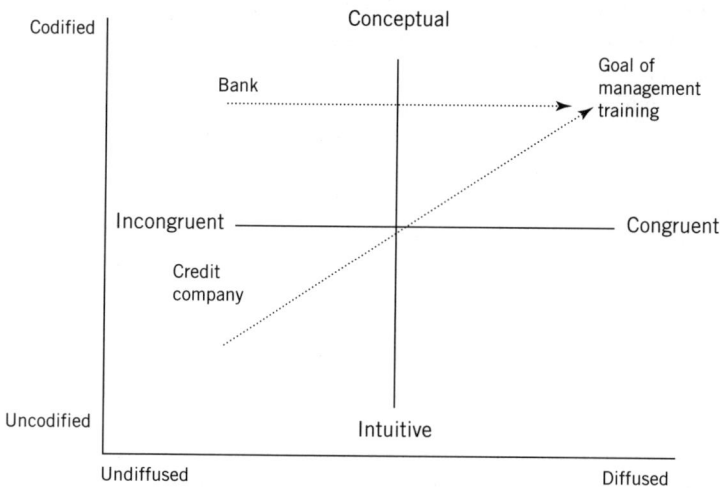

type of knowledge in alliances, it was also aware that the unique aspects of uncodified information were not easy to copy. This was the basis upon which it set about developing a learning organization. At its undiffused end of the continuum, uncodified knowledge is personal knowledge. When it is diffused among a general population it becomes common sense. This is the 'common sense' only of a group with a common culture, such as a work organization, an ethnic group or a country. The old approach of BP in its upstream activities was to highly codify information regarding the risks of developing an oil field. The new approach was to rely less on this and more on contingencies and 'action learning' as they developed in the field. This experience could then be generalized to the exploitation of other fields. Highly codified diffused information becomes 'public knowledge'. It is in the public domain because it is contained in textbooks, websites and other text-based media. Andersen Consulting (which was discussed in Chapter 3) has introduced a knowledge management system called 'Knowledge Xchange', an intranet-based system for writing up experiences and posting them to the intranet site, to enable access to other consultants anywhere within Andersen's worldwide organization (Davenport and Hansen, 1998). This is an approach that seeks to codify experience and then diffuse it throughout the organization so that consultants may learn from the experience of colleagues. Much recent work in knowledge management has focused more on 'tacit' knowledge (Boisot's, 1987, uncodified information) and its interaction with explicit knowledge (Boisot's, 1987, codified information). This is understood less, as was noted above.

Intuitive knowledge has been studied under various guises, not least in connection with the learning process and the way managers actually approach learning and management. A distinction between 'thinking' and 'intuition' is contained within the Myer-Briggs Type Indicator, a personality questionnaire that is used extensively in the United States and Britain. Agor (1985) has formalized these concepts, also borrowing from the literature on right-brain, left-brain dominance, into his 'Intuitive Management Survey' which seeks to distinguish between managers who predominantly use a 'thinking' style based on deduction, objectivity, facts and problem solving by reductionism, and an 'intuitive' style based on induction, subjectivity, feelings, and solving problems by looking at the whole and using hunches. This aspect was recognized some time before by Revans (1965), as was seen above.

There is some evidence that these 'styles' may be influenced by culture. The issue of learning styles across cultures was discussed above. Jackson (1996) suggested differences among country cultures in the way that learners sort and judge information (intuitively or rationally), and the way they make decisions (personal and subjective judgements or logic and scientific methods). The samples of British learners were the most intuitive and the Polish less so. The French, British and Taiwanese showed the highest preference for subjective judgements, and the Polish and Lithuanians for using logic. Although not backed up by empirical evidence, Lessem (1989) provides a typology of cultural differences related to different approaches to knowledge, learning and management.

Lessem looks at the evolution of business and management over time and across the globe, characterizing approaches to management in the West (United States), East (Japan), North (Britain and Europe), and South (Africa). He looks at *entrepreneurial* management (the early stage of a company's development, typified by the West); *executive* or *rational* management as a second bureaucratic stage typified by the North, but also borrowing heavily from literature and business schools in the West; *developmental* management, often a third stage of breaking down bureaucracy and developing quality, and typified by the East; and finally *transformational* or *metaphysical* management aimed at higher ideals, and being a final, but continuing stage, which is typified by a few international companies and possibly in the South.

These different cultural approaches may determine both the competences that managers should have, and the nature of their results, but in particular show the way they are likely to process information. Lessem terms these four 'domains' of management. Table 6.1 combines and summarizes his categorization.

Table 6.1 Cultural attributes of managers in knowledge management (adapted from Lessem, 1989)

Function	Entrepreneural	Executive	Developmental	Transformational
Physical	Hard work	High productivity	Intense interactivity	Energy flow
Social	Raw enthusiasm	Effective teamwork	Quality circles	Corporate culture
Mental	Native shrewdness	Management control	Manager self-development	Process and change
Emotional	Sheer willpower	Competitive strategy	Cooperative strategy	Business interfusion
Analytical	Improvisation	Formal organization	Corporate architecture	Natural management
Intuitive	Market instinct	Analytical marketing	Planned evolution	Unlimited possibilities
Imaginative	Imagination	Systematized innovation	Corporate renewal	Spiritually based vision

To be an effective entrepreneurial manager you need certain 'primal' (Lessem, 1989) attributes of hard work, enthusiasm, shrewdness, willpower, an ability to improvise, an instinct for the marketplace, and imagination. Instinctive processing of information is likely to be useful here, as was the case with the credit company above, and may be a knowledge and learning style of North Americans as well as entrepreneurs generally.

It is only at a more mature stage in the development of an organization that a manager needs to rationally plan for optimum performance of the organization and turn attention inwards towards greater operational efficiency. Teamwork, control, strategy and analysis are all attributes which are required in this situation. Again, if Lessem's assumptions are correct, the more rational features of decision making and analysing data may be evident in mature organizations in Europe.

Only when organizations are unable to compete on a purely production basis does attention turn to the quality of product and quality of life that managers need to be developmental in approach. Quality circles are a typical feature of this type of organization; and self-development is an attribute that can lead to corporate self-renewal. It is perhaps at this stage in North America and Europe that organizations start to develop concepts of the learning organization and knowledge management in order to compete effectively, when they can no longer compete on quantity of production, or even simply explicit knowledge, since this is capable of codification and fast transmission around the globe, and hence copying by competitors. It is likely that organizations then start to reflect on their 'knowledge resources', including their tacit or uncodified knowledge, in order to successfully exploit what is regarded in companies such as BP as providing a competitive edge that is unlikely to be copied. This type of 'development management' may well be a feature of Japanese management from which Western companies take a lead.

Metaphysical management needs higher ideals such as transformations (for example contributing to world peace or conservation of natural resources) at a global level or a 'higher order' concept of corporate culture. Lessem (1989) points to 'the South' as being more likely to give birth to this type of concept. It may well be that this approach is based on the type of 'humanism' discussed in the Introduction of the current text. It was seen in Chapter 5 that Japanese companies such as SMI have a philosophy of valuing 'humanity', yet Lessem's ideas may transcend this. However the development of knowledge management theory has come from both the 'West' (certainly IBM has invested much money in this concept through initiatives such as the Institute of Knowledge Management: e.g. Snowden, 1999), and from Japan (notably from the pen of Nonaka and colleagues at the Graduate School of Knowledge Science in Ishikawa: e.g. Nonaka et al., 2000).

If the aim of the learning organization is to provide a process and means by which organizational members can continually learn and adapt to changing circumstances by adding to the intellectual and skills base of the organization; then theories of knowledge management provide an understanding of the nature of requisite knowledge (both conceptually based and action based) in organizations. The nature of the understanding of the competitive basis of a company has changed to reflect an emphasis on its 'intellectual capital'.

From the initial concept of the learning organization as a system of inputs, throughputs and outputs (Argyris, 1992) by which organizations could transform themselves in much the same way that Lewin (1951) described force field analysis in the early 1950s (through a process of unfreezing attitudes, changing ways of doing things, and refreezing attitudes, and akin to the 'unlearning' organization of BP, which Donegan, 1990, describes), a move has been made away from the 'mechanical' metaphor (within which is encapsulated the competences approach) towards the 'organic' metaphor (Snowden, 1999). In this, theories of knowledge management have attempted to incorporate the management of tacit knowledge that was regarded as outside the ambit of training and often the learning organization concept. Hence Nonaka et al. (2000: 7) define knowledge not in the absolute sense of 'truth' in Western tradition, but as 'a dynamic human process of justifying personal belief towards the "truth"'. They propose a model of knowledge creation that incorporates the conversion of knowledge from tacit to explicit (the SECI process: socialization, externalization, combination and internalization), the shared context for knowledge creation or *ba*, and knowledge assets that are the inputs, outputs and moderators of the knowledge creation process.

Knowledge creation is conceived as a spiral which interacts between action and cognition, emotion and logic, body and mind, tacit and explicit, micro and macro, and chaos and order. For example creativity is achieved on the borderline between chaos and order. Knowledge conversion is the interaction of tacit and explicit knowledge through: socialization (tacit to tacit knowledge), which creates new tacit knowledge through shared experiences by, for example, informal social meetings where trust can be established and mental models shared; externalization (tacit to explicit knowledge) which makes previously tacit knowledge available to others, such as through quality circles; combination (from explicit to explicit knowledge), which creates more complex and systematic sets of explicit knowledge, easily disseminated through reports and computer media for example; and internalization (explicit to tacit knowledge), which is closely related to 'learning by doing', and putting into action things learned in training courses so that they become part of the way people do and understand things.

Knowledge is also converted and created in context (*ba*), which Nonaka et al. (2000) categorize as 'originating *ba*' involving individual face to face interaction to establish trust among individuals; 'dialoguing *ba*' offers a context for externalization and sharing collectively on a face to face basis; 'systemising *ba*' is a virtual collective interaction context for explicit knowledge, using for example information technology; and, 'exercising *ba*', which provides an individual virtual interaction and a context for internalization through written media or simulations.

Through these interactions in context, knowledge assets are created (Nonaka et al., 2000): 'experiential assets' comprise tacit knowledge shared through common experience and include skills and know-how, care and trust, energy and passion; 'conceptual assets' comprise explicit knowledge that is articulated through images, symbols and language, and include product concepts, design and brand equity; 'systemic assets' comprise systematized and packaged explicit knowledge including documents, manuals, databases and patents; and 'routine assets' comprise tacit knowledge that is routinized and embedded in actions and practices, and include know-how of daily operations, organizational routines and organizational culture. Again, a number of years before, Revans (1965) was grappling with the concept of knowledge as an outcome of action.

Implications for managers: potential cross-cultural problems with the learning organization concept

The learning organization concept is based firmly on a systems model with a focus on the purpose of the system pursuing executive goals. Although many of the assumptions about this model are taken from ideas about the developmental nature of Japanese organizations (see Lessem, 1989) and what makes them successful, it is firmly grounded in an Anglo-Saxon concept of the commercial organization based on the maximization of resources (particularly in economically unfavourable conditions and when there is a need to downsize, delayer and empower; in uncertain commercial conditions; and in conditions of rapid change). There is therefore a tendency to reflect an instrumental approach to people in the organization rather than a truly developmental approach in the humanistic sense. South African companies, for example, are going through a process of downsizing and massive societal changes. The concept of the learning organization is an appealing one as the message is that this can help to transform an organization, to make it more responsive to change in the wider environment and global competition. Yet to build a 'learning society' there is a need to develop more people inside organizations, not less. It is unlikely that the (Anglo-Saxon) model of the learning organization can cope with the wider societal need to develop people, not only in South Africa (where Peter Senge has already been consulting) but also in a number of transitional societies (see Chapter 9).

The model is also based on the concept of participation, empowerment and responsibility of training resting more firmly on the individual (often as part of the group). This may be difficult to implement in higher power distance cultures, higher uncertainty avoidance cultures, and may be unnecessary in some collectivist cultures where the concept of complementary competences within the work group, as well as the developmental approaches are already well entrenched (more so perhaps in Japan than other collectivist societies: see Chapter 5).

Questions for managers

1 How can BP best protect its unique know-how in view of its policy of allying with other, possibly competing organizations, within its concept of the learning organization?

2 By moving from a reliance on the explicit knowledge of written reports, towards an emphasis on implicit knowledge that can be shared and adapted, how can BP operate this successfully in different cultural contexts, where the sharing of implicit cultural knowledge may be problematic?

3 How successful would BP's principles and practices of the learning organization be in your country?

An agenda for research: the cross-cultural challenge

It is unfortunate that most of the current work on knowledge management is being developed in a kind of 'culture free zone', perhaps in an endeavour to develop it as a universal theory. However, the concept of learning and knowledge management contains tremendous potential to incorporate and understand multiple perceptions of reality, including those across cultures. Yet it has been argued in this chapter that the initial concept of a learning organization, which attempts to develop a continuous experiential learning process, is a product mainly of an Anglo-Saxon mindset, and certain of its precepts may not be appropriate in cultures that are dissimilar. For example, employing Hofstede's (1980a) cultural dimensions, a high uncertainty, high power distance culture may favour an instructor-led content-focused approach to learning, rather than a learner-based process-focused approach.

It was noted above that little empirical work has been undertaken to try to understand these aspects of learning across cultures. That which does exist (e.g. Jackson, 1996; Hayes and Allinson, 1988) suggests that there are differences in the ways in which people from different cultures process knowledge. There may also be differences in the way that people understand knowledge in terms of their concept of the meaning of 'truth' as Nonaka et al. (2000) have pointed out, and studies such as the Chinese Cultural Connection (CCC, 1987) seem to support this empirically.

The second generation of the 'learning organization' may well be 'knowledge management'. Certainly this is beginning to add to our understanding about learning capabilities in organizations. Yet little or no work has been undertaken on it within the context of different cultures, and through cross-cultural research. This is an area that should be developed, and some questions for researchers are suggested below.

An important aspect in the idea of a learning organization is that it should be capable of rapid adaptation to its (international) environment. This requires a flexibility to respond to both geographical contingencies as well as temporal factors involved in rapid change. This required flexibility in the international context is now dealt with, in Chapter 7.

Questions for researchers

1 What are the likely cultural barriers to developing the learning organization concept in countries other than Anglo-Saxon ones?

2 What aspects of management and organizational learning are transferable from Anglo-Saxon countries to other countries?

3 How can knowledge management systems be employed across cultures to better understand and incorporate implicit knowledge within each cultural context?

The flexible organization: the European Union model

The European model

In a recent article on innovative forms of organizing in Europe and Japan, Pettigrew, Massini and Numagami (2000: 259) write that 'the pace of innovation is generally much faster in Europe than in Japan. This pattern of more incremental change in Japan and a more radical change in Europe is overlaid by a tendency for firms in both regions to seek new forms of organising by simultaneously altering their structures, processes and boundaries.' Perhaps what differentiates the European from the more homogeneous context of Japan, and indeed the United States, is the degree of lateral flexibility, change and innovation (across national boundaries, cultures and socio-economic and legal systems) that is required alongside the need for temporal flexibility (for innovations related to progress and development of technologies, social and economic changes over time). Brewster, Hegewisch and Holden (1992: 2) allude to this other dimension of the need for flexibility when they state that

> HRM in Europe is complex. There is no other region in the world
> where so many different histories, cultures and languages exist in such
> a relatively small space. Each European country has its own approach
> to the employment of people; its own laws, institutions, trades unions,
> education and training provisions, and managerial culture. In many
> European countries these approaches operate at a number of
> geographical levels. Overlapping this complicated picture there is now
> the unique supranational legislation of the European Community.

There is no doubt that organizations in many parts of the world are undergoing changes in order to instigate more flexible modes of operation. New work practices are evolving to meet the combined needs of more effective and competitive organizations, and to respond to requirements to humanize work in line with the developing needs of people in organizations: whether this be from a perspective of making best use of human resources in the face of downward trends in the working population, or as a contribution to 'valuing humanity', as was discussed in Chapter 5. Yet in Europe the lateral dimension is probably more prominent than in other regions. This does not mean to say that it does not exist in other regions. What it does mean is that much thought has been given to the types of models that have been developed in Europe to meet this special perspective: the management of people and change across national boundaries to provide synergies by capitalizing on cultural differences.

chapter seven

This has affected areas such as management development, high performance teams, and innovative new organizational structures. In all these areas the overriding requirement has been for flexibility.

A good example of this is seen in the management education approach developed since 1973 by EAP (now ESCP-EAP following a merger with another Paris-based school) European School of Management, a graduate management school of the Paris Chamber of Commerce and Industry with integrated campuses in Paris, Oxford, Madrid and Berlin (where it is a joint venture with the Senate of Berlin). Its core programme has been a pre-experience three-year, three-country, three-language master's. Students are drawn from all over the European Union and beyond (for example, increasingly from the former Soviet bloc countries, as well as from Asian countries). Students spend, in their cohorts, a year in each of three different countries. Instruction is in the language of the country, and in each year students spend a trimester (about 12 weeks) in an internship in the respective country. As they stay with their cohorts for three years, they share their experiences in all of the countries. Although classes provide some national input in the different management and business disciplines, there is an emphasis on international, cross-border, and cross-cultural approaches. Much of the training is experiential, involving consultancy and research projects. Teamwork encourages flexibility and multinational working. Above all the overriding experience encourages flexibility of approach and working across different countries and cultures, rather than instilling country-specific knowledge. Graduates typically obtain well-paid international positions anywhere in Europe, and often outside Europe.

This unique model differs significantly from the 'sojourn' model that is often typical of American international management education, where students spend a semester (or sometimes a few weeks) in a foreign country. The concept of 'foreign' has not been in the mindset or in the vocabulary at EAP.

The objective of this chapter is to examine the needs for both geographical (lateral) and temporal flexibility in work and organizational practices as a result of requirements to respond to cultural differences as well as rapid changes in technology and wider societal changes. The real (cross-) cultural context is the European Union, and particularly the way that Digital Equipment Corporation (an American company) has changed its working practices to meet the contingencies of operating in Europe.

Digital Equipment Corporation (Europe)

Digital Equipment Corporation's (DEC) manufacturing plant in Ayr, Scotland, at the end of the 1980s had to respond to the need to adapt the American organization to the commercial requirements of the European market in computer technology. To highlight the problems of organizational adaptation that DEC faced, McCalman (1989) quotes from Konosuke Matsushita (see also Chapter 4) on Western-style management.

> We will win and you will lose. You cannot do anything about it
> because your failure is an internal disease. Your companies are based
> on Taylor's principles. Worse, your heads are Taylorized too. You

firmly believe that sound management means executives on one side and workers on the other, on one side men who think and on the other men who can only work. For you, management is the art of smoothly transferring the executives' ideas into the workers' hands.

DEC's Ayr plant was opened in 1976, and by 1989 employed over 1,200 people. Its initial production concept was based on the traditional role of American branch plants in Europe: to configure, assemble and test systems for the European customers, adding little value to products that were made in American plants.

However, this role did not meet the needs of a highly competitive market that was extremely important to the American company in terms of dollar revenue. A need to be adaptable, and flexible to meet customers' needs, and a political pressure to increase its local sourcing of components meant that the company had to rethink the way production was organized (McCalman, 1989).

DEC adopted the approach of 'high-performance work design' in order to meet the requirements for new product development from the Ayr plant, the pressures of typically a three-year product cycle, and a volatility of the market from the early 1980s which made forecasting from one quarter to the next very precarious. As well as securing extra funding to evolve from final assembly to test, to complete manufacture, they had to find a production process which was flexible enough to handle variation in demand as well as attaining the objective of meeting unit costs which were competitive with other DEC plants, particularly with those in the Far East. Employees were retrained and autonomous work groups were set up to respond to the need for flexibility and skills acquisition, to meet product and market changes. Management styles were rethought, as the situation demanded a supportive rather than a directive style. There was a turning away from the concept of mass production (and perhaps Taylorism) towards a belief that change was a natural process that could be managed by means of a flexible workforce and production organization. McCalman (1989) describes six dimensions of this change process:

1   *Focus*. There was a clear management view of future products and the organization design required to manufacture them, with a shared vision which helped to sell the changes both upwards and to the workforce.

2   *Support policies*. Employees were encouraged to develop their skills through a skills-related reward system. Job demarcation was rare. As such, employees were encouraged to develop in areas in which they were not immediately engaged and to contribute to the business.

3   *Work organization*. Autonomous work groups were established, each with around 12 members, with full responsibility for product assembly, test, fault finding and problem solving and maintenance, using flexitime without clocking in and out, and being responsible for their own discipline. Each member was encouraged to develop skills and pass them on to others in the team.

4   *Management style*. The new style involved supportive back-up for the teams rather than directive coordination. Those managers who found this diffi-cult could move to other parts of the company. Team leaders had the job of encouraging group autonomy and then withdrawing from the group. Decision

149

making in the groups was slow at first, but after a while they learned to resolve problems and call on management experience where required.

5 *Project management*. Project managers were designated as responsible for obtaining the new product line, to liaise with colleagues to persuade them that the approach to organizing was appropriate, and to gain a competitive edge.

6 *Involvement*. The process of engendering ownership of the process was started long before the changes were implemented. A project team was established to do this some 12 months prior to the new production system. Regular meetings were held to promote and develop enthusiasm and commitment, and the new language of 'flexible working', 'product-ownership' and 'front-to-back responsibility' was frequently employed.

Through this new organization of autonomous work groups, management in Digital identified key characteristics that facilitated high performance, namely: a willingness to change; speed of communication; employee 'ownership' of product and process; multifunction career patterns; and better business awareness and priority-setting multi-skilling which enhanced flexibility.

The context of management and organizations in Europe

The current author has previously described the context of European management and organization (Jackson, 1993c) as being characterized by: increased technological change; integration of a variety of cultures; a need for different types of management structures such as international project teams and networking organizations; the decline of a young workforce due to demographic changes and the need for organizations to be more flexible and people-oriented; a changing of organizational and cultural 'rules' and an interfusion of such rules and cultures requiring both organizations and individuals to adapt.

Whilst not being unique to the European context this description of the strategic and operating environment does characterize some of the important aspects of the context of European management. Tijmstra and Casler (1992: 31) had noted, for example, the increasing merger and acquisition activity on an international basis in Europe: 'Since 1985 mergers and acquisitions in the European Community have increased eight-fold. Where in 1985 less than 15 per cent of this activity involved a foreign partner, in 1989 nearly 50 per cent of all M&A activity included an international partner.' Similarly, joint ventures and alliances greatly increased over the same period. The nature and scope of such activity is likely to be more concentrated and complex than in other economic regions such as the United States home market, and possibly the Japanese. In order to effect such change across countries with widely different cultural traditions and language, the extensive deployment of technology has been necessary to aid communication, as is the use of different types of organizational structure, as Bartlett and Ghoshal (1989) note (Chapter 2).

European management (after Jackson, 1993c) within this context can perhaps be characterized as having a variety of perceptions, objectives and motives of individuals; often a resistance to change which needs to be overcome;

a need to consider individuals' objectives, which may be quite varied, in the context of the organization's objectives; a need to consider and marry up the individual styles of managers with the culture and styles of the organization; different organizational 'policies' of management performance (a need for this to be adequately defined, and agreed, but to remain flexible enough for the changing context).

With the geographical scope of organizational change it is likely that this is more complex than when undertaken simply on a national basis, and more fraught with problems of differing perceptions, attitudes, objectives and motives to take into consideration, as well as the added problems of resistance to change. The problems of different styles of management may compound difficulties of integration. The different 'policies' on management performance also will have to be understood. Management by Objectives (MBO) has previously been mentioned as a method used for management appraisal for a couple of decades in Anglo-Saxon countries, but not so appropriate, for example, in a French company environment (Chapter 1), particularly when linked with pay structures. This suggests that methods and criteria for performance evaluation should be clearly defined, while keeping a degree of flexibility. Flexibility may also apply to the differing styles that managers need to adopt. Jackson (1993c) has suggested that this should be reflected in the way managers operate. For example, there is a need to develop the appropriate management skills to meet the needs of the individual (in relation to management styles and the 'performance policies' of organizations); a need to develop not just the 'how' of management skills, but also the 'why' of management action (that is, understanding the environmental and organizational context, and the cultural content, as well as the skills of management performance); and the need to develop attitudes and flexibility towards managing change, and managing across cultures.

Thurley and Widenius (1989) contrast 'European' management with American and Japanese management. They contend that American management theory is firmly built on the tenets of scientific management, using a systematic approach to improving task performance. An individualist approach allows classical management theory to define roles in terms of specific jobs and responsibilities, where managers are individuals with their own interests and personalities. In order to serve organizational goals, group norms are fostered through a human relations approach. In this respect change management requires a planned approach to changing structures and cultures. Further, organizations define the business strategies required to achieve market position and design structures to fit these needs. Japanese management emphasizes equality as the basis for competition and cooperation (Thurley and Widenius, 1989), basing its practice on collective responsibility where all members feel responsible for the organization. Individuals do not own their jobs, as they may have to do anything, needing training to perform a variety of jobs. In this spirit, employees are trusted to get on with their jobs and have their potential stimulated. Employees are protected by the organization as they are vulnerable, while life careers are planned. There is a recognition that everything changes and management should be pragmatic, and flexible enough to change to the new circumstances. Finally, the work ethic is connected with the individual's interaction with the work group. It is through the work group that employees gain their identity and associate their activity with the *michi*, or 'the way'.

151

Thurley and Widenius (1989) therefore characterize these differences between Japanese and American management theory and practice as: work security versus individual freedom; organizational loyalty versus job competence; consultation and involvement versus management authority; and work group innovation versus specialist know-how. They are concerned to develop a 'functional' model of management in the European context that reflects the different cultural values and legal institutional practices in Europe. They therefore present European management as: emerging, and not yet existing except in limited circumstances; being broadly linked to the idea of European integration, which is continuously encompassing more and different countries; reflecting key values including pluralism and tolerance, although not consciously developed from those values; being associated with a balanced stakeholder philosophy and the concept of social partners.

It is possible to summarize the European context of management and organizations (after Jackson, 1993c) as follows:

- There is no national identity across the European Community as there is in Japan and the USA; for example there is no equivalent of the 'American Dream'.

- There is no common language or culture.

- Change is more complex than in America or Japan, particularly with the further integration of Eastern and central European countries, and this is in some ways artificial in creation: manufactured by the architects and politicians of the Single European Market, signifying the higher level of creativity needed to manage in this environment.

- There is increasing cross-border activity through mergers and acquisitions, joint ventures and direct investment situations requiring approaches to management such as project management and networking.

- There is increasing emphasis on the use of technology as a means of competing (such as e-commerce opportunities) and communicating (such as extensive use of intranet systems).

- There is a continuing demand for linguistic skills, in addition to more traditional management skills.

- In sum, there is a need to manage increasing diversity (between cultures rather than trying to create a uniform culture), ambiguity and complexity, and an increasing need to create more flexible organizations and methods of working in order to cope with both diversity and change.

Within this context the management of people may be rather more complex than in American models of human resource management, and higher levels of flexibility may be required compared with Japanese approaches.

A European model of people management

Brewster (1995: 3), in developing a model of European human resource management, indicates that the North American concept of HRM has been built on a belief in organizational independence and management autonomy and freedom of action. The European situation, he contends, is different:

> European organizations operate with restricted autonomy: constrained at the international (European Union) level and at the national level by culture and legislation, at the organizational level by patterns of ownership, and at the HRM level by trade union involvement and consultative arrangements. There is a need, therefore, for a model of HRM that goes beyond seeing these features as external constraints, and integrates them into the concept of HRM.

The features to be considered in this model he proposes are as follows:

Culture and legislation National culture is reflected in legislation, and the USA has far less legislative control than European countries over employment relationship. European HRM is influenced by state regulation and companies have a narrower scope of choice than American ones. This includes:

- regulation of recruitment, dismissal and employment contracts generally;
- legislative requirements on pay;
- formalization of educational certification;
- public funding of labour market programmes (including training, retraining, job transition support, job creation for youth and the long-term unemployed);
- quasi-legal nature of industrial relations including the right to trade union representation, and co-determination arrangements in some countries;
- social security provision;
- more state intervention in the economy;
- at the European level the European Union Charter of Fundamental Social Rights (Social Chapter of the Maastricht Treaty).

Patterns of ownership Public ownership is still generally more prevalent in European countries than the USA, and patterns of private ownership are different, including major companies in southern Europe being held in family hands, and in Germany being owned by a tight network of banks with a consequent lower pressure for short-term profits and disincentives to drive competitors out.

Trade union involvement and consultative arrangement American HRM has been regarded as anti-union, yet in most European countries union membership is high, and often where it is not (such as in Spain: see also Chapter 1) employers or industries are governed by collective bargaining agreements. Often pay bargaining is outside the direct control of managers of individual organizations.

153

Employee involvement   This is commonplace in European countries, with workers' councils required by law in some countries. In the Netherlands and Germany employee representatives can resort to the courts to prevent managerial decisions in areas such as recruitment, termination, and changing work practices. This is something quite contrary to US practices, which maintain management prerogative on such issues. In addition board-level representation of employees is a legal requirement in many countries. Employers also often go beyond the legal requirements to provide information to employee representatives. Communication upwards often goes through the work councils or trade union representatives. These aspects are encouraged at the European Union level as well, where there is a commitment to maintain the role of employer and trade union.

Brewster (1995) concludes that many of the American approaches to HRM reflect a unitarist concept of the organization and have been subject to criticism in Europe. He also rejects an approach that sees HRM as purely contingent on organizational strategy with little account of managerial action, and little account of the aspects outlined above. He contends therefore that a model of European HRM should interact with business strategy, and with the external environment of national culture, power systems, legislations, education, employee representation and other issues outlined above. Such a model should reflect the differences between countries and the interaction of the HRM strategies of multinational firms with the national HRM context (see Figure 7.1).

Figure 7.1
Brewster's
(1995)
European
model of HRM

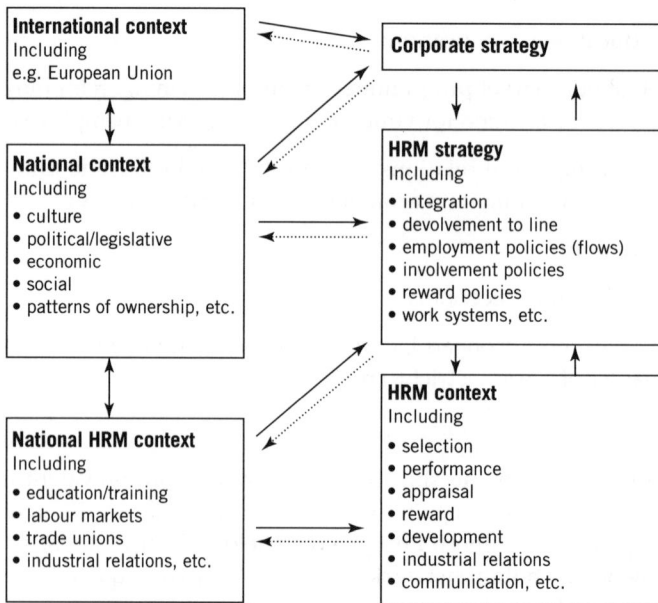

Note: dotted lines indicate that the organization and its HRM strategies and practices in turn interact with and are part of the environment in which they operate.

The model is an attempt to counter the acceptance of American-based models in the European context, by taking account of the different degrees of managerial independence, the different approaches to working with employee representatives, the different levels of government involvement, and the complex links between HRM and economic performance (Brewster, 1995).

Organization and work flexibility

In particular, it may be said that a discussion of the nature of management and HRM practices in Europe leads to a conclusion that organizations, management and work practices should respond to increasing complexity and the need to be flexible in approach. Scott Morton (1995), in discussing the need to address the external fact of the increasing turbulence of the business environment, and the internal fact of continuing changes in information technology, identifies a number of types of organizational forms (after Quinn, 1992) which are emerging:

- *Starbust*. Organizations such as Johnson and Johnson have successfully developed an organizational form that is designed to encourage creativity and innovation. As new products or services are developed they are split off from the parent organization to form separate subsidiaries, partly owned by the parent but free to develop entrepreneurially through outside capital if they wish. Core competences are nurtured within these subsidiaries along with entrepreneurship and the ability to manage risk, and providing the next generation of products and services. This may be inappropriate for large-scale heavy investment products (Quinn, 1992).

- *Cluster organization*. Clusters or teams are developed to carry out specific key tasks. These are permanently based around key activities rather than being *ad hoc* teams, but they then form and reform smaller task clusters to solve specific problems. People are able to move across organizational boundaries using their skills as they become necessary. Volvo and GE are example of companies who have used this type of organizational form to increase effectiveness, and it seems very appropriate for highly trained, well-motivated people undertaking constantly varying tasks (Quinn Mills, 1991).

- *Spider's web*. This form of networked organization is very flat with little hierarchy with a high level of communication between individuals and the small groups involved in key tasks or projects. Consulting firms are good examples. The independent 'nodes' of this type of organizational form contain the accumulated knowledge of the organization, and operate largely without formal authority. Where there is a centre it collects and transfers information between the various nodes rather than instigating it.

- *Internal market*. The key example of this form is Semco in Brazil (Semler, 1994), which emerged from the chaos of military dictatorship, hyper-inflation, labour unrest, import restriction and high business taxes, and took some eight years to transform from a more traditional organization. The company's products are diverse, and such items as machinery used by biscuit manufacturers are sold all over the world. The company has no hierarchy. Employees bid for opportunities that are posted on a noticeboard. They may form temporary mini-companies under the umbrella of the factory building to manufacture the product by assembling the resources any way they choose. The parent company undertakes the necessary innovation activities to generate ideas and opportunities.

It may be that these examples are still unusual, but they underline the point that organizations are having to adapt their forms and adopt new approaches in order to address the need to become more flexible and adaptive to differing economic and cultural circumstances. Muzyka, de Koning and Churchill (1995) outline some of the processes of organizational transformation that have arisen over the previous decade to adapt and develop new ways of organizing and working:

- *Re-engineering*. This describes approaches to improving efficiency by lowering costs in order to survive in a competitive environment (the word was first used by Hammer and Champy, 1993 and similar approaches which focus on process efficiency have been advocated by Constanza, 1992 and Goldratt, 1992). It parallels attempts by industrial engineers to make factory-floor operations more efficient by increasing output per input, and borrows terminology from this area. The approach is systems focused with underlying assumptions of efficiency of process through a more streamlined organization. Although it makes attempts to involve the workforce more effectively in the change process and to engage organizational knowledge, it is instrumental in its focus on increasing organization efficiency through definite processes and only marginally addressing new opportunities and engaging the workforce in the process.

- *Restructuring*. This approach was designed to address the failure of corporate resource allocation in providing value to shareholders (Blair, 1993). This could include 'fat' management or such problems as misallocation of resource investment. It seeks to tighten financial discipline through restructuring of ownership and debt/equity structure, and through dividing fiscal responsibility into smaller units, intensifying financial incentives, downsizing, and flattening hierarchies. This involves a top-down approach of cutting up assets, laying off staff and removing layers of management (often labelled 'turnaround' management). Changes in behaviour of the company were expected with divesting or outsourcing of activities that could not be undertaken more cheaply than the external market. This top-down approach does not engage the workforce in the process, and commentators have noted a short-term gain leading to longer-term adaptation problems as a result of removal of slack in the organization. Again this approach is instrumental and directed exclusively at improving efficiency (Muzyka et al., 1995).

- *Renewing*. Here the assumption is that transformation can take place through 'liberating' people in an organization by encouraging them to think and act more openly. It includes aspects such as the benchmarking and total quality management of Moss Kanter (1989) and the liberation management of Peters (1992). Companies can improve their efficiency, effectiveness and innovativeness by empowering employees by allowing them to make decisions to the level of their full ability and not simply their job description. This involves a long-term and sustainable change in values as well as behaviour. Muzyka, et al. (1995) comment that although this approach specifically sets out to engage the workforce in change, and recognizes that historically the failure to do this has weakened opportunity, knowledge and organizational energy, it lacks a guiding direction in terms of results and process, and has little accompanying structure.

- *Regenerating*. This approach is offered by Muzyka et al. (1995) as a way of taking elements of both instrumental approaches that focus on efficiency and 'motivating' approaches that seek to engage the workforce in the process of change. It also provides the direction and objectives of change that such approaches as re-engineering try to provide, as well the motivating and knowledge-engaging aspects as approaches such as renewing provide. It is a continuing process rather than a 'turnaround' or temporary measure to address particular problems or circumstances.

The organizational and work structure implications of these processes are indicated by Bowman and Carter (1995) by reference to Mintzberg's identification of five basic parts of the organization:

- *strategic apex*: who controls the organization;
- *the operating core*: the operational heart of the organization;
- *the middle line*: the line managers connecting the operating core to the strategic apex;
- *the technostructure*: staff analysts who help to achieve the standardization of outputs, work processes and skills;
- *support staff*: who carry out suporting activities such as staff restaurant, public relations and building maintenance.

Changes in these areas are effected by challenges to traditional, hierarchical and functional organizations, as follows:

- *Delayering and downsizing* (more euphemistically, 'rightsizing'): organizations have reduced staff. Delayering strips out the middle line and downsizing first reduces support staff whose services are often outsourced, and then reduces the technostructure, and sometimes moves into the operating core (DEC may be cited as an example of this). Sometimes the corporation has helped create a supplying firm where none existed (Bowman and Carter, 1995, provide BP Exploration as an example of this).

- *Empowerment*: as a result of delayering, and popularized by such writers as Tom Peters, there has been a move to empower more junior levels of staff (perhaps to take on the responsibilities of more senior colleagues who have been delayered). This has given rise to self-organized, autonomous work teams (as in the example of DEC at the beginning of this chapter) which are supported by effective information systems. This has (at least in part) challenged the traditional role of the middle line, in particular their coordination and super-visory roles. This has led more specifically to pressure on staff in the operating core to become more flexible in terms of their employment contracts as well as their capabilities.

- *Restructuring*: such processes as re-engineering, flexible manufacturing and just-in-time systems have led to restructuring in the operational core. These processes tend to span existing operating sub-divisions and encourage the formation of cross-functioning teams in order to improve cooperation and coordination.

Firms are therefore becoming leaner and smaller, previous ways of organizing the operating core are being challenged, and power is becoming more decentralized to staff in the operating core who are expected to make decisions based on effective information systems, and to have more task flexibility. This in turn requires a move away from traditional employment contracts.

The extent to which innovative forms of organizing are being introduced, and the nature of these new forms, were investigated in Europe in comparison with Japan, and comparing the position between 1992 and 1996, by Pettigrew et al. (2000). Although there is still a predominance of the multidivisional organizational form of the largest firms in Europe, there is evidence that innovative forms are emerging among large and medium-sized companies. Pettigrew et al. suggest that there is also some evidence of a link between innovative forms and company performance. In line with changes suggested in the literature they investigated new forms of organizing along three dimensions: structures, processes and boundaries.

Structures   In line with competitive pressures, and with hierarchical layers of middle managers becoming too expensive, organizations are delayered. This addresses the need for better information flows and for quicker responses to the need for flexibility and innovation. This has also led to decentralization of both operational and strategic aspects. Companies are moving to more flexible project-based forms that bridge functional divisions and have a more horizontal character (Pettigrew et al., 2000).

Processes   As a result of the need for flexibility and knowledge within the learning organization (see Chapter 6) effective and intensive communication and exchange of information is needed both horizontally and vertically. This requires heavy investment in information technology. This in its turn enables greater flexibility in terms of participation and polycentricity. In order to facilitate these processes human resource management has become key, and new HRM practices have emerged to support horizontal networking as well as maintaining organizational integration. This involves bringing people together across functions in seminars and company-wide conferences, instilling a sense of corporate identity, and cultivating cross-unit teams and communication (Pettigrew et al., 2000).

Boundaries   With lower hierarchies and more horizontal relationships, organizations are more likely to be decreasing in scale and increasingly focusing on a narrower span of activities. They are focusing more on core competences, and shifting to smaller decentralized units in order better to compete in hyper-competitive environments. This involves strategic downscoping: abandoning of conglomerate strategies and concentrating on core areas of competitive advantage. Value chain activities which produce little value, and non-core activities such as training and R&D are increasingly outsourced. A corollary of this process is the use of strategic alliances to enhance or complement the firms' competences. Organizational boundaries are therefore being drawn around a narrower band of activities (Pettigrew et al., 2000).

In 1992, Japanese organizations had steeper hierarchies, more operational decentralizations and vertical communication linkages, greater use of IT, more strategic alliances, and focused more on a dominant business rather than a range of businesses compared with their European counterparts. There were no differences in the use of project forms or the use of horizontal linkages between sub-units, or in strategic decentralization. Although some of these differences persisted in 1996, such as taller hierarchies and higher use of IT in Japanese companies, differences had disappeared in the extent of operational decentralization, vertical linkages and strategic alliances. New differences that had emerged were in the increasing adoption of project forms in Japan, more European companies developing horizontal linkages compared with Japanese firms and more European firms developing a set of related businesses, rather than a single business or conglomerate arrangement. Although organizations in Japan and Europe have been moving in the same direction, there were differences in the pace of change, with European firms changing more rapidly, and Japanese firms changing slowly and incrementally. Of particular note is the extent to which European firms were developing horizontal links in 1996 (25.6 per cent compared to 18.7 per cent in Japanese companies in the survey). Over a third of companies in both samples in 1996 said that they were introducing new human resources practices including the development of internal labour markets, corporate-wide mission building, team building and developing internal networks for knowledge transfer. Many of the organizational processes such as decentralization, developing vertical linkages, adopting new HRM practices and engaging in strategic alliances, which are now being employed by European firms, have traditionally characterized Japanese companies. However, Pettigrew et al. (2000) reject a simple convergence thesis. European organizations have been adopting a more radical change process, particularly in the area of developing horizontal links, strategic decentralization and engaging in strategic alliances. These have given rise to multidimensional organizational forms different from those in Japan.

Implications for managers: revisiting DEC (Europe)

It is possible to deduce from the above discussion that horizontal linkages and lateral hierarchies (Galbraith, 1994) and communication are becoming particularly important in regions such as Europe, where there is a need to develop flexibility and innovative processes. This is in keeping with the necessity to facilitate the transfer of information and to share and generate new knowledge within the concept of the learning organization (see Chapter 6). In order to look at emerging practices in this area it is possible to revisit the European operation of DEC (McCalman, 1996). Earlier in this chapter we saw the way that DEC organized its manufacturing plant in Ayr. Cross-functionality was introduced at plant level to achieve a higher level of flexibility in order to respond to change and variation in the European market for computer products. In the early 1990s DEC also had to respond to the pressures of competition throughout Europe and to introduce horizontal linkages across its European operations in the UK, France, the Netherlands, Ireland, Germany and Switzerland (with its European headquarters situated in Geneva), to develop innovative solutions to operational issues. McCalman (1996) describes the specific example of the setting up and operation of a cross-functional and cross-cultural project team tasked with developing a Europe-wide customer order delivery system that guaranteed delivery to the customer within 10 days. What was a complex logistic planning process was to be devised laterally by this management group, which would meet regularly at different European locations.

In establishing the project team a major consideration was that the task had to involve a lot of people across Europe, in order to fully understand the process that required one supply base and delivery to a number of countries. In each country differences had to be understood, which were unique or common enough to make an impact on the process. The project manager therefore had to select the team based on his or her understanding of the company and where he or she thought the skills lay within it. Through networking it was possible to establish this where the manager did not know.

Little attention was paid to hierarchical level and who was responsible for what, and more emphasis was placed on who had the skills and energy to make the changes. Individuals were approached, and if they were interested, then their boss was approached.

The team finally consisted of 10 members with three from the manufacturing plant in Ayr, two from the other UK operations, two from Switzerland, and one each from Germany, France and the Netherlands. However, at the same time the project team also had to continue to work on their own functional responsibilities within their subsidiary.

The project work was time consuming in terms of weekly meetings. In between times use was made of networking. People were tasked to go away and complete particular areas and then report back. The importance of cross-cultural teamwork was emphasized, and there was a desire to accomplish tasks as a team, and to assist others in this on an ongoing basis. Members were encouraged to ask others for help if they needed it. There was also a willingness to subordinate operational subsidiary goals to the benefit of the European operation as a whole. As part of this, and an outcome of the project, people in the different subsidiaries were asked to abandon local custom and ordering behaviour in order to introduce common language in the ordering process so as to streamline it. A typical reaction from team members was that the project process helped to develop a different perspective that reflected the scale of the company's operations in Europe.

This helped towards understanding the unique aspects of local operations and behaviour, and how these might be overcome in a project of this nature. A number of concerns emerged in managing lateral hierarchies (from McCalman, 1996):

1 It is difficult to manage this process logistically and structurally. Control is difficult and success is highly dependent on the enthusiasm of the team rather than on formalized procedures. A certain amount of 'bureaucracy busting' is necessary. Care should be taken in the selection of people.

2 The control and use of power may be problematic. There is little 'formal' power available to sanction members in the case of failure. Managers were selected irrespective of position in the hierarchy. This raises questions of reward systems and how performance is assessed in lateral hierarchies. Presumably, a solution is that companies gradually introduce project working of this nature into the total responsibility of the manager rather than regarding it as separate, as in this case in DEC.

3 As there is a continuing need for this type of working across borders and cultures, thought should be given to common decision premises based on the managing of different cultures, value systems, languages, business environments, industrial relations and management techniques. McCalman (1996) concludes that from the experience of DEC, where there is a need to address an innovative task, it is better where divergence occurs earlier rather than later in the process, and that this is recognized and managed within the team.

4 For managers to operate effectively they need to learn to think more strategically and outside ordinary line responsibilities of operational fire fighting. This type of project work can facilitate this type of perspective and thinking.

5 There is also a need to think from different perspectives and at the different multifunctional, corporate and subsidiary levels. This requires managers to be open-minded, flexible and adaptable.

6 They therefore need to work at the strategic level associated with change, adaptation and development and the operational level associated with the realism of budgetary constraints and vertical management pressures. This should be built into the development process to assist the development of strategic awareness. Exposure to different jobs and nationalities is likely to aid this.

Questions for managers

1 What could be some of the problems if DEC tried to implement autonomous work teams, as they did in Scotland, in countries whose culture is higher in power distance and in uncertainty avoidance? What would be the difficulty of implementing this in your country? What would be the implications for motivation and reward systems?

2 DEC's experience with implementing cross-border project groups suggests conflicts with the concerns of local operations. How could this conflict best be resolved?

3 In view of the need to make the organization meaner, leaner and to give employees more flexible contracts, how can a company like DEC balance the instrumental needs of shareholders' interests with the humanistic needs of fulfilling the potential of its people?

An agenda for research

Much of the literature in this area is from Western countries and focuses on areas that seem to be effective in North America and Western Europe. Little or no research has been undertaken on the way flexible structures operate in different cultural environments (although Pettigrew et al., 2000, may be an exception at the strategic level, and with limited geographic scope). A research agenda may address some of the following items:

- Whilst delayering and downsizing may be aspects of organizing which are contingent on responding to the needs of economic downturn, shareholders' interests and efficiency, they may be less effective when there is a requirement to focus on the longer term, to provide job security to loyal workers (as in the case of Japanese HRM), to develop for the future prosperity of a society the capabilities to run and work in an effective organization (as is the case of transitional and emerging economies), and/or where there is a need for an effective social infrastructure to act as a safety net for redundant employees (as is often the case in most developed countries). Yet there is evidence that such trends are current in countries other than developed countries (see Chapters 9 and 10).

- Empowerment may only be appropriate in low uncertainty avoidance, individualistic and low power distance cultures, and where information and status are not protected.

- Autonomous and cross-functional work teams may only be appropriate in a lower power distance, low hierarchy culture, where autonomy of functional units is not protected, and which favours matrix forms of organization and sharing of information.

These are areas which need specific research in order to develop understanding of the desirability, effectiveness and nature of flexible organizational forms and work practices across different cultures (e.g. from a headquarter perspective), and different perspectives on flexible working in a situation like the one described for DEC, from a subsidiary point of view.

Questions for researchers

1 Is there a relationship between cultural values in specific countries (e.g. collectivism, power distance, instrumentalism, humanism) and the way (indigenous) organizations respond to changes in technology, economy and society? Do multinational companies take account of cultural contingencies in their countries of operation when implementing organizational change?

2 Are organizational forms and work practices involving lateral and temporal flexibility in the European Union transferable to other regions across the globe?

3 What specific practices, such as autonomous and cross-functional teams, and principles, such as empowerment, are best suited to which cultural contexts? How are these practices (with their relationships with cultural values) best introduced by management in cross-cultural teams that may have members from very different country cultures?

The joint venture organization:
the Chinese model

With Peter Xu Lu*

Chapter 7 discussed the need for flexibility of organization, lateral hierarchy, and alliances to bring in expertise or capabilities that are no longer part of organizations that have concentrated on their core competences. Since China's opening-up policies in the late 1970s the only way of doing business has been through some form of joint venture: for the Chinese company there may be a perceived need to develop advanced production capabilities through connections with Western or Japanese companies; and for foreign companies wanting to do business in China, this is seen as the only way of opening up a potentially vast emerging market.

Of course not all joint ventures take place in China. In this chapter the 'Chinese' model is discussed in connection with joint ventures. This is only because so many joint ventures are taking place in this country and that by this process China is rapidly moving away from the 'communist' way, and towards a market economy. This may mean that organizational and management cultures and principles are becoming more hybrid in nature. To illustrate some of these processes, Peter Xu Lu describes the case of the Blue Sword Group in Sichuan Province, its development as a relatively successful state-owned enterprise, and then its problems and rapid failure in an international joint venture.

The objective of this chapter is to investigate the implications of joint ventures for the management of people. This is of particular interest, as through the growing need for organizational flexibility, and the opening up of new markets, managers increasingly have to manage people within joint ventures. The cultural context discussed is that of China, because of the numbers of international joint ventures there. In particular, motivational and reward systems are examined in the Chinese context, and the way these are managed in joint ventures. Often this takes the form of foreign managers managing an indigenous workforce. It also takes the form of Chinese and Western managers trying to understand each other, and trying to work together, sometimes not successfully, as is seen in the case of Blue Sword in its venture with a Belgian partner.

The Blue Sword Group

Background of the company

Blue Sword Group used to be the Chengdu Beer Factory and was established in 1986. Its headquarters and main factory is located to the northwest of the beautiful, richly endowed Chengdu Plain, 59 kilometres from Chengdu, the capital city of Sichuan Province. The factory has an area of 350,000 square metres and 2,800 employees, among whom 573 are managerial personnel and engineers with medium or senior technical titles.

From taking over a small unknown beer factory that had gone bankrupt ten years earlier, Blue Sword has now become the largest manufacturer of beer and beverages in the southwest of China, with an annual capacity of 60,000 tons. The production scale of the enterprise is developing very fast. Altogether it produces 30 kinds of products in four categories. The industry structure, with beer as the leading product, includes soft drinks, medicine, food, packing, printing and international trade and commerce, with total fixed assets of 980 million yuan. In 1998, the sales revenues had reached more than RMB 200 million yuan.

Blue Sword is a comparatively advanced enterprise compared with others in its sector in China. All of the production systems employ advanced equipment, technology and management expertise imported or introduced from America, Italy, France and Japan.

A Reformed enterprise

The reason for Blue Sword's development appears to be economic reform and the country's opening-up policy. However, its achievements also appear to be a result of Blue Sword's own efficient management systems. According to Mr Zeng Qingrong, this is the real reason for Blue Sword's success. It has formed its own strong organizational culture and management styles. The main factors include the following.

Independence: no 'mother-in-law' From Figure 8.1 it can be seen that even though Blue Sword is regarded as a state-owned enterprise (SOE), it has successfully shifted from a transitional socialist management system to a marketing-oriented management system. There is no official organization or government department (in Chinese, this is called the 'mother-in-law') directly controlling the enterprise.

Figure 8.1 Organizational structure of Blue Sword (Party Committee Office of Blue Sword Group, June 1999)

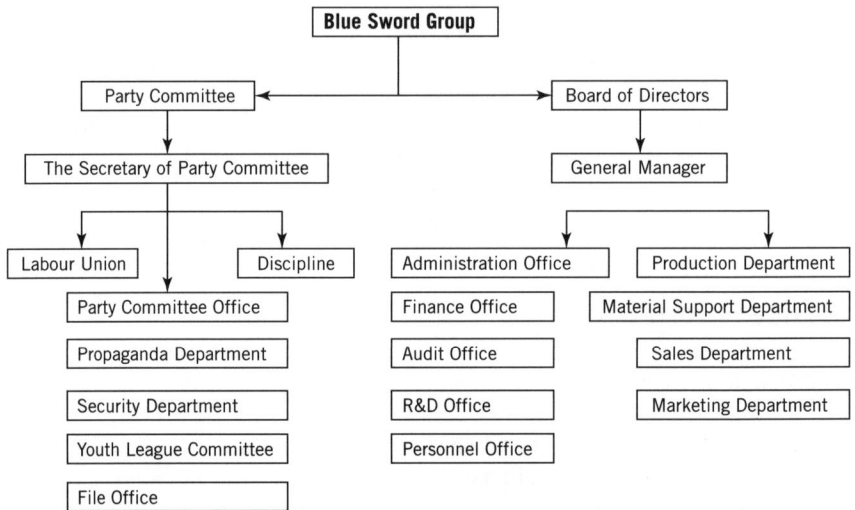

In the Blue Sword Group, the general manager is responsible for all the business operational activities. However, being a Chinese SOE, Blue Sword still has to keep the traditional post of secretary of the Party Committee. Now this post is called the 'second hand' instead of the 'first hand' as it was in the past (i.e. the person who holds the highest position in the leadership). The 'second hand' is actually Mr Zeng Qingrong. It is clear that Mr Zeng Qingrong controls most of the organizational operations. The result is that the organization can make its own decisions for the business operation without pressure from outside. As Ms Tan Lingping, the assistant to the chairman of the board said, 'the Blue Sword Beer Company was established on a bankrupted enterprise. We cannot depend on instruction from above any more. To be responsible to ourselves is the only way that we can survive.'

'The policies of two cats': personal responsibilities Deng Xiaoping had a famous saying: 'No matter a white cat or a black cat, the one that can catch the mouse is a good cat.' By this he meant that a person should be judged and evaluated only according to his or her achievements, instead of his or her background.

Unlike in other Chinese state-owned enterprises, all the managers from senior to junior positions in Blue Sword have obtained complete authority over their duties. Their ability and achievements are evaluated according to the profit they can make for the company. So they have obtained the type of authority that is often unheard of in other Chinese SOEs, such as the right to sack any employee who they think is incompetent to do the work. Mr Zeng Qingrong, writing in the Chinese language pointed out in the *Journal of the Office of Policy Research* (April 1999), 'Managers must be persons who take responsibilities and who shoulder all troubles at the same time. Managers who fail to run an enterprise in profit are committing a crime.' He also declared himself a 'capitalist' instead of 'normalist'. According to him, the reason that most Chinese SOEs have gone bankrupt is that the managers had been restricted by and assessed on normative values and socialist ideology instead of taking responsibility for the enterprise.

'The business market is like a battlefield': the market as the lifeline of the enterprise In the Blue Sword Group, the management system has been formulated as being closely attached to the demands of the marketplace. All management activities are undertaken according to market need. The company is continually developing new, readjusting products and giving up certain products in line with changes in the market. Employees' promotion is also according to their achievements in the market. Mr Guo Xuming was a salesman in 1992. However, because of his contribution to Blue Sword's market position – its beer sales occupy the largest market share in Sichuan – he was promoted to vice-general manager of the Blue Sword Group.

The decision-makers at Blue Sword always compare the business to a battlefield. Only those who make the right judgements, conduct in-depth forecasts into the future and make timely preparations can take the advantage in the marketplace and win through (according to Mr Qingrong, writing in the *Journal of the Office of Policy Research*, April 1999).

165

Being loyal to the organization?   Perhaps the most important factor in making Blue Sword more efficient than the other Chinese SOEs is its people. The company requires that all employees should be loyal to Blue Sword Group at all times: the decision-makers believe that only employees who are faithful to the enterprise will readily face setbacks or failure in a spirit of devotion. One of the strategies to achieve this aim is that all managers and staff in the Blue Sword Group hold shares in the enterprise. The staff get annual dividends from these shares. The level of shareholding is dependent on the position of each member of staff: the higher position they hold, the more shares. Benefits derived from this are connected with the profit of the enterprise, but also with a member of staff's loyalty to the enterprise.

Another strategy is to offer opportunities for self-development to managers and employees, especially to the younger ones. Every year the company selects dozens of junior managers and young employees to attend universities in order to undertake training programmes, even degree courses. Most of them can be promoted when they finish studying. Some distinguished managers have even been sent to study abroad. There are some problems concerning this motivation strategy. Some of the younger managers 'tiao cao' (abandon one occupation in favour of another) to other companies as soon as they finish their studies. Continuing loyalty to the enterprise is one of the conditions for younger employees to be sent for training.

The joint venture: towards failure

In 1994 nearly 80 per cent of the beer market had been occupied by Blue Sword beer in Sichuan Province. However in order to meet the challenges of extreme market competition, and to develop new markets and a competitive edge, Blue Sword was lacking in money. The decision-makers of the company realized that to import advanced management practice and to meet international management standards it would have to form an international alliance. At the same time it would be easier for an international company to enter into the Chinese inland market if it established a joint venture enterprise with Blue Sword. Based on these reasons, at the end of 1994 a French investment bank that the company had consulted suggested the Belgian Interbrew S.A. as a joint venture partner for Blue Sword.

However, the story of the success of Blue Sword Beer Company in China and the international reputation of the Interbrew company did not avoid problems and risks. Due to the different understandings of organizational management, and cultural compatibility problems, the frustrations of a short-lived joint venture could not be avoided. The problem of different management styles that many Western multinational companies have encountered in China also seems to have caused the failure in this case. The following is an examination of some of these problems.

'Same bed, different dreams': who controls the joint venture?   In 1994, Mr De Keersmaeker, chairman of Interbrew S.A., visited the Blue Sword Company and agreed in principle to establish a joint venture. 'We were very excited by the

166

cooperation at that time', said Ms. Tan Lingping. 'Interbrew is the fourth largest beer manufacturer in the world. The joint venture can help us update our technology and management systems. We expected that our beer would appear in the supermarkets of Western countries.'

The involvement of an international company that was keen to develop the Chinese market, the Chinese local government which hoped to boost the local economy and a successful Chinese SOE, which was determined to become an international company, might have safeguarded the initial stages of negotiation and joint venture establishment. However, the expectation of further construction, operation and expansion of the business, and the nature of personnel management could not be outlined in detail in the contract that would bind all the parties together. According to the contract, Interbrew S.A. would invest 35 million yuan in the joint venture and control 60 per cent of the shareholding. The Chinese side could not use the brand name Blue Sword any more. The products of this brand had to be sought under the name of Interbrew.

Because of different understandings of the purposes of joint venturing, both the Chinese local government and Blue Sword wanted to have a say in decisions. Against a background in which the majority of shareholdings belonged to Interbrew, the final decision on organizational management was not always made by Interbrew, however. The influence of the Blue Sword organizational culture and the political power of the Chinese government could not be underestimated. For instance, in terms of marketing strategies, Interbrew insisted that the main products should be focused on the Chinese market and the scale of product investment should be mainly on the low to medium level. However the Chinese side was keen to improve the quality of the products to meet international standards, and to export the product. As Mr Zeng states in the *Journal of the Office of Policy Research* (April 1999) 'We wanted to march toward the international market. Our goal was to realize the internationalization of management and operation; striving to become an international consortium and to make a greater contributions to the promotion of national industry.'

However, the Belgium company viewed things otherwise, and wanted to make profits as soon as possible. The question was raised: 'Who is in control?' On many occasions, arguments and disagreement occurred not only about business direction, but also about people management.

'The best plan — buy popular support': people management Perhaps the most important factor in ensuring the success of joint ventures in China is people. More and more multinational companies operating in China have realized that joint venture business is in fact a 'people' business. People's expectations and aspirations must be identified before any joint venture is established.

In order to establish the management necessary for the joint venture organization, at the plant level Interbrew sent several expatriate managers from Belgium and some Hong Kong Chinese who had a firm understanding of Western management concepts but who were not too far removed from Chinese society and culture. The expatriate managers were provided with housing and cars. The annual salary paid to each expatriate manager was above US$100,000. 'That amount of money was the total annual payment of all our employees at that time,' Ms Tan remarked. Furthermore, severe problems were created by the domination by expatriate managers: most local Chinese managers felt that they had been ignored and that they had very limited chances of being promoted to higher levels of management.

As soon as the joint venture was established, the conflicts between the Chinese employees and foreign expatriates, expatriate (Hong Kong) Chinese managers and local Chinese managers, increasingly emerged. Interbrew wanted to redeploy the Chinese managers and recruit new Chinese employees. However this policy was totally against the old personnel system of Chinese enterprises. Employees, especially manual workers, had almost exclusively been recruited in two different ways: because local government had to reduce the pressure of high unemployment rates, the workers who used to work in bankrupt SOEs had priority to be re-employed; old employees of the enterprise often arranged that their sons or daughters or even other relatives would work in the enterprise via their relationship. Interbrew insisted that the enterprise should recruit employees publicly.

A distinctive gap had also been created between the foreign management and local staff in aspects of housing, salary and career advancement. There were many complaints about the joint venture from the Chinese employees at that time. 'Most of the managers complained that they would become cheap labour and slaves,' said Ms Tan. Chinese managers also claimed that the Western managers did not understand Chinese culture and their situation. In order to save costs, the old welfare systems including housing, health care and pensions had to be modified.

Interference from the 'mother-in-law'

The local government had as one of its major roles to encourage the establishment of enterprise in the locality. Its expectation was to build an international investing environment through the example of the Blue Sword and Interbrew joint venture. However, many unexpected problems occurred almost as soon as this venture was established. The local government received appeals not only from the employees who had lost their jobs, but also from retired workers who were worried about their pensions and health care.

In 1995, the government intervened. In accordance with the newly estab-lished law of evaluating enterprise assets and brand, the value of Blue Sword Company's asset and brand should have been RMB 600 million yuan. Based on this calculation, the Belgian company's level of investment to dominate the joint venture management and product brand was found to be unreasonable. The local government also modified some local regulations on employee policy in foreign-invested enterprises and on conditions for the future development of foreign-invested companies.

Even though Interbrew appealed against the method of evaluating assets and brand, they agreed to terminate the joint venture without conditions. This short-lived joint venture collapsed in less than one year from the date that both sides had signed the contract.

Reasons for the failure

There may be other factors that may have caused the failure of this joint venture: the background of the Chinese general managers; the level of local government influence; or the role of the former Chinese management group. However, based on the information available, it could be concluded that at least some of the failure was due to the lack of knowledge of Blue Sword's original organizational culture. Blue Sword was very different from other nearly bankrupt Chinese state-owned enterprises. It had formed its own organizational culture that had been widely accepted by its original managers and employees. Government interference may be seen as the external cause of the failure. Misjudging the existing characteristics of Chinese managers and employees by the Belgian management may have contributed more directly towards the ending of this 'bitter marriage'.

Chinese work values

Hofstede (1980a) did not include the People's Republic of China in his IBM study, although more recently he adopted the Chinese Cultural Connection (CCC, 1987) Confucian dynamism as a fifth dimension (Hofstede, 1991), which adds limited information to our current knowledge of China's work-related values. Even the more current work of Trompenaars (1993) is surprisingly silent on such key areas as collectivism–individualism when it comes to China. Of course Hofstede (1980a) draws on data from Hong Kong and Taiwan to describe Chinese characteristics. But there is a need to be wary of generalizing from these societies that have been exposed to Western ideas and practices for some time. However, it is likely that such value dimensions as collectivism–individualism, power distance, uncertainty avoidance, masculinity–femininity, as well long term/short-term ('Confucian dynamism'), have some relevance in the mainland China context and can help us to understand those aspects of motivation which are related to work values.

Power distance, for example, may be regarded as high in China, with the top stratum being unapproachable, but with distances between middle management, supervisors and workers being smaller (Warner, 1993; Locket, 1987). A person who advances through the system beginning as a worker, then moving up to foreman and finally middle management will gain comparatively little power influence. Power structures are not well installed because of a lack of managers, and may take shape as a result of necessity. The respect for hierarchy and authority may be rooted in Confucianism, together with a regard for age as a source of authority: this is largely unknown in organizations in the West.

The level of uncertainty avoidance in China is not so clear-cut. Hofstede's (1980a) work indicates a lack of need to avoid ambiguity in Chinese cultures, and this may reflect the fact that China itself (as could be argued of Hong Kong) is relatively free of a highly regulated legal code, and has traditionally been ruled by men (power distance) rather than by laws (uncertainty avoidance), but more recent work (Chimezie et al., 1993) indicates a strong avoidance of uncertainty among Chinese, with a strong desire to maintain social order with a degree of predictability. But Hofstede (1991) argues that uncertainty avoidance, which is linked to the question of 'truth', may be an irrelevant concept, as truth is not a relevant issue in Eastern thinking. The Chinese manager may well be motivated to save 'face' and to tell the other person what they want to hear, rather than what may be regarded as the absolute truth in Western eyes.

Masculinity–femininity is also a value dimension for which there is little direct information in relation to China. Chinese cultures in Hofstede's IBM studies had medium scores for this dimension. The concept of masculinity represents an emphasis on competition and the centrality of work in one's life. Japanese managers, for example, score high on masculinity (Hofstede, 1991). The Meaning of Working study (MOW, 1987) also indicates a high centrality of work for Japanese individuals. This is an area of information which is lacking in the context of China.

As one would expect, collectivism is high in Chinese cultures, with the main group of reference being the family (collectivism is target specific: Hui, 1990). This is rooted both in Confucianism and in the ancient land system that ensured the farmer and his family were immovable for economic reasons. Mao attempted to weaken this influence, but perhaps it will be the increasing economic prosperity of China that may further weaken collectivism. A different approach is worth noting here, in that Chen, Meindl and Hunt, (1997) suggest that increased economic success may be paralleled by a weakening of horizontal collectivism or interpersonal cohesion, and the strengthening of horizontal collectivism or corporate loyalty and identification. Hofstede (1991) indicates a positive correlation between individualism and per capita GNP. Individualism may well be on the increase in China (Nevis, 1983) as no doubt it has already been in Hong Kong. The implications for this in motivational terms may be a higher emphasis on individual achievement rather than the mutual reliance of the group or collective.

Rather than the short-term achievement orientation of many Western societies, China is characterized by long-term values (Hofstede's, 1991, fifth dimension) such as thrift and perseverance. This is believed to sustain steady economic growth (Hofstede and Bond, 1988), as has been borne out until recently by the 'economic miracles' of some of the Asian Pacific countries. Certain 'quick fix' management approaches, suggested by many Western management specialists, may not be appropriate in China. Different perspectives on time between China and the West also have implications for the perception of objectives: the achievement of short-term objectives as an indicator of individual achievement may not be appropriate. This has implications for the introduction of individually based reward systems founded on goal achievement. A connected factor is that of locus of control (from Rotter, 1966): Eastern cultures have a fatalistic view of destiny, where cause and effect are more likely to be attributed to external factors rather than factors that can be controlled by the individual. With a view that the individual has little control over short-term objectives, goal-based individual reward systems may not be appropriate.

Many researchers believe that the value system in China is changing. For example, Cyr and Frost (1991) argue that Chinese workers are shifting towards a value system that is more goal-achievement oriented rather than egalitarian. Certainly, labour and management reforms have had an impact on organizations in China. Warner's (1996a) summary of this is shown in Table 8.1. Certainly, many of these aspects were seen in the case of Blue Sword.

However, an empirical study of work values in eight different countries including China (Elizur et al., 1991) indicates a low importance in China of

Table 8.1 Differences as a result of labour-management reforms in China (Warner, 1996b)

System characteristic	Status quo	Experimental
Strategy	hard line	reformist
Employment	iron rice-board (interventionist)	labour market
Conditions	job security	labour contracts
Mobility	job assignment	job choice
Rewards	egalitarian	meritocratic
Wage system	grade based	performance based
Promotion	seniority	skill-related
Union role	consultative	coordinative
Management	economic cadres	professional managers
Factory party role	central	ancillary
Work organization	Taylorism	flexible
Efficiency	technical	allocative

'instrumental' values, such as pay, benefits, convenient working hours and working conditions. Taiwan scores high on the same instrumental values, which may indicate that the low importance of these factors in China results from several decades of socialist influence rather than any fundamental Chinese cultural characteristic (assuming it is possible to separate these). Moreover, Vertinski, Tse, Wehrung and Lee (1990) point out the greater weight traditionally placed upon ascribed rather than achieved status in Chinese society, being a reflection of Confucian values. The empirical evidence from the People's Republic of China does not provide unequivocal evidence that China is moving towards an achievement society, and this has implications for the sort of people management policies which may be effective in East–West joint ventures in China. This was evident in Blue Sword, where recruitment practices resulted in conflict between the Belgian and Chinese partners.

International joint ventures in China

The Chinese Communist Party Central Committee gave economic reform top-level priority during its 'Third Plenum' at the end of 1978. By 1979, foreigners were permitted 'to establish equity joint ventures together with Chinese companies, enterprises or other economic organizations . . . within the territory of the People's Republic of China, on the principle of equity and mutual benefit' (PRC, 1987).

Since the beginning of these economic reforms in 1979 the Chinese economy has exploded, with an average annual growth rate in GNP of 10 per cent over the last decade and the attainment of 20 per cent in the coastal areas designated 'special economic zones' (EIU, 1994). Foreign direct investment more than doubled between 1987 and 1990 (Kelley and Shenkar, 1993), despite a slow-down after the Tiananmen Square incident, with an estimate of more than 150,000 joint ventures in China. Much of this investment comes from Hong Kong (68.2 per cent in 1992) and other countries of Eastern Asia, with European countries, and even the USA (with 4.6 per cent in 1992) badly represented.

Despite this economic growth, there are indications that productivity has been a problem. This may have implications for the attractiveness of China to foreign investors, despite low labour costs. A study undertaken in the mid-1980s

171

indicated that productivity levels were 60–70 per cent of those in Hong Kong (Locket, 1987). A recent study (Turcq, 1995) indicates a steady rise in productivity relative to wage increases over the ten years from 1980 to 1990. But many of the problems and failures of international joint ventures in China have been associated with problems in the area of human resources management, and particularly in performance motivation and staff retention (Henley and Nyaw, 1990; Child et al., 1990; Child, 1994; Wang, 1992; Kelley and Shenkar, 1993; and Wang and Satow, 1994).

Hence, Bjoerkman and Lu (1997) report that at a recent round table discussion with the government of the PRC, 59 per cent of participants from foreign-invested enterprises (FIE) concluded that recruiting and retaining managers (a substantial input into human resource management) was the most significant problem facing FIEs in China. This represented twice the number who considered Chinese bureaucracy to be the major issue. Findings drawn from a study of 67 Sino-foreign international joint ventures by Lu, Child and Yan (1997) show the highest cause of perceived difficulties to be differences in management styles (according to 26 of the 51 foreign managers surveyed), and the second highest perceived cause of difficulties being human resource management including such areas as payment, welfare and arrangements of accommodation (18 out of 51 foreign managers). In this study, Chinese managers saw as the highest cause of difficulties expatriate managers without knowledge of the Chinese environment (29 out of the 56 Chinese managers surveyed), and the second highest cause different management styles (18 out of 56 Chinese managers). This is reflected in the problems associated with the failure of the Blue Sword joint venture. In both sets of accounts within the 67 international joint ventures, human resource management and related issues such as management styles were seen as the main causes of difficulties within the general management of such enterprises.

Over the last two decades Chinese state enterprises have undergone a number of market-related reforms, as was seen in the Blue Sword case, in order to develop institutions pursuing profit and productivity rather than ideological, political or specifically social goals (Boisot and Child, 1988; Chen, 1995, Jackson, 1992; Walder, 1986). With the changing face of China's social and economic infrastructure, work and management attitudes may be changing, and perhaps they must change in order to facilitate additional increases in productivity that will encourage further investment from the West. But this does not mean that Western human resource management techniques can simply be imposed on joint venture operations.

An important aspect of managing international joint ventures in China is the reconciliation of differences between expectations of the objectives of the joint venture and practices of people management. Sweeney (1996) compares common conflicts of objectives in joint ventures (Table 8.2). These differences were seen in Blue Sword's expectation of enhancing production techniques through cooperation with a Western partner, to develop international quality standards, and to expand to Western markets. The expectations of Interbrew were to develop a focus on the Chinese market with minimum investment in product development and quality standards, and to focus more on quantity.

With one of the biggest sources of difference between the joint venture partners being the management of people, Sergeant and Frenkel (1998) indicate some of the major problems in this area (Table 8.3). Again, the issues of

Table 8.2 Differences in objectives between Chinese and foreign partners in international joint ventures (adapted from Sweeney, 1996)

Objective of joint venture	Chinese partner	Foreign partner
Financial outcomes	to increase foreign exchange reserves to invest for future development	to repatriate profits over the long term to maximize long-term returns
Investment	to minimize initial investment	to provide an acceptable minimum investment
Process of negotiation	holistic heuristic	sequentially, step-by-step
Nature of the contract	adaptable short-term ambiguous	enforceable long-term precise and unambiguous
Planning	to obtain congruence between state plan and aims of joint venture	to obtain maximum flexibility
Inputs	to focus on domestic suppliers	to minimize poor quality to minimize unpredictability
Outputs	to generate foreign exchange to increase exports	to access Chinese domestic markets to develop Chinese domestic markets
Strategic intent	short to medium term domestic and international	short to long term domestic and international
Operations emphasis	stress on quality	stress on quality
Personnel requirements	maximum number of local employees	fewest people possible for acceptable output maximum productivity
Management style employed	traditional	modern

recruitment came to the fore in the Blue Sword/Interbrew joint venture, where the Belgian partner insisted on going to the open market. This may have been inappropriate, not only from the point of view of insensitivity to local practices, but also at the pragmatic level of accessing skilled staff from other state-owned enterprises.

The new labour law (effective January 1995: Warner, 1996b) to which Sergeant and Frenkel refer may well have an impact on human resource management in international joint ventures as it provides:

- workers with the right to choose jobs, to be paid and to have rest and holidays and protection in the workplace as well as receiving training to improve skills;

- no employment for children under 16;

- no discrimination by race, nationality, sex or religion;

- women with the same rights as men;

- minimum wage levels to be set by local government;

- contracts between employer and worker which set out pay, conditions, tasks to be performed and how the contract may be terminated;

- permission for enterprises on the brink of bankruptcy to reduce staff if agreement can be reached with the trade union after consultation of all staff;

- an average working week of 44 hours with one day off per week;

- an eight-hour working day;

- women not to work in mines and conditions of extreme temperature, and after the seventh month of pregnancy when maternity leave of 90 days should be allowed;

- dispute committees to be established in the workplace and to include employers and workers (Warner, 1996b).

Table 8.3 Human resource problems in Chinese international joint ventures (IJV) (adapted from Sergeant and Frenkel, 1998)

HRM	Issues
Employee recruitment	Rapid wage increases, high staff turnover and poaching of staff common because of shortages in the labour market for skilled manual and blue-collar workers Nepotism and over-hiring Difficulty of transferring staff from state enterprises as approval needed and liability for economic damage may result in compensation paid by the new employer
Reward system	New labour laws permit companies to set their own wage levels resulting in disadvantage to Chinese organizations as IJV tend to pay much more Wage disparity between skilled and non-skilled Reward packages complex because of social benefits (which are increasingly being taken over by the state, allowing more flexibility to IJV) Difficulty in introducing pay differentials for workers of similar status (because of disruption to interpersonal harmony, and distrust of performance appraisal: evaluations in state enterprises based on ideological principles and *guanxi*)
Employee retention	Difficult for IJV because of shortages of well-trained local staff, but now being overcome by more control on compensation and other motivational techniques
Work performance and employee management	Lack of initiative of Chinese staff due to socialization Time not seen as a scarce resource Little emphasis on quality Lack of work ethic Managers rarely rewarded for high performance Managers risk averse and not innovative (risk of failure and losing face) Difficulties in dismissing non-performers
Management–employee relations	The right to join trade unions Trade unions not adversarial and help to facilitate operations by arranging courses and cultural activities Unions may become more adversarial with new laws and possibility of collective bargaining
Expatriate relations	Often problems of preparation of expatriates in Chinese IJV Balancing foreign and local staff can be a problem

This legislation, whose effects would not have been felt until after the dissolution of the Blue Sword joint venture, should provide more flexibility for employers in the nature of contracts given and the reward systems possible. It has effectively abolished the traditional job assignment and labour allocation process, and this and other legislation gives far more flexibility to international joint ventures in their recruitment. The issue of reward systems and other motivational mechanisms which are used and which are appropriate is an aspect of Chinese international joint ventures, which Jackson and Bak (1998) take up.

Motivation and reward systems in Chinese international joint ventures

Jackson and Bak (1998) suggest that motivation of Chinese workers can be understood in terms of Katz and Kahn's (1978) categorization of 'rule enforcement', 'external rewards' and 'internalized motivation', as follows.

Rule enforcement

Rules and role prescriptions may be regarded as a form of role protection in the Chinese context, with job descriptions carrying little motivational content in terms of tasks or objectives to be achieved, but acting as an insurance against being asked to take on additional and unknown duties and against being overworked and avoiding the risk of punishment. There is therefore a need to structure work tightly around well defined parameters which are documented, communicated and accepted by employees and supervisors, with an emphasis on role protection as well as task performance.

External rewards

Material incentives have been used by China's economic reformers in order to stimulate performance and there is evidence that money is important in China as a motivator, as individual bonuses have existed in China since 1978 and performance-related bonus incentives schemes since 1983. However, there has been a tendency towards low differentiation of pay in an egalitarian reward system, reflecting a need to minimize competition and foster harmony in the workplace: a reflection of a strongly collectivist culture. Limited pay differentials are often based on length of service. State enterprise employees' wage structures are extremely complex and based on a whole number of different subsidies, bonuses and allowances. Employees may be reluctant to leave this type of system for a less socially supportive one as there is an expectation that the enterprise will take care of employees through housing and other social benefits, which must have a strong loyalty effect. Systems of pay in joint ventures should therefore retain a strong element of reward for loyalty and seniority, as well as 'belongingness' elements such as housing allowances.

Internalized motivation

A major source of internalized motivation in China has been political indoctrination and campaigning, including 'emulation campaigns' in communist

China involving 'labour heroes' in an attempt to appeal to high performers who might otherwise feel inhibited to perform in an exemplary manner in an egalitarian culture. In a related way Japanese companies in China send their best workers to Japan in order to learn from example and from being exposed to a foreign culture and encourage a willingness to change. Building a sense of belongingness and loyalty in Chinese workers creates a good opportunity to develop internalized motivation from developing corporate identity through a strong organizational culture. Foreign companies may have a kudos for Chinese workers, and this could be built on to encourage long-term loyalty, as could effective supervision involving doing by example. New patterns of behaviour (including creativity and innovation) could be encouraged by emulation, both in the workplace and on training courses in China and, where appropriate (particularly for managerial and supervisory staff who can act as role models) abroad. A focus should therefore be placed on building corporate identity through effective induction and subsequent training programmes in order to promote 'the way we do things around here', as well as developing supervisors who can act as role models in developing and changing work-related behaviour towards that supported by the corporate culture.

Intrinsic job motivation

In a study by Child (1994) employees were found to be satisfied with the intrinsic job content and challenge, and with opportunities to enjoy social relationships in the workplace, yet there was dissatisfaction with prospects for advancement and promotion. There may therefore be considerable motivational potential in creating opportunities for employees to advance. This could well be in the formulation of a career path for those who have successfully taken on board those work behaviours which are seen as appropriate to the organizational culture, and who themselves can act as role models in supervisory and management positions.

Jackson and Bak (1998) then investigated what Chinese joint ventures and foreign-invested enterprises actually do to motivate their employees through a study of 13 different enterprises in Beijing. There finding were as follows.

Rule enforcement

The way responsibility is given and the way performance is directed:

- *Responsibility.* There is a guarded attitude towards giving too much responsibility, as workers like guidance and older workers in particular prefer clear instructions. Motivation rises when more responsibility is given to employees in their own area, but this comes with experience. There are few precise job descriptions being used, and instructions seem to relate to the job at hand. General rules of conduct exist in some companies. One company made its rules clear in a two-day induction session: no spitting, no smoking, how to dress and cut your hair (an in-house hairdresser is employed).

- *Goal setting and appraisal.* Several companies use goal setting extensively, and see it as useful. This involves the setting of individual targets, face-to-face performance discussions, and weekly to annual appraisals, depending on the company.

- *Pressure and punishment.* Direct punishment was found only in the hotel sector, where some companies punish their staff for bad behaviour and not working. Deductions from salary or bonuses are seen to give positive results. For some offences up to three warnings can be given before dismissal. Penalty schemes for non-attendance at training sessions are also in operation. The use of pressure and punishment of this kind was not identified in companies outside the hotel industry.

- *Praise.* Companies do not praise their employees very often. Individual praise in front of the group is not often used deliberately except in the hotel industry. A view elsewhere is that this may be negative or embarrassing.

External rewards

Incentives involve packages which include, to a greater or lesser extent, money, bonus systems, and welfare benefits.

- *Money.* Generally money is seen as important for recruiting and retaining employees, but not as a real motivator. It is seen as a hygiene factor in that it keeps staff in the company.

- *Bonus systems.* It is considered that bonuses relating to individual performance would improve motivation, but this view is not widespread. One company pays a fixed salary only. Some companies offer performance-related bonuses. One company has established smaller units or profit centres where performance measurement is undertaken monthly, on which basis a bonus is paid to employees within the profit centre, with an element of the bonus also reflecting the performance of the company as a whole.

- *Welfare package.* This is seen as necessary but is not believed to motivate. The provision of housing in state companies causes problems when foreign companies do not provide housing. By moving to a foreign company employees lose their house. There is therefore pressure on foreign companies to provide housing or an associated benefit. Company provision of local housing also may cut down on commuting time, which may benefit productivity. Some companies provide housing loans. As Chinese workers give up benefits when they move to a foreign company, this has implications for recruitment.

Internalized motivation

There is some evidence that efforts are being made to engender corporate loyalty and belongingness through internalizing factors of motivation.

- *Identification with company.* Managers from at least two companies thought that working for a foreign joint venture or Fortune 500 company engendered pride in its employees. One company also involves employees more by use of a suggestion box, a communication letter, service campaigns, honesty campaigns, a smiling campaign, and badges and certificates for best workers.

- *Training*. Most companies report some form of training as part of their motivational programme, including lunchtime learning. On-the-job training for one company takes place in China, whilst their top engineers are sent to Europe for one month a year to attend special courses. One company has set up a (transient) business school in China based at local hotels for a few days at a time, with a view to setting up a permanent classroom in the near future. One hotel reported having to compel staff to attend training courses. Punishment is given for non-attendance at training courses in this instance.

- *Setting a good example*. The supervisor or manager often tries to set a good example to employees, and this is seen as motivating employees to do the job, as often when the boss is away employees are reluctant to work.

- *Staff outings and activities*. Several companies regard staff outings as motivators.

Intrinsic motivation

The term 'intrinsic motivation' is used by Jackson and Bak (1998) to refer to the total employment experience.

- *Working conditions*. Results were mixed. Chinese workers are used to a lower standard from state-owned companies and tend to have low expectations. Air conditioning, for example, was believed by one company not to be overly important. In another company employees in the hot summer prefer to stay in the cool office rather than to go home. There is also a view that Chinese employees expect a European working environment if working for a European company, and therefore expectations are generally high.

- *Job rotation and enrichment*. Lip service seems to be paid to job rotation and enrichment schemes, as there was little evidence of these being used, or when used being particularly effective. In one company, supervisors and managers have resisted implementing such a scheme.

- *Social life at work*. There seem to be no mechanisms used to encourage and foster the social dimension of work at the workplace, and this aspect seems to be left to extra-mural activities.

- *Promotion and career in company*. Rapid promotion through an extensive staff ranking system is seen in one company as a very important motivational mechanism. As the company is successful in China, it can offer more opportunities with the growth of the company. All other companies were silent on the positive use of career planning and promotion as a motivational tool.

Implications for the management of joint ventures

Huo and von Glinow (1995) provide an interesting comparison of specific human resource management practices between the USA, People's Republic of China and

Taiwan (Table 8.4). Their suggestions for introducing human resource management practices into China are that for selection job interviews can be used as a starting point in building a long-term work relationship by providing useful information about the organization to the candidate. For rewards systems, merit pay can be used sparingly as can differentiating non-monetary rewards by employees' performance. For performance appraisal there is a suggestion not to use too many objectives or tedious appraisal procedures or forms, and that participation or inputs should only be encouraged if employees have shown an interest in this. Participative management, they suggest, can be used judiciously but may backfire if workers are reluctant to participate in organization-wide decisions.

Table 8.4 Comparison of human resource management practices in the USA, PR China and Taiwan (adapted from Huo and Von Glinow, 1995)

HRM practices	USA	PR China	Taiwan
Selection	Job interview is an essential step for filling major positions	Most jobs are still allocated by the government or the university based on credentials Interview is not yet common	Credentials are more important than anything else Similarity to the recruiters in education and social background is a critical advantage
Reward system	A wide variety of rewards are used in the incentive system	The range of wage and salary is narrow Bonus is not based on individual performance Pay is more motivating than in the USA	Intrinsic rewards are getting more important for the new professional Money is still very important for labour workers
Performance appraisal	Two-way communication and counselling are widely used in the performance appraisal system	Superiors have absolute authority to evaluate subordinates Standards of performance are vague and generic	Input from the workers is increasing Superiors still have absolute authority
Participative management	Participative management is welcome and encouraged, but is not particularly prevalent yet	Collective leadership is widely used Participation of workers in major decisions is superficial and symbolic	Workers are only interested in taking part in decisions that directly affect their benefits, e.g. workplace safety, health insurance and wage levels

Jackson and Bak's (1998) recommendations for (Western) foreign partners in international joint ventures in China are as follows:

- Organizational rules and procedures should be well documented and communicated in order to reduce risk and ambiguity. This should provide a strong element of 'security' for employees by informing them of rules of conduct, the parameters and scope of their jobs, and expectations in terms of performance and quality. This reflects a need to protect employees by the use

179

of defined roles and rules. This should be reflected in human resource practices by:

- providing clear job descriptions as well as clear instructions for specific tasks. As confidence levels grow alongside experience in a foreign company, participation in the decision-making process could produce high levels of motivation, for carefully selected employees;
- experimenting with praise and goal setting in order to raise confidence levels.

- Structural reward systems should include a 'loyalty' element which inculcates 'belongingness', and reflects seniority, rather than directly addressing an achievement motive which may not be as relevant as in a Western setting. This should include provision such as housing allowances. Additional human resource practices should include:
  - ensuring money is commensurate with an employee's standing in the organization, as this may well be seen as a measure of success for individuals and for their family.

- A strong corporate identity should be fostered, and a human resource policy should reflect a desire to inculcate both common work values, and a belongingness to the company through:
  - developing effective induction programmes which draw the new employee closer to the company;
  - developing subsequent training programmes which reflect the way things are done in the organization, while taking care not to concentrate too heavily on training for skills which are easily transferable to other enterprises;
  - focusing on developing role models: supervisors who have been trained in the way of the company can gain standing in the organization by representing the values and practices of the organization;
  - as a foreign manager, working hard, not coming in late, not drinking tea all day, and expecting Chinese employees to copy your positive behaviour;
  - not getting too hung up on job enrichment programmes: these seem to have only limited success when they focus on individualistic values. Focusing on team working may be more productive.

- Attention should be paid to developing clear career paths as part of human resource planning, as well as through a need to develop loyalty, identification with the organization, required work-related behaviour and intrinsic motivation for the total work experience. Human resource managers should therefore:
  - present clear options for career development: this seems to be a major motivator, although significantly lacking in current motivational design. Career paths should be particularly visible for those who can develop as effective role models.

At a more general level, in the management of international joint ventures, Pucik (1988) argues that one of the main challenges anywhere is the organizational learning capacity (see also Chapter 6) of the partners within the joint venture. This is bound up with human resource issues that he spells out as obstacles to organizational learning (Table 8.5).

Table 8.5 Obstacles to organizational learning in international strategic alliances (Pucik, 1988)

HR function	Key obstacle
HR planning	strategic intent not communicated
	short-term and static planning horizon
	low priority of learning activities
	lack of involvement by the HR function
Staffing	insufficient lead-time for staffing decisions
	resource-poor staffing strategies
	low quality of staff assigned to the alliance
	staffing dependent on the partners
Training and development	lack of cross-cultural competence
	unidirectional transfer of know-how
	career structure not conducive to learning
	poor climate for transfer of learning
Appraisal and reward	appraisal focused on short-term goals
	no encouragement of learning
	limited incentives for transfer of know-how
	rewards not tied to global strategy
Organizational design and control	responsibility for learning not clear
	fragmentation of the learning process
	control over the HR function given away
	no insight into partner's HR strategy

An interesting aspect of this which often has implications for Western joint ventures with Chinese partners, or partners from developing or transitional countries, is that except for local knowledge, the Chinese partner is often seen as having nothing to offer the Western partner. There is a unidirectional transfer of know-how, perhaps based on the assumption that Western management methods are somehow more effective. This is well reflected in the view of Sweeney (1996) who summarizes the differences between international joint venture partners in China in terms of wider people management related issues. This paints rather a pejorative picture, which perhaps is not very helpful in formulating policy and practices within joint ventures, or in the development of further research in this area. He suggests that the Chinese model is characterized as people having limited accountability, careers being unplanned, bottleneck communication, limited customer focus, hierarchical decision making, limited delegation, reactivity and a lack of planning, lack of equal opportunities, overbearing bureaucracy, limited HR planning, reactionary leadership, lack of participation, static management style, and a lack of teamwork, among other attributes. The Western model, for Sweeney (1996) figures positively on all these factors.

The Blue Sword joint venture depicted a number of misunderstandings between the Western and Chinese partners. It is likely that such practices as recruitment of family members was seen in the negative 'nepotism' sense. Such a view is likely to have played its part in the demise of the joint venture. Not only does this approach hamper understanding between joint venture partners, it also restricts useful and informative research in this area.

Questions for managers

1 How could the problems in the Blue Sword joint venture, leading to its eventual failure, have been avoided?

2 How should the Belgian management in the joint venture have handled the issue of recruitment?

3 How should the management of the joint venture have managed reward and motivational systems within the company?

An agenda for research

Much research has been undertaken in the last decade on management in China, and in the area of joint venturing in China. This chapter has reflected some of that research. However, as can be seen, much of this research has been from a Western perspective, and implicitly or explicitly judges Chinese management against the same criteria that would be used in the researcher's own country. Often, where Chinese collaborators are involved in such research, at worst they are used as data collectors, or if contributing to interpreting findings, tend to conform to the paradigms and ideas of the Western partner (perhaps another form of Chinese–Western joint venture). A major question that is ripe for research is, 'What can a Chinese concept of people and management offer to the Western world, or to global managing generally?' This will be taken up in the final chapter within the context of this whole book, which derives the lessons of looking at different perspectives on the management of people, and forming a general principle on which could be based the future of cross-cultural management research: the extent to which indigenous knowledge is identified, incorporated into research and managed in cross-cultural organizational situations.

Questions for researchers

1 What are the main factors in successful international joint ventures in China, and what are the main factors in failed joint ventures?

2 To what extent are Western HRM principles and practices being applied in Chinese enterprises, and how successful are these? How do they contrast with Chinese indigenous approaches, and to what extent are they being combined into hybrid forms of people management (either successfully or unsuccessfully)?

3 How can reward and motivational systems be successfully employed in international joint ventures in order to meet the needs and aspirations of an indigenous workforce?

Note

The case study of Blue Sword was contributed by Peter Xu Lu.

The transitioning organization: the post-Soviet model

chapter nine

The post-Soviet model

After a decade of 'transitional' management initiated by the collapse of the Warsaw Pact and the Soviet system, it is still possible to talk about the post-Soviet era as one of transition. However, the word 'transition' implies a change from one form to another. Whatever that new form may be in connection with the former Soviet countries, it may be that this has not yet been reached. The ideal form is often presented as some adaptation, if not a direct adoption, of the free market system of countries such as the United States, or perhaps more appropriately the Social Democratic systems of Northern Europe. Within Eastern and Central European countries the International Monetary Fund has often been setting the agenda (Glenny, 1993), with this being firmly set toward a free market economy.

The objective of this chapter is to examine the interaction of Western and post-Soviet people management systems and practices. Of particular relevance is the interaction of German organizations and immediate neighbours such as the Czech Republic, and the previous centre of the Soviet system, Russia. To place this in the context of real cultures and real management issues, the joint venture of Volkswagen-Skoda is considered as a corporate mediator between German people management culture and Czech culture.

Volkswagen–Skoda joint venture

The training department manager at Skoda Automobilova, Barbara Gutmann (1995) describes the situation following the beginning of the joint venture between Skoda and Volkswagen. This was viewed by Volkswagen as support for the transformation of the former socialist republic, as well as an important step into the Eastern European markets. Volkswagen recognized that the 100-year-old Skoda had high levels of professionalism among its 18,000 staff. However, at the same time there was a perception that there was a lack of economic knowledge and experience, initiative, responsibility and management skills; that management had been restricted to authoritarian methods of order and obedience; and that employees were careful not to be noticed. Although effort and initiative could be seen in people's private lives, there was a lack of commitment and willingness to take decisions in the workplace. Sometimes the expertise that the expatriates brought was encountered with scepticism. Despite this there was a high level of motivation and readiness to learn.

Gutmann, herself an expatriate, recounts that the joint objective was to transform Skoda into a customer-oriented learning organization. There was therefore a central question of how to eliminate deficiencies and get the most out of both parties' strengths, and how to undertake know-how transfer. Rather than filling the top positions with German expatriates the company wanted to effect this transfer by project work, coaching and tandem management. Project work involved bicultural teams in a limited time-span of three to six months, led by a local manager who was responsible for the project results. There was also a small team of three expatriates who were available to support the projects. Projects within the HRM department included designing a new organizational structure for the HR function, producing management guidelines, a management appraisal system and creating a Skoda management culture. Tandem management involved one key position being filled by an expatriate manager, and one by a local manager, usually for three years. During this time the expatriate would act as a knowledge mediator and coach in order to develop the local manager so that he or she could manage the department independently. As the local partner became more competent, the expatriate would withdraw more and more. Negative factors in this process were concerned with the incompatibility of the partners, cultural insensitivities and perceived arrogance of the expatriate as the expert and senior partner. Successful cultural and personal integration had been helped by the early involvement of the people concerned. For example Volkswagen initiated a programme of 'look-and-see' trips for potential expatriates. Universal bilingual communication was introduced, although there was evidence of this being bypassed with Germans speaking German, and the Czechs falling back on the 'old boys' network' (Gutmann, 1995: 23). Temporary assignments for local managers to other group companies were also seen to contribute to accelerated integration.

Cyr and Schneider (1998), using the thinly veiled name of Karnovac automobilova, highlight in more detail some of the issues involved in the integration of the German and Czech partners. These included the following:

- *Cultural sensitivity*: too many German regulations, attitudes and behaviour had been transferred (much of this and the following attitudinal information comes from a staff survey involving Czech and German managers); there was a lack of respect by expatriates of what had worked well in the past in the Czech company, matched by pride from local managers in, for example, working long hours to achieve targets; but there were also commonalities between the two cultures: common historical roots, the high level of industrialization of Czechoslovakia after the Second World War; and a concern for technical aspects rather than styles, and positive social policies.

- *Communication*: language was indicated as being a problem, but also the desire for information to enable locals to perform their jobs was not always forthcoming.

- *Staffing*: there were some problems in recruiting staff of the right calibre and attitudes (willingness to work and improve oneself, and to work as part of a cooperative team, and to take risks); the unemployment rate was low in the area and the company had a policy of avoiding major layoffs where possible, so there was a high degree of job security.

- *Training*: there was a strong commitment to training to enhance efficiency, creativity, work quality and productivity. This included the tandem training outlined by Gutmann (1995), and visits of Czech staff to plants in Germany. Foreign language training was also available.

- *Reward systems*: this was differentiated between Czech and German managers, with expatriates being on higher salaries. This led to some resentment. There was a bonus system for Czech staff. Under the old system this had relied on one's relationship to decision making. There was still a feeling that pay did not adequately reflect performance, nor was there a fair chance for promotion. Short-term rewards were deemed more effective than longer-term ones. This was because people lived from one month to the next. A new salary structure was introduced in 1993 based on the Hay system which allocates points for aspects of a job, such as difficulty and level of expertise required. Job descriptions were more flexible in the Czech system as there had been less of a distinction between blue- and white-collar workers. The new system established 12 salary scales according to job classification, performance increments for all based on an annual assessment (based on quality, transfer of know-how, initiative, problem solving and efficiency), a bonus system based on quality and productivity and a one-month bonus based on attainment of annual organizational goals. Social benefits such as subsidized vacation facilities and company apartments, lunches, medical insurance and interest-free loans, were available to staff.

This joint venture, its successes and problems, should be assessed in the context of German systems of management, as well as in the historical perspective of Soviet systems of control and management.

German people management

The former West Germany is depicted by Hofstede (1980a) as relatively low in power distance (below the USA and on a par with Britain), fairly individualistic (but far less so than the USA, the Anglo-Saxon countries, the Scandinavian countries, and slightly below France), fairly masculine (on a par with Britain), and medium in terms of uncertainty avoidance (certainly much higher on Hofstede's index than the Anglo-Saxon countries, and the Scandinavian countries). Smith et al. (1996) using Trompenaars' (1993) data place the former West Germany relatively high on egalitarian commitment (in contrast with conservativism) and midway on the dimension of utilitarian involvement/loyal involvement (see Chapter 1). In contrast, the former East Germany is positioned relatively high on loyal involvement (in contrast to many of the other former Soviet bloc East and Central European countries), and relatively high on conservatism (in line with many of the other Eastern and Central European countries). The two former German countries occupy quite similar positions on Schwartz' (1994) conservative dimension (low), intellectual and affective autonomy (high), egalitarian commitment (high), but not hierarchy (low for former West Germany, medium to high for the former East Germany.

It may be that from evidence of the latter study (which may represent values more generally in the community, being drawn from schoolteachers who in

Schwartz's view are the custodians or carriers of societal culture) prevailing cultural values in the two Germanys were more similar and more pervasive during the iron curtain years than is suggested by data from studies of organizational employees and managers. Yet Germany is also diverse, from north to south and from west to east, and has a history of shifting allegiances and borders. Guy and Mattock (1991) have suggested that it may be just this changing topography of the country, its historically and geographically insecure borders, that has fostered insecurities and doubts about a German-ness which is not certain (see also Warner and Campbell, 1993). This national insecurity may give rise to a need for orderliness and risk reduction. Gannon and Associates (1994: 67–8) use the metaphor of the symphony to describe:

> the coming together of various musical divisions of style and perspectives, such that those between entire sections of strings and the brass, and between the individual flutist and percussionist, are melded and moulded by the conductor to produce a unified sound . . . for the greater good that is the music, individual preference is subdued to the wants of the conductor and the needs of the symphony . . . the soloist's time of improvisation is brief, and the conductor soon signals that it is time to return to the history of the piece. It is this discipline – the voluntary submission of the individual to the whole, the guidance of the conductor, and the shared meaning of the music – that allows the symphony orchestra to flower and flourish.

Table 9.1 Comparisons of German and British management culture (Hickson and Pugh, 1995, after Ebster-Grosz and Pugh, 1991)

Element of management culture	German	British
The financial system favours	Long-termism	Short-termism
The marketing function emphasizes	Sales and financial analysis	Marketing and market response
Consumers look for:	High quality performance	Value for money and economy
Advertising is	More explicit and technical	More implicit and humorous
Vocational qualification of staff	Comprehensive system covering all levels	Middle level missing for technical training
Top management qualifications	Highly technical with less work experience	General, with more work experience
Work attitudes of staff	Adherence to procedures	Personal initiative
Decision making	Risks calculated, decisions slower	Risks uncalculated, decisions faster
Management emphasis on	Reliability	Flexibility
Management values	Efficient operations	Strategic awareness

There are many similarities of culture between Germany and Britain, yet a study by Ebster-Grosz and Pugh (1991) which looked at chief executives from the two countries found they experienced difficulties in cross-national co-operation. The differences that were expressed are summarized in Table 9.1.

The main features of the context of management and work values in Germany appear to be:

- *A social market economy*: instigated in former West Germany after 1945 which established a principle of intervention in and regulation of the economy in order to encourage and facilitate freedom of competition, free access to markets, freedom of investment and freedom of consumption, including the provision of redistribution of the market income (GDP) through progressive income tax and socio-political measures to safeguard the survival of weaker economic entities and protect natural resources. This includes obviating concentrations of power which are uncontrolled by competition, provision of a welfare state and principles of social justice to balance social disparities (Blum, 1994).

- *Integration of two systems*: unification of the two Germanys meant converting a former command economy to the social market economy of the former West Germany. This has involved privatization of state-owned companies and the injection of capital in order to make them internationally competitive, large-scale investment by the government to redress social inequalities, and changes in mindset towards international integration and away from an inward-looking domestic market positioning (Blum, 1994; Lawrence, 1994). This has created a number of tensions and issues that will be looked at later.

- *Education*: a highly structured system with a distinction between universities providing traditional scientific education and *Fachhochschulen* focusing on the practical application of scientific subjects; a comprehensive vocational training system through apprenticeship contracts with companies or with vocational training institutes supervised by chambers of handicrafts and commerce for young people, with practical training within these systems complemented by part-time theoretical education in vocational and technical schools; comprehensive adult training; with junior management recruited from the universities and increasingly from the *Fachhochschulen* (Blum, 1994).

- *Trade unions*: despite more recent decline in membership, they are powerful partners in collective bargaining, but also exert influence in political and social life. This structural power is largely based in their institutional participation through co-determination laws and workers' councils (Fürstenberg, 1998).

- *Co-determination*: aimed at controlling economic power by giving labour and capital a more equal status and bringing democracy to companies. Employees are represented at above-company level in self-governing health and pensions funds. At company level elected worker representatives serve on governing bodies such as the supervisory board of companies with over 1,000 employees. This has equal employee and shareholders' representatives with the right of nomination of employee representatives by the trade unions (although for companies of over 2,000 decisions involving issues of prime importance to the company such as winding-up, capital increases and changes in company objectives are excluded from co-determination). At plant level co-determination is through works councils which are involved in decision making in such issues as changes in working conditions, production methods, holiday scheduling, recruitment, redundancies and transfers, with management retaining the sole right of decision, with certain rights of appeal (Garrison and Rees, 1994).

- *Influence of the banks*: Heavy involvement of the major banks in companies facilitates continuity of ownership and provides support for long-term strategic planning. The emphasis on yearly profits and their effect on share prices, and thus the market value of the company, is less than in Anglo-Saxon countries and on a par with Japan. The implication of this is a longer-term planning emphasis as opposed to an emphasis on short-term results (Blum, 1994; Hickson and Pugh, 1995).

The implications for the styles of organizational and people management, as they developed in the former West Germany, and now in the unified Germany, may be profound. These, together with cultural factors give rise to a management style that Lawrence (1994) describes as follows:

- *A formal interactive style*. Formal modes of address, behaviour and dress are used.

- *A relatively weak informal organizational system*. Unlike in Anglo-Saxon countries, the 'formal' system of prescribed structures, systems and rules is normal in German organizations.

- *Neither bureaucratic nor authoritarian*. Formal modes of behaviour, and the weakness of an informal system, does not mean a love of bureaucracy and concern for authority. Studies have suggested the opposite, with lower hierarchies and fewer rules than France and Britain, and a willingness to criticize superiors.

- *Predominance of subject-based education in management training*. Managers tend to be graduates, with possession of a doctorate common, and managers are typically qualified in law, economics or engineering with a predominance of the latter. There is a predominance of training within the company rather than outside and this tends to be oriented to particular jobs and functions; it is more technical and less concerned with the general management processes of communication, coordination, decision making and control.

- *A neglect of American-style managerialism*. A lack of emphasis on those general aspects of management normally emphasized in Anglo-Saxon countries, although criticized by American commentators, does not seem to have disadvantaged German management.

- *A specialist rather than generalist understanding of managerial work*. Management is seen as an element of a job, not the job itself, with the emphasis being placed on the specialism and the knowledge and skills required for a particular function such as design, manufacturing, personnel or sales in a specified industry.

- *An emphasis on 'Technik' as both means and ends*. The importance of engineering knowledge and craft skills that go into production is evidenced by the high standing of engineers in society and in companies, and by the emphasis on production and the relative investment in this area.

The implications for human resource management seem to be as follows (Blum, 1994):

- *Recruitment*. With an emphasis on specialized skills and the possibilities of enhancing qualifications within the company through further training, recruitment is often first through internal sourcing with the involvement of the works councils, and then through external advertising.

- *Performance management*. Structural instruments such as wages and salaries, job design and the management of cooperation between individuals and groups are employed; the 'Harzburg model' involving job descriptions and management instructions containing principles of operation are the main tools used, although this is increasingly seen as over-bureaucratic and regular performance appraisals which have been neglected in the past are being introduced.

- *Reward systems*. Wage levels are complex and involve issues of wage fairness with principles laid down in collective wage agreements, labour–management agreements and individual contracts of employment; job rating is used to evaluate job content and requirements, relating them to standard performance and used as the basis for wage scales. Social benefits may also account for as much as 50 per cent of indirect personnel costs.

- *Human resource development*. Further education often follows after the initial dual system of craft and commercial apprenticeship which involve in-house and vocational school training.

- *Termination of employment*. This involves a number of safeguards, with redundancies necessitating the involvement of the works council.

Having explored German management systems and context, particularly in view of the ramifications of unification, it is now necessary to look at the historical context of Soviet management, in order to review the interactions of Western (including German) systems with the remnants of the Soviet systems of control and management.

Soviet management and organization

In the Soviet Union and its satellites the planning, management and control of enterprises were undertaken within the framework of the Soviet command economy and system of state ownership and management. The most common property form was the bureaucratic state-owned enterprise (Kornai, 1992), which covered key industries such as mining, energy production, foreign trade and finance, and which enabled the domination of non-state and non-key industrial sectors. The state-owned form constituted the property of the 'whole of the people' and could be defined by:

- the disposal of its residual income into the central state budget (the definition of what is residual income is itself decided by the state);
- it not being an object for purchase or sale, lease, gift or inheritance; and
- property rights of control over the activity of the enterprise being exercised by the state bureaucracy, normally directly by the lower levels of the hierarchical bureaucracy.

189

Another important property form was the cooperative, particularly within the agricultural sector. Kornai (1992) suggests it can be characterized as follows:

- Members were not free to refuse to join or to leave the cooperative, or to employ outside labour or be employed as outside labour.

- The leadership was only formally elected by the membership, and was often an appointed member of the bureaucracy, which in turn was dependent on upper levels of the bureaucracy.

- The leadership had no authority to make independent decisions about using the cooperative's income, alienation of the cooperative's means of production and how the means of production would be used.

In fact, in the cooperatives, decisions were taken at the upper levels of the bureaucracy, and provided little distinction from direct state ownership.

Kossov and Gurkov (1995) describe the state system of governance of enterprises within the USSR as being at two levels:

- functional committees having no direct supervision of enterprises, but responsible for overall policy and planning (*GosPlan*) and certain subordinate aspects of economic life such as supply (*GosSnab*), labour (*GosTrud*) and science and technology (*GKNT*); and

- branch ministries to which enterprises were directly subordinated, and which were responsible for translating directives of the functional committees into concrete operating decisions for the enterprises. Branch ministries were of three types:
  - *soyuznye* (all-Union, controlling enterprises directly from Moscow);
  - *soyuzno-respublicanskie* (Union-republican, linked to affiliated ministries within the Soviet republics where there was a need for more management decentralization in industries such as food-processing with numerous smaller enterprises; and,
  - *respublicanskie* (republican, having their headquarters in the republics, and directly supervising sectors which were focused on local needs such as intra-republic transportation, and which were subordinate to the Union-republican ministries).

The supervisory functions of the ministries comprised:

- strategic planning of enterprises following directives from functional committees, and involving such areas as mergers of divisions, developing and financing of new facilities and diversification of products; research and development; and

- operational planning including annual production targets, product mix and wages; and staffing.

The latter included the appointment of senior enterprise managers by direction of the supervising ministry. This ensured that enterprise managers were dependent and accountable to the functional committee bureaucrats in Moscow. In turn, the most successful enterprise managers were recruited to the branch ministries.

In parallel with the state governance system was the party system. Because of the territorial principle of party structure, every enterprise had two bosses who often had conflicting interests: the branch ministry and the local committee of the Communist Party. The minister's goal was for each enterprise to achieve targets based on state directives; the party boss viewed industrial enterprises as 'cash, material and labour cows' according to Kossov and Gurkov (1995) and often forced enterprise managers to send their workers to harvest, construct houses, and to work on other local projects such as road maintenance. This led to additional waste of resources, and increased costs.

Kornai (1992) describes the coordination mechanisms (which involved both vertical and horizontal linkages), operating on and within enterprises, as follows:

- *Bureaucratic coordination*. This best describes the vertical linkages existing within the control mechanisms imposed on enterprises, although this did not conform to the classic model of hierarchy as has been seen in the overlap between state and party apparatus. In both state-owned and cooperative enterprises, management was dependent on functional ministries, and subordinate to the (political) needs of the Soviet Union bureaucracy.

- *Market coordination*. The extent to which horizontal market linkages existed within the formal sector was minimal, or non-existent. Enterprises could be typified as having a lack of relationship with the product market, a direct relationship to central planning which not only controlled the flow of products but also directed the allocation of resources and labour, placed geographical and other restrictions on production and deployment of labour, set prices by central banking, and directly controlled foreign trade. Informal and distorted aspects of market relations existed between supplier and user enterprises, where, as a result of shortages of the means of production, an enterprise might try bribing representatives of supplier firms in order to obtain material or components, and sometimes train staff to make these transactions.

- *Self-governing coordination*. The nominal character of cooperative enterprises was of self-governance, but only vestiges of a system of proposals or criticisms from below pertained in practice. It is unlikely that such horizontal linkages were a feature of the management system.

- *Ethical coordination*. This would apply to the motivation of those in enterprises who were prepared to give up their personal time and make sacrifices for the good of the enterprise. The extent to which this is based on altruism, a feeling of community, political conviction or pressure from above is difficult to assess.

- *Family coordination*. Despite the eroding of the traditional family in many of the Soviet republics, there is evidence that family traditions and ties had survived despite Sovietization and collectivization, particularly in the Central Asian republics. The extent to which family coordination mechanisms operated informally within and between enterprises is however likely to have been limited given the nature of bureaucratic control, but may have been a factor in promotion practices alongside party and bureaucratic considerations.

The motivation for managers of enterprises to perform may be varied. Kornai (1992) suggests the following motivators under the Soviet system:

- political and moral conviction in party ideals and the enterprise plan's objectives;

- identification with the job and satisfaction gained from a job well done;

- power, prestige, and material benefits;

- a quiet life free from problems with superiors and subordinates; and

- fear of punishment.

It is likely that these motivators acted on the management of enterprises in varying forms. To a large extent managers' motivation depended on their degree of conviction to party ideas and ideals, and to the strategic and operating objectives handed down from the state bureaucracy. Despite criticisms of this economic-political system, it should be remembered that in the space of less than 50 years from the time of the Russian Revolution in 1917, it dragged large parts of the Soviet Union out of feudalism into the modern era. It was perhaps through its inherent contradictions that it finally collapsed as a system and as an ideological competitor to capitalism.

Soviet management in East Germany

Within East Germany (DDR) the Socialist Unity Party controlled 'the legitimate means of force', as well as education and the media (Lawrence, 1994), and the trade union movement (FDGB) which contained 95 per cent of the DDR workforce. The central planning model was characterized by four main principles:

- the articulation and coordination of a range of production facilities through a central plan;

- economic policy which was socially directed and concerned with the good of society rather than the optimization of the economy;

- an emphasis on long-term strategy rather than short-term profitability;

- a replacement of pecuniary motivation by social-ideological commitment.

In the 1970s the DDR began to catch up with West Germany. It was ranked the world's ninth largest economy, with GNP per capita figures higher than Britain (Lawrence, 1994). By the 1980s international borrowing had increased and economic decline had started.

The education system was directed towards meeting the needs of the economy, with university entry being on a subject quota basis and graduates allocated to jobs by the state. Manufacturing sites (VEBs or 'people's own companies') were judged on outputs required by the central plan: the plan being demanding and not easy to fulfil and requiring the resourcefulness of those managing and working for the VEBs. Managers would normally be party members, but this was not essential. Being politically 'clean' was more important. In addition the usual criteria of qualifications, personal qualities and experience were necessary to become a manager, as well as resourcefulness and skills necessary to fulfil the requirement of the plan.

Although works directors enjoyed many of the prerogatives of their Western counterparts, they were free of many of their constraints. They would not have to be involved in devising strategy, making profits, quality control, new product development or environmental controls. Management of the VEBs concerned implementation rather than initiation. Decision making was slow and compromise driven, and the works director was less powerful (autonomous) than his Western counterpart. Apart from problems of an over-demanding plan, and dependency on suppliers who suffered similar problems of inefficiencies, the workforce also presented problems of poor discipline, tardiness, absenteeism and taking prolonged breaks (Lawrence, 1994).

Soviet personnel management

Personnel matters were largely administered by government departments within the Soviet system (Koubek and Brewster, 1995), as follows:

- The personnel policy department administered by the party and staffed by party appointees was responsible for evaluating the political reliability of employees of organizations, and to a lesser extent their expertise, performance and professional attributes. It was responsible for selection, placement, promotion, training and development, and termination along party lines.

- Departments of labour and wages administered compensation and the organization of work, with a brief to implement rather than make policy in this area.

- Special departments organized training and development of employees, responding not to organizations' needs but to tasks imposed by the central authorities. Employees often saw such training negatively as it did not have an impact on their work, reward or promotion prospects.

- Personnel departments administered personnel records and the compilation of statistical records. This system generally throughout the Soviet system produced an extremely thorough record of labour statistics.

Human resource planning followed the system of central planning, with some inputs from organizations at the formulation stage of state plans. Planning was directed towards full employment and often imposed additional jobs on organizations. Organizations in their turn attempted to increase the number they employed in order to attract central funding. This led to over-staffing.

At the organizational level, departments often administered aspects of employee care such as benefits including housing, kindergarten, sport and leisure activities and canteens; and sometimes also were involved in employee training, health and safety. The trade unions, which themselves were closely linked with the Communist Party, were also involved in employee care, but had little actual

193

influence in other personnel issues including collective bargaining (Koubek and Brewster, 1995).

Koubek and Brewster also point out that there was a lack of any objective performance appraisal system, and instead a formal system of 'political reliability appraisal' existed which only marginally included the performance and capabilities of the individual. They suggest that the reasons for this are based in three sources:

- socialist egalitarianism which resulted in wage levelling;

- full employment policies, and therefore lack of concern with negative appraisal, as salaries varied very little and there was no danger of unemployment;

- scarcity of labour owing to full employment in a planned economy, making an employee with poor performance better than a vacant job.

Post-Soviet people management

The former DDR has now been taken over by the former West Germany, with the disappearance of the concepts of the state-owned enterprise, central planning, party representation in the workplace and control of the trade union movement, mostly replaced by organization and management norms of the former West Germany. Most of the VEBs have been bought, many by West German concerns. Similarly the social provisions such as child and medical care administered by the old VEBs have been closed, sold or privatized. Works councils have been established and co-determination laws extended to the old DDR. The main implications for former DDR companies have been:

- the loss of markets in the former Soviet bloc, with its collapse, but evidence that this may still be a key factor in the positioning of some companies;

- a reduction in the workforce of enterprises which were deemed as over-manned, with an emphasis on efficiency and productivity; this had an impact on lower absenteeism and better work discipline;

- changes in the relative importance of various functions: production was slimmed, with a shift towards quality, reliability and differentiation; purchasing was slimmed as it is easier to handle through the use of computer technology; a need for sales and marketing; a more important role for personnel with a concern for non-allocated recruitment, and compensation; and an emphasis on research and development;

- a change in management, with managers of former DDR enterprises still often the same people who operated under the old system, but perhaps then in more junior positions. Somes managers have been recruited from the West, to fill sales positions where there may be a lack of experience; they are better paid with greater pay differentials than existed in the old system, and have greater freedom of decision making, and can exert more control downwards; managers are less encumbered by rules and interference; and they need to work harder under greater pressure to succeed;

- a loss of job security for workers; however, they have obtained pay rises, and those who have retained their jobs have greater purchasing power and have to work harder;

- a change in ethos: efficiency rather than bureaucracy; higher workforce discipline; different attitude to employees involving less paternalism and more instrumentalism; a greater differentiation between manager and managed; and a possible decline in the quality of human contact which is subordinated to the efficiency of the organization or to ambition (Lawrence, 1994).

The former East Germany may be unique in its position as a former Soviet bloc country in that it has been reunited with the former West Germany. It is likely to take on more of the characteristics of the management of people and organization of the former West Germany. Principles of social justice within the social market economy of the unified Germany may be protecting employees and former employees from the harsh realities of a free market economy. The German system of control of excesses of power through intervention in the economy, workplace democracy and social provisions, while costly, may be appropriate to facilitate this type of transition. For the other former Soviet bloc countries, the question 'transition to what?' may be appropriate.

Srica (1995) suggests that the new circumstances in Eastern and Central Europe have created an impetus for change and opportunity, and points to several comparative advantages of the post-Soviet situation:

- *Fresh motivation*. The changing environment presents fresh opportunities for new ideas, enterprises and motivating challenges.

- *Willingness to learn*. Attempting to shake off obstructive old habits produces a genuine desire to learn new ways, not only from the West but from East Asia as well.

- *Talent for improvisation*. This arises from the need to overcome problems of a lack of infrastructure, inadequate organization and bureaucratic controls over the last decades.

- *Large potential market*. Shortages in the former Soviet bloc have created a huge potential market.

- *Education system*. Central European countries have maintained a high standard in higher education, developing well-educated specialists, largely in the German tradition.

- *Competitive wages*. The cost of labour is far lower than in 'developed' countries.

- *Emerging entrepreneurs*. The dynamic environment has provided good examples of entrepreneurial endeavour.

- *Emigrant links*. Many of the emigrants moving to the United States and Western Europe have been established businesspeople, educators and scientists, all of whom may provide important links between the West and Central and Eastern European countries.

- *Suppressed creativity*. Suppressed talent during the Soviet era is now surfacing as these countries enter into the mainstream of world developments.

- *Favourable environment.* Particularly the proximity to the European Union, and potential membership within it, may provide favourable conditions for development.

Yet Srica (1995) indicates that there are still attitudinal problems that need to be overcome. These include:

- a lack of participation in decision making and initiative by employees;
- a high level of employee turnover and absenteeism and a lack of identification with hard work;
- manager–employee relationship deteriorating over time;
- too much short-term, situational thinking, and a lack of long-term planning;
- a neglect of quality in relationship to international competitors;
- a lack of management responsibility concerning ecological issues and the utilization of scarce resources.

It should not be forgotten that the Central and Eastern European countries are heavily indebted and need to use their resources in the form of exports to service these debts; that they are in a cleft stick between the need to shed staff from over-manned and inefficient operations and the need to train and develop a workforce in order to drive forward the economy (Glenny, 1993; Srica, 1995). In part this may be understood as an interaction between the concept of people as a means to an end (instrumentalism) and as an end in themselves (humanism) as was discussed in the Introduction. The antithesis of these two positions may well lead to issues at the 'micro' level in the interactions of managers and staff, and at the 'macro' level in terms of building the transitional economies. This is also discussed in relation to the 'developing' countries of the 'post-colonial' world in Chapter 10.

Apart from the possible implication of this antithesis in understanding the temporal and geographical interactions of people management systems and building appropriate new or hybrid systems, there is the problem of discerning the different influences that may impact on emerging systems. These may include aspects of the former Soviet systems, the impacts of Western approaches (including differences in approach between, for example, the US and German systems), and aspects of the traditions and culture of countries such as the Czech Republic prior to Sovietization (with all the difficulties this may entail). Another factor, of course, is one of relative power (normally financial) in the interactive process. This may not simply be the objective power of a company such as Volkswagen, but also the power of 'Western' management know-how and technology, as perceived by the people in transitional countries who seek this expertise: appropriately or inappropriately. Some of these issues may be discerned in the Czech context.

People management in the Czech Republic

The Czech Republic has a long tradition of industrialization and entrepreneurship that precedes the Soviet era, and was one of the most efficient of countries within the Soviet system. This was an aspect that the Czechs saw they had in common in the German–Czech joint venture described above (Cyr and Schneider, 1998). Some of the issues discussed in conection with the Skoda–Volkswagen case can also be seen in Koubek and Brewster's (1995) suggestion of six major influences on HRM practices in the post-Soviet Czech economy:

- Exposure to market forces has focused attention on the cost of human resources as a high proportion of operating costs.

- Specific training needs are coming to the fore: language, computer, sales and marketing skills.

- The loss of entrepreneurially minded staff from larger organizations back to family businesses has focused attention on recruitment, retention and compensation.

- The entry of foreign organizations with more attractive compensation packages and work is also causing problems of retention in state-owned and just-privatized organizations, and there is a need to look for means of stemming this out-flow.

- Attempts to address over-staffing through various methods which did not reflect future skills and operational needs have highlighted the need to develop other methods of human resource planning.

- The interest in developing know-how, often through foreign sources, has led to the development and uptake of training in HRM through the universities and through foreign companies.

Koubek and Brewster (1995) report on an extensive survey of companies in the Czech Republic that focuses on human resource management practices. Through this they highlight certain issues of concern, and of optimism.

Causes of concern

- *Recruitment and redundancy.* Skills shortages as a result of loss of employees and lower wages in the state- and former state-owned organizations has led to targeting of school leavers, the long-term unemployed, older people and disabled people, and the internal recruitment of managers; as well as to a focus on reducing labour costs through redundancies (although voluntary redundancies were possible).

- *Trade unions.* Some enterprises may view the increasing influence of trade unions as a problem, with trade unionists seeing the future of trade unions as uncertain.

Causes of optimism

- *Training and development.* This has been a relatively well developed yet formalistic tradition in Czech organizations. Organizations are investing most in the training of managers and professionals and technical staff. Key areas are seen as computer training, foreign languages and management under market conditions and marketing, with a relative neglect of training in personnel management skills.

- *Pay and benefits.* Evidence suggests a significant departure from the old centralized mode, particularly for managers, professionals and technicians, with pay for clerical and manual workers still established in state-wide systems (as in most of Western Europe), and reflecting anti-inflationary measures; variable pay is increasing, with other incentives including profit sharing and merit/performance-related pay; social benefits are often still offered, including child care facilities and grants for recreation for children of employees.

- *Flexibility.* Organizations are introducing new working patterns and abandoning some traditional ones, influenced by economic transformation and savings in labour costs; however, part-time working has decreased with women bearing much of the redundancies, yet fixed-term contracts have increased.

In the German–Czech joint venture described above there was a strong desire to establish the organization as a learning organization (see also Chapter 6). However, much of this was concerned with the need to train people in the skills necessary for a more competitive marketplace, and to effect the transfer of knowledge from the German to the Czech partners. Cyr and Schneider (1998) note a disparaging of what could be learned from the Czech partners. Generally the HRM function is perceived as secondary to other functions, and is not seen as having a strategic role. Koubek and Brewster (1995) suggest that the focus on labour costs, training shortfalls and the need for redundancies has raised the profile of HR management, but it is still distrusted as a hangover from communist days. They suspect that with stabilization of the economy the role will be further downplayed as a strategic issue, and there seems no evidence that line managers are undertaking the strategic role of human resource management.

There is evidence of similarities in approach between the German model and a possible emerging post-Soviet model, which values aspects such as a strong social safety net to protect people from the ravages of a free market economy. There is also evidence that the human resource function may be underdeveloped. Yet Gutmann (1995) contends that HRM is coming to the fore in the German–Czech joint venture, and actually taking a leading role in the effective transfer of knowledge between the two partners. However, there is still a question as to the extent to which it is desirable to transfer management practices from one culture to another. While there may be more empathy between, for example, the German and emerging Czech model, the insensitivities of transfer may militate against the effective development of a hybrid system based on the best of practices of both systems that would be appropriate to the Czech situation and could best help staff to develop.

This raises some practical issues for Western managers working in post-Soviet countries. Some of these are now taken up in the context of Russia.

Implications for managers: Western companies in Russia

Russia is positioned fairly high on Smith et al.'s (1996) scale for utilitarian involvement (as against loyal involvement), which indicates a perceived instrumental relationship with one's organization. The Czechs (or at least ex-Czechoslovakia) are considerably higher in utilitarian involvement than Russians. Russia is also higher on their conservatism dimension (against egalitarian commitment), indicating possibly a high level of vertical collectivism. The Czechs exhibit moderate conservatism only on this dimension.

May, Bormann Young and Ledgerwood (1998) identify a number of key issues or problems of Russian human resource management that they believe Western enterprises can help to address. These are as follows:

- Underestimation of the complexities of a free market, with a tendency to rely on imported solutions. Western managers, they recommend, should encourage a blend of HRM involving both free market practices and Russian culture.

- A lack of commitment to the organization. Western managers can help to foster organizational commitment through promoting the organization as a stable ongoing entity, which employees and managers can help to build.

- Lack of personal accountability and responsibility. Rewards can be tied to effort.

- A disregard for health and safety management. Managers can be encouraged to take a proactive approach to these issues, and a holistic approach that ties in these issues with the company's profitability and competitiveness.

- Confusion surrounding compensation and benefits, with a lack of information and benchmarking. Comparative data for benchmarking needs to be collected and disseminated.

- Strained labour–management relations that are deep-rooted. Long-term benefits, they believe, can be obtained through appropriate employee training on company survival, and both managers and employees can be held accountable for task accomplishment.

Shekshnia (1998) notes however that human resource management practices have changed within Russian subsidiaries of Western companies and documents these changes from 1994 to 1997 (Table 9.2).

There is no doubt that Western styles of people management are gaining in influence and importance. This may be simply through a lack of alternatives. The dangers of accepting these wholesale are noted by May et al. (1998), and perhaps more attention should be devoted to developing specifically indigenous forms of people management in the former Soviet countries. This may be difficult, given historical circumstances, and the appropriateness of adopting German approaches should not be excluded.

Table 9.2 Changes in HRM practices in Russian subsidiaries of Western companies (Shekshnia, 1998)

HRM activity	1994	1997
Strategy	Virtually non-existent and an *ad hoc* approach	Clearly articulated at some companies and linked to business strategy
HR management systems	Non-existent as a coherent entity, single unconnected elements	Built around business objectives and constantly evolving along with the organization
Staffing	A major issue and problem, using a word-of-mouth approach	Formal system utilizing a wide range of methods
Development	Involved only training, and mostly business/market awareness with substantial investments made	Formal system which includes career planning and management development, skills-oriented training and in-house training centres
Evaluation	Introduction of formal systems	Formal periodic appraisals, and MBO
Compensation	Involved struggles with inflation and blind salary setting	Market-driven system with upward salary trends and increasing sophistication

Questions for managers

1   What are the main problem areas in the German–Czech joint venture of Volkswagen–Skoda described above, and how can they be accounted for by reference to differences in culture? What part is played by the difference in power balance between the two parties?

2   The transfer of management knowledge from the German to the Czech operations may be problematic not only because of the power position of the German partner, but also the hunger for Western know-how by the Czech partner. How can this relationship best be managed? How relevant are German approaches to the Czech situation? If the Western partner were American, would this make a difference to the relevance of management know-how being transferred to the Czech partner?

3   How would the situation be different if Volkswagen were to establish a joint venture with a Russian company? What people management principles and practices should be put in place?

4   How can the development of a learning organization help in the success of the joint venture, and what form should this take?

An agenda for research

Mills (1997) suggests that a stakeholder approach be used to research the transformational process with regard to human resource management in the former Soviet countries. She suggests that the main stakeholders in this process that will influence philosophy underpinning HRM practice will be:

- *National government.* This applies particularly to the legislative framework under which firms operate in such countries as Czech Republic, including company, employment and social legislation that contribute to defining employment relations.

- *The banks.* As major shareholders in privatized companies, and creditors of technically bankrupt companies, banks have a say in systems of ownership and control, and the nature of the company policy towards its people (in terms of downsizing, and employment levels).

- *Enterprise owners.* In view of transition to private control, ownership questions will be open to debate, and will include a combination of state, banking, private and foreign interest. These owners, and their mix and composition, will affect the policy regarding people in the organization.

- *Foreign investors.* These often bring fixed ideas about HRM in terms of organizational culture, management philosophy and practice.

- *Management and employees.* Motivations and behaviours, and particularly responses to changes, may be critical factors in the ways emerging HRM policies and practices take shape.

- *Trade unions and employer associations.* These act as pressure groups and can influence employment relations depending on their relative strengths.

This may be a useful starting point. Coupled with it must be a thorough analysis of the different (cultural) management systems, which this chapter has begun to look at, that impact on emerging forms, together with an understanding of the relative power arrangements (both objective and subjective) among the different stakeholders who may be propagating these different systems. For example, banks (including the overriding influence of the International Monetary Fund on economic and structural policy: Glenny, 1993) may take a macro-instrumental approach to people in organizations focused on a need to downsize. Trade unions in East and Central European countries may take a more developmental approach, as may some governments, to the need for organizations to develop people for the future of the economy. Some approaches may be more successful than others in providing both transformations and ongoing appropriate management systems. For example, US firms may take as their model a free market one, whereas German companies may take a social market approach that may provide the necessary social safety nets, as well as better fulfilling people's expectations.

Management and educated elites in the former Soviet countries may expect Western policies and techniques to fulfil the needs of emerging economies. This may also be considered as part of power relations among the various stakeholders, in terms of subjectivities created by the influence of Western education and the increasing influence and dominance of Western systems of management. This aspect requires further investigation in the context of transitioning organizations and the transformation of economies in the former Soviet countries.

Some of these issues, in terms of power relations, and subjective power manifested in the perceptions of managers in emerging countries, are investigated in the next chapter in relation to the 'post-colonial' organization.

Questions for researchers

1 In post-Soviet countries, which are the main stakeholders in the transfer of management know-how, what are their particular interests, and how does this influence the nature of knowledge transfer in international joint ventures?

2 What is the relationship between the relative power and influence of the various stakeholders, and cultural factors in the development and implementation of people management systems in post-Soviet countries?

3 How relevant are German people management practices and approaches to the situation in the Czech Republic and other post-Soviet countries? How do these approaches differ in relevance to other Western countries? What are the key factors in success and failure of joint ventures and knowledge transfer between Western and post-Soviet countries?

chapter ten

The stakeholder organization:
the post-colonial model

The post-colonial model

In emerging or 'developing' countries it is difficult to identify specific management and organizational cultures that have not been heavily influenced by Western practices. This chapter focuses predominantly on African (particularly South African) and Indian management. African management practices have been strongly influenced by Anglo-Saxon or French practices. Indian management has been influenced by Anglo-Saxon practices. One of the main arguments of this book is that the interplay of indigenous and Western influences produces an antithesis between instrumental (Western) approaches to people management and humanistic (non-Western) approaches. Employees in Africa, for example, who go to work in the morning, may be stepping into an alien environment on entering the organization. While African approaches to people management are still emerging, Indian human resource development (the preferred term in India) has tried to reconcile the two influences. This type of approach may well be applicable in other emerging countries, not least the African countries, as well as in the so-called 'developed' countries.

The objectives of this chapter are to examine the way management in post-colonial countries has tried to reconcile instrumental and humanistic approaches to managing people, and to manage the relationships between different stakeholders. It also seeks to investigate this within hybrid forms of management that have developed as part of cross-cultural interactions at different levels. After looking at approaches from South Africa and India, three quite different South African organizations (Eskom, AECI Explosives and Germiston City Council) provide the real context of management issues. In discussing the management implications of balancing stakeholder interests, the case of Colgate Palmolive in South Africa is also discussed.

People management in South Africa

South Africa has a relatively long history of foreign investment by companies that are heavily influenced by Western management techniques. The country was partially isolated from the global economy by sanctions against apartheid and through protectionist and interventionist policies. Since the beginning of the 1990s this has changed, and South Africa has been launched onto the world stage of global competition. Apartheid as a system had an internal logic: a perceived need to keep black Africans out of the predominantly white cities and the system of migratory labour which kept wages low for blacks and protected skilled jobs for whites. The economy was built on the primary production of gold and diamonds, which did not create an internal market for goods. This again kept wages low. It also did not require a large skills base. Lack of educational provision for black Africans also led to under-education, much illiteracy and a low skills base. South Africa is thus left with a workforce (and potential workforce) that is ill equipped for a highly competitive marketplace. Organizations, particularly in the public sector, were over-staffed. There is still a lack of foreign investment, owing largely to continuing high levels of criminal violence. A typical organizational response is to downsize (Jackson, 1999).

With such an underdeveloped skills base, downsizing and delayering (and the associated process of 'empowerment') may not be appropriate if a longer-term perspective is taken, as there is a need for organizations to be a means to developing people for the future. The government has tried to address these problems:

- The Reconstruction and Development Programme (RDP) in part tries to meet this need and has a large commitment to educational provision and people development.

- Government pressure has increased for the upward mobility of black managers, particularly in the public and parastatal (publicly owned utilities) sectors.

- Approximately 11,300 affirmative action posts have been allocated in the public sector since April 1994 (Horwitz et al., 1996).

- The recent Employment Equity and Skills Development Bills of 1997 are aimed at redressing racial and gender-based employment inequalities, and require companies with more than 50 staff to formulate plans to develop a workforce whose racial composition reflects that of the country (Jackson, 1999).

Despite these continued efforts to invest in people and skills, there is evidence that South African organizations are disinvesting in people:

- The number of people completing their artisan training in 1992 was 5,588: less than half the 1985 figure.

- Private sector organizations in South Africa spend only an estimated 2 per cent of payroll per year on education and training, compared with 6–8 per cent in the leading industrial nations (Horwitz et al., 1996).

- There are lower levels of tertiary education in technical and scientific subjects than in other (developing) countries and this is likely to affect the skills pool.

- The new Growth, Employment and Redistribution policy (GEAR) which was presented to parliament in June 1996 has continued to attract criticism from the trade union movement for its implications for reductions in public spending and monetarist leanings (Jackson, 1999).

At the macro level it is possible to detect the interaction between instrumental and humanist values. These include short-term versus long-term imperatives;

downsizing versus job creation; status quo resourcing versus affirmative action; and monetarist versus interventionist policies.

At the micro levels of management attitudes and practice, organizational orientation and people development, the differences between regarding people as a resource and a means to an end, or as a value and end in themselves may be a cultural issue which needs reconciling in South Africa and other post-colonial economies. In the South African context of managing a predominantly black African workforce, this may mean rethinking the meaning and implications of 'human resource management'.

Jackson (1999), provides insights into what is being done in South African organizations to address some of these issues.

Eskom

The 'parastatal' organization Eskom is the main supplier of electricity in South Africa with 40,000 employees. It is governed by the government-appointed Electricity Council, which determines overall policy, planning and objectives. It also appoints the management board. Whilst a monopoly, it has a brief to encourage domestic competition for itself, and at the same time position itself in the global marketplace as a key player beyond southern Africa. It has a strong commitment to the development of its people, not least because of the recognized need for an educated workforce to operate and maintain its sophisticated technology, and appropriate management to take it into the future. Its development focus is therefore on basic education, opportunities and the ability to manage change. Its policies reflect this. Affirmative action is seen as central to its objective for at least 50 per cent of managerial and supervisory staff to be black South Africans by 2000. This stood at 6.1 per cent in 1994 (*Personnel Management,* December 1994).

It is also involved in a number of community projects, and plays an important part in the RDP-led initiatives such as electrification. It has a policy to enable its employees to own their own home, and the company already owns some 14,500 employee houses. With this stock, and the conversion of its single men's hostels for married people, it is encouraging workers to bring their families to live permanently with them. All employees receive a housing allowance based on their salary band. Eskom also runs its own medical scheme with 28,540 members and over 43,000 dependants subsidized by the scheme. Management–union relations are being built through encouragement of more participative management by establishing forums at a number of levels from the strategic level through to business unit forums and work team sessions where issues are addressed locally. Joint task forces have been established to look at Eskom's long-term viability as a top performing utility; trade union involvement in decision making; business training and development of shop stewards; trade union representation on the Electricity Council; education, training and development; optimal sharing of information and financial disclosure; and accommodation.

Currently its investment in education and training amounts to about R450 million. The emphasis is mainly on technical skills. It is also aiming to employ 370 black trainees on bursaries each year, although this does not exclude other trainees on these schemes. In addition, Eskom planned to spend R90 million over a two-year period in order to minimize illiteracy among the estimated 11,000 employees without basic education.

Its organizational department operates a number of management development programmes:

- the Manager's Challenge Programme, which is designed to stretch and challenge the company's most promising managers, and to address the more contextual and business issues;

- the Business Leader's Programme, which addresses the needs of the changing roles of newly appointed managers and professionals, and develops business understanding and leader skills in the changing environment;

- the Accelerated Development Programme, which focuses on developing business leaders from people who are identified as being able to help Eskom achieve its business objectives; this is focused particularly on the benefits of self-development for black employees.

Despite these positive steps, there may still remain a basic mistrust of a predominantly white management. There may also be concern among white employees about the effects of affirmative action. Inefficiency may be a result of over-staffing, and the necessary downsizing of the company may provide cause for concern for the future.

AECI Explosives Ltd

AECI Explosives Ltd is a joint venture between ICI plc and AECI Ltd. ICI holds a 51 per cent interest, with the joint venture company being incorporated within ICI's explosives division, and the chairman based in London. It is a leader in explosives products (detonators, packaged explosives, bulk explosives, initiating systems and ammonium nitrate) within the continent of Africa, and its main customer is the mining, quarrying and construction industry.

Its major business objectives are: market-driven innovation of products; winning in quality growth markets worldwide; inspiration and reward of talented people; exemplary performance in health and safety; responsible care for the environment; and pursuit of operational excellence.

Its people policy objectives include: providing a safe working environment; equality of opportunity; attractive compensation packages; emphasis on training and development; developing an atmosphere of trust and mutual respect; encouraging innovation; fostering open communication; implementing management processes to support these policies; conforming with the relevant laws.

The company is rule driven with formal written instructions at all levels: company directives, company standards, departmental procedural instructions, job descriptions, quality plans, operating instructions and test methods. The company has embarked on an internal literacy project with a target of full literacy by 2005. However, no very clear policy on affirmative action seems to have been formulated. There also seems to be little or no involvement in community or social obligation projects, although an environmental remedial project is under way where land that the company has contaminated is being cleared up.

A management competences model has been adopted, which is supported through various management training and development activities. This is based on four clusters: 'thinking' (conceptual, strategic, innovative and analytical thinking); 'self-management' (learning, self-development, adaptability, flexibility, self-image, self-control, tenacity, thoroughness, interpersonal awareness and independence); 'influencing' (impact, persuasion and strategic influencing); and 'achieving' (critical information seeking, efficiency, development, concern for standards, results orientation).

The company still has vestiges of high power distance and mistrust from the past. With old labour-intensive technologies and increased competition, there may be a need to reduce waste and increase efficiencies. This may involve further downsizing, which in turn could lead to a flattening of hierarchy and a move towards greater participation in decision making. In the meantime this seems to be creating uncertainty in job security, which could contribute to lower productivity.

Germiston City Council

The amalgamation of Germiston, Palm Ridge, Bedfordview and Katlehong local authorities in 1994 produced the Transitional Local Council of Greater Germiston. It has 40 elected councillors. Members drawn from their ranks sit on an executive committee of 10 councillors and some 59 section committees. The chief executive officer acts as liaison between the 13 different departments. These cover such functions as engineering services (basic utilities such as water, electricity and sewerage), social services, community services and law enforcement. Operational objectives that are pursued across the departments are: uniformity in standards of service provision; the rendering of prompt, efficient and effective service; involving residents at all levels in the process; and winning the trust of residents and ensuring that the culture of non-payment for services is discontinued within the foreseeable future.

The transitional council is currently investing substantially in developing and training its employees, and is attempting to move away from an autocratic style of management to a more participative approach. Currently it is facing a number of challenges. A strong commitment to affirmative action seems to be causing a feeling of threat amongst previously entrenched employees, and expertise is being lost in some areas. This has been to the detriment of the efficiency and effectiveness of some of the departments which are short of skilled staff. Services are also being affected by strikes in some areas.

The communication of decisions, taken by central government and the provincial government, which influence the work of the council, seems to be an area where there are shortcomings and perhaps a certain mistrust among employees. Following the amalgamation of a number of local authorities with large numbers of people from disadvantaged sections of the community, some under-funding is apparent, with subsequent effects on areas such as additional resources, personnel and training.

The council has a well-developed system for recruiting and inducting employees at two levels: general orientation, and departmental orientation. However, there is no well-defined appraisal system, and poor performance is addressed more by sanction and disciplinary procedures than through a well-developed appraisal system.

In summary, these three case studies show two discernible approaches: downsizing to respond to financial constraints and commercial imperatives; and responding to the social and developmental needs for affirmative action.

The organizations appear to be attempting to reconcile the antithesis between an instrumental and a humanistic view of people. However, despite indications of 'best practice' from these three organizations the current nature of managers and organizations in South Africa may militate against reconciling such differences (Jackson, 1999).

The question remains, however, what is being reconciled? Although there is current good knowledge of Western people management styles and practices, those of Africa are less well articulated.

African people management

There is a need for African managers to manage effectively in a multicultural workplace, increasingly across national borders, and with management influences from both Western and non-Western traditions. Parallels can be drawn with the developments in multicultural management across Europe. Both continents have huge historical divisions and enmities. Europeans and North Americans often see 'Africa' as an entity with a single culture. Equally fallacious, of course, is the perception that Europe comprises similar cultures. Cultural diversity can be seen as a strength. This principle can be applied to African management and is the perspective taken as the basis for this text. By conceiving an antithesis between an *instrumental* approach to management, and a *humanistic* approach, it is possible to provide explanations of the dynamics of management in post-colonial countries, particularly the conflicts and contradictions in the process of change, and the attendant industrial relations problems that are often inherent in African economies.

By using this construct some of the pitfalls of applying a 'developing–developed' country analysis (Jaeger and Kanungo, 1990) can be avoided. Apart from the pejorative nature of this dichotomy, many emerging African countries contain elements of both. The other pitfall that can be avoided is that of applying a simplistic individualism–collectivism model (Hofstede, 1991) to cultural analysis in explaining differences between indigenous and imported views of human relations. Often this dichotomy is used to explain differences between Western (developed) and Eastern (developed and developing) cultures, and may not be directly applicable to an analysis of Western and non-Western approaches in emerging economies in Africa and beyond.

Jaeger and Kanungo (1990) present a distinction between management and organization in 'developed' and 'developing' countries. This represents developed countries, in terms of a relationship to the economic and political environment, as having a relatively high predictability of events, and a relative ease in obtaining resources, with developing countries having a low predictability and relative difficulty in obtaining resources. In terms of cultural characteristics, they depict the organizational situation in developed countries as relatively low in uncertainty avoidance, with high individualism and low power distance, a relatively high masculinity (Hofstede, 1991), and relatively high abstractions and low associated thinking (Kedia and Bhagat, 1988). In associative cultures people make associations between events that do not have a 'logical' basis. Abstractive cultures tend to think in terms of cause–effect relationships in a 'rationalist' mode of explanation. Socially this is reflected in communication that is context-specific and decisions that are related to relationships (associative) as distinct from more universalistic communication and decisions based more on the application of abstract rules and principles (abstractive). Hence developing countries are depicted as low in abstractive and high in associative thinking, relatively high in uncertainty avoidance, low in individualism, high in power distance and low in masculinity.

Jaeger and Kunungo (1990) further depict the internal work culture of developed countries as reflecting a view of human nature as assuming an internal locus of control, where creative potential is regarded as unlimited, and people are regarded as malleable and changeable, and where decisions are more future oriented and action is focused more on the longer term. This contrasts with the external locus of control of developing countries where events are considered as not within the individual's control; where creative potential is regarded as limited, and people are generally fixed in their ways and not malleable or changeable; where decisions are focused in the past and present rather than the future; and action is focused on the short term. Guiding principles of behaviour in organizations tend therefore to reflect a proactive task orientation in developed countries, but a passive-reactive orientation in developing countries. Success orientation is pragmatic in developed countries but moralistic in developing countries. People orientation in organizations in developed countries tends to be more participative, yet authoritarian and paternalistic in developing countries. Jaeger and Kunungo (1990) also suggest that because of the associative thinking in developing countries, there is more a tendency for behaviour in organizations to be context dependent, rather than the developed country orientation towards context-independent behaviour orientation where explicit and universal rules apply to a situation rather than the situation and context determining the responses to it.

However, Human (1996) contends that this 'maximalist' approach to classifying culture leads to ideal types that tend to be value laden. These have serious implications for the way people see themselves and how others perceive them. These perceptions, which have a tendency to create positive or negative self-fulfilling prophecies, influence performance and development. Human is also concerned that whilst such theorists refer to the dynamic and changing nature of culture, their cultural dimensions are not put into a context of change. This leaves the approach open to the interpretation that it sees cultural differences as unchanging. These charges may be levied against any such categorization of cultural difference (e.g. Hofstede 1980a) but may be particularly pertinent in a depiction of a contrast between 'developed' and 'developing' countries. As a basis for considering the development of indigenous approaches to management in 'developing' countries (one of Jaeger and Kunungo's concerns), the perceptions created may not be useful: fatalistic, resistant to change, reactive, short-termist, authoritarian, risk reducing, context dependent, associative and as basing decisions on relationship criteria rather than universalistic criteria.

There is also the danger in this approach that the objective of development is to make the 'developing' world more like the 'developed' world, and that this should be reflected in the way managers are developed and the ideal way of managing an organization. The construct of *instrumentalism–humanism* goes some way in reconstruing the perceptions arising from the developed–developing dichotomy.

Collectivism-individualism

In this context it is necessary to consider a cultural construct which provides an understanding of cultural differences, and is related to a concept of instrumentalism–humanism. The individualism–collectivism dichotomy is not overly judgmental and does not provide a sharp distinction between developed and developing societies but rather between Western and non-Western societies. However, it may fall short of an adequate explanation of the antithesis between such cultures in a dynamic such as exists in African countries.

The collectivism–individualism dimension has a long pedigree, and constitutes a fairly robust construct as it appears in many cross-national studies undertaken over the years that explore cultural dimensions of management values (e.g. Hofstede, 1991; Trompenaars, 1993). Following a survey of social scientists working in this area, Hui and Triandis (1986) concluded that there is a general consensus that collectivism can be defined as:

- concern by a person about the effects of actions or decisions on others within a wider collective;
- sharing of material benefits within a social network of reciprocity;
- sharing of non-material benefits such as time and affection;
- willingness of a person to accept the opinions and views of others through normative social influence which lead to conformity, and maintaining harmony;
- concern about self-presentation and loss of face, and gaining approval of the collective;
- belief in the correspondence of own outcomes with the outcomes of others through interdependences, where a person's misbehaviour may bring shame on the whole collective; and
- a feeling of involvement in and contribution to the lives of others.

Is it possible to apply these seven criteria of collectivism–individualism directly to the African situation? In particular, is it possible to describe an antithesis between Western and non-Western views of people as an antithesis between individualism and collectivism? The South African popular management literature (e.g. Koopman, 1991) highlights the differences between the 'communalism' of African cultures and individualism of white cultures within South Africa. Much is being written about the spirit of 'ubuntu' (e.g. Mbigi, 1997; Boon, 1996). This popular literature supports a view that African culture has a collectivist propensity, and despite a lack of research literature on collectivism–individualism in Africa, generally traditional African society may be regarded as low on individualism (Blunt and Jones, 1992).

Despite the long pedigree of the collectivist–individualistic construct, it has come under criticism for its lack of explanatory adequacy, for confusions in the literature owing to its width of interpretation, and even because of pejorative interpretation in its application to cultures (Schwartz, 1994). In trying to more tightly define the value orientations involved, Schwartz (1994) prefers the term autonomy/conservatism (see Chapter 1), and this may be closer to the concept of instrumentalism–humanism. Persons in the former cultures are seen as autonomous entities endowed with individual rights and desires and relate to others in terms of self-interest and negotiated agreement. In the latter culture the person is viewed as being part of the social fabric, and their significance is derived from participation and identification with the group in a shared way of life. However, data from this study is not very helpful in respect of African countries. The only African country included, Zimbabwe, scores medium to high on conservatism.

Something even closer to the construct used here is found in one of the two main dimensions in Smith, Dugan and Trompenaars' (1996) reanalysis of Trompenaars' (1993) data: utilitarian involvement/loyal involvement. This defines the way in which individuals relate to social entities in terms of a calculative involvement or an obligation-based commitment. Three African countries are included in the study, Ethiopia, Nigeria and Burkina Faso, and all score relatively high on loyal involvement.

Other cultural dimensions that have a bearing on African cultures are as follows:

- *Power distance* (Hofstede, 1991). African cultures are generally seen as tolerating higher levels of inequality and hierarchy. This has implications for the level of participation in organizations and styles of managing people. However, there are bound to be differences in power distance between African cultures, as there are in European cultures.

- *Uncertainty avoidance* (Hofstede, 1991). African societies are considered high in uncertainty avoidance. Western (mainly American) views of change management which increase participation and uncertainty and work well in low uncertainty avoidance cultures may not work very well in African organizations.

- *Centrality of work* (MOW, 1987). Some African countries may be considered to be high in femininity and low on work centrality. This has implications for the results-focus of many Western management practices, which might not be appropriate to an African context.

- *Universalism–particularism.* An inclination to apply the rules according to friendship and kinship relations has implications for recruitment and promotion policies in organizations in some African countries which may be at variance with practices in countries such as the United States and Britain, but not all European countries.

- *Achievement–ascription.* Quite often more traditional societies accord status according to ascription. Again, this may influence recruitment and promotion policies that may be at variance with practices in some (but not all) Western cultures.

An attempt has been made to describe African culture, but to point to the need to reconceptualize the dichotomy between Western and 'developing' countries in terms of 'humanism' with a positive connotation. By so doing it may be possible to understand what 'humanistic' cultures have to offer people management practices in other parts of the world. In order to develop this understanding, it is necessary to explore the nature of Indian people management and to analyse the way it has tried to reconcile the antithesis between Western instrumentalism and Indian humanism.

Indian people management

India's economic transition can be traced back to before 1991, the year of economic liberalization. Today, it is a complex mixed economy characterized by a multiplicity of sectors, multiplicity of objectives, and a variety of adjustment mechanisms to solve the conflicts between various sectors. The present day mixed economy of India has evolved through a series of policy formulations and legislation aimed at restrictive practices and protectionist measures and finally to the new economic policy, announced in July 1991 by the government, which has far reaching implications. After years of protection from foreign competition, India has now been exposed to competitive markets both internally and externally, as a result of the policy of liberalization. These changes have resulted in increased competition, leading to lower prices, higher operating costs with accompanying slow or declining industrial growth, and growing expectations of organizational stakeholders: managers' expectations of their staff, customers expectations of the organization, expectations of staff towards their managers. In order to meet these challenges Indian organizations have had to develop strategic competitiveness through attention to the management of people and organization.

Culture and Indian managers

England's (1975) study of the personal value systems of over 2,500 managers in Australia, Japan, Korea, India and the United States supported an assumption that despite the value differences among managers in the five countries and value diversity within each country, there is a common pattern of translation of values into behaviours across the countries. While pragmatists have an economic and organizational competence orientation, moralists exhibit a humanistic and bureaucratic orientation. The study reports that the percentage of pragmatists is 67 per cent in Japan, 57 per cent in the United States, 53 per cent in Korea, 40 per cent in Australia, and only 34 per cent in India. The degree of moralistic orientation was 9 per cent in Korea, 10 per cent in Japan, 30 per cent in the United States, 40 per cent in Australia and a relatively high 44 per cent in India. The study reports and highlights the values associated with Indian managers. These include a high degree of moralistic orientation; a valuing of stable organizations with minimum or steady change; a valuing of status orientation; and valuing a blend of organizational compliance and organizational competence.

The implications of such values to the management of people in Indian organizations appear be that

- Indian managers are more responsive to the human and bureaucratic consequences of their actions;

- they are more influenced by positions and approaches which utilize philosophical and moral justifications;

- they are more responsive to internal rewards and controls;

- because India has a larger proportion of moralistic managers, change in managers is likely to be slower and more difficult.

Another study undertaken in the 1970s (Smith and Thomas, 1972) of cross-cultural attitudinal differences between American and Indian managers identified the following differences in the area of authority and influence:

- Indian managers at both middle and senior levels in organizations profess a belief in group-based, participative decision making, but have little faith in the capacity of workers for taking initiative and responsibility. American managers on the other hand place a relatively higher faith in the capacity of individuals to take responsibility, and a lower faith in group-oriented participative decision making.

- In contrast to American managers, Indian managers favour labour and government intervention in the affairs of the organization.

- Middle-level managers in India espouse a greater belief in change and are less conservative than their American counterparts at this level.

According to Hofstede's (1980a) data, Indian culture is relatively high on power distance, medium in collectivism (on the same level as Spain and Japan), medium in masculinity (same level as Belgium, with a score not far below the United States), and low on uncertainty avoidance. Smith et al. (1996) place India midway on their conservatism–egalitarian commitment dimension, and towards loyal involvement rather than utilitarian involvement.

Indian management responses to liberalization

According to one popular account (Khanna, 1996) trends in Indian management since liberalization have been as follows:

- CEOs are aiming their internal and external processes directly at customer satisfaction.

- People are becoming the principal instrument in delivering service to the customer, particularly as the service industry grows in importance.

- Corporations are discovering that their core capabilities lie not in particular products or product categories, but in unique expertise.

- Successful techniques are focusing directly on people instead of technologies or processes, operating on the principle that devising systems for getting the best out of people will automatically maximize corporate performance.

- Although previously top management of the company usually controlled the resources at the company's disposal, in the changed economic environment a corporation's knowledge resources are increasingly seen to be the brains of its people: not all of this can be codified in rule-books and manuals.

Indian management practitioners and academics have developed a distinctive approach to human resource development (HRD, a term preferred to HRM as a means of distancing from Anglo-Saxon practices which emphasize the *resource* side of the equation: Sparrow and Budhwar, 1995). HRD approaches are increasingly playing a role in organizational responses to issues arising from liberalization. Accustomed to operating in protected markets, organizations are having to learn to combine the virtues of conflicting paradigms, rather than relying exclusively on a single set of preconditioned theoretically right policies. HRD therefore addresses the need to arrest deteriorating values by building up organizational and cultural strengths, broadening the philosophy of tolerance and sacrifice and displaying deep concern for people (Rohmetra, 1998). HRD as a 'humanistic' concept and a subsuming norm that guides management approaches to employees has come to assume a critical role in Indian management thought and practice. As a management philosophy, HRD involves a paradigm shift from the old approach of control to the new approach of involvement and self-development (Silvera, 1988).

It is similar to the concept of the rights and duties of human beings which democratic constitutions the world over consider inalienable from human nature, and has similarities to the United National Development Programme's concept of a nation's human development. HRD is therefore a humanistic concept that places a premium on the dignity and respect of people and is based on a belief in the limitless potential of human beings. It stresses that people should not be treated as mere cogs in the wheel of production, but with respect.

It proposes that human beings should be valued as human beings, independent of their contribution to corporate productivity or profit. The various underlying attitudes symbolizing respect for people's dignity, trust in their basic integrity and belief in their potential, should lead to the creation of a climate in companies where individuals find fulfilment in work and seek newer horizons for themselves and the enterprise (Rohmetra, 1998).

HRD practices in Indian companies attempt to blend Western and Eastern ideas and systems of people management. This concept of HRD (from Pareek and Rao, 1992) attempts to be more comprehensive and meaningful than utilitarian concepts evolved in Anglo-Saxon countries. It has come to denote a planned way of developing and multiplying competences, and the creation of an organizational climate that promotes the utilization and development of new competences. Culture building is seen as a part of its agenda.

Implications for managers: indigenous knowledge and the stakeholder approach

The attempts at building an Indian model of HRD may be a more conscious attempt at hybridization of post-colonial organizations than is happening in Africa. The thesis that colonial institutions were tacked onto African civil society

(Dia, 1996), and that the nature of organizations and management in 'developing' countries (Jaeger and Kanungo, 1990) are simply the remnants of colonialism (Jackson, in press), is one that is gaining currency. It is unlikely that the organizations described by Jaeger and Kanungo (1990) in the 'developing' world generally, and by Blunt and Jones (1992) in Africa are in fact 'indigenous'. At worst they are structurally post-colonial remnants, and at best they are hybrid forms. In Africa this may well be a result of influences from different systems of management that Jackson (in press) has described as 'post-colonial', 'post-instrumental', and an 'African renaissance'. Tables 10.1 and 10.2 provide a typology of these management systems in their 'ideal' forms, together with a comparison of an 'East Asian' system which may provide a perceived alternative system for organizations in Africa. It was noted earlier (Introduction) that Western organizations from countries with mature HRM systems are unlikely to operate a purely 'hard' instrumental approach to managing people. A 'post-instrumental' concept is therefore more appropriate, although this remains an area for further research (see below) into the nature of this system as operated in diverse African environments, or indeed in other post-colonial countries.

The nature of management in Africa, and many other post-colonial countries, is cross-cultural. South Africa, for example, has 11 official languages representing the major ethnic/cultural groups, and India has 18. Rather than introducing Western HRM and other management approaches wholesale, in an attempt to universalize management across cultures, an understanding of the cross-cultural process that increases integrative effects and decreases disintegrative effects may lead to more effective approaches to managing people. This may best be understood from the point of view of developing synergistic hybrid organizational cultures, in order to develop effective management through cross-cultural participation. This is a true stakeholder approach: giving voice not only to the objectively defined stakeholders (for example those identified by Mills, 1997: Chapter 9 in this book), but also to indigenous knowledge systems which are currently being explored, for example, under the aegis of the *ubuntu* movement in South Africa (Mbigi, 1997). This is the 'African renaissance' identified in Figure 10.1 below (see pp. 216–18). Fanon (e.g. 1967) was concerned not simply about the more overt effects of colonization, but particularly about the need to decolonize the mind. One may not be able to speak truly of, for example, an 'African' approach to management that draws on African thought prior to colonization, but it may be possible to think outside the Western instrumental 'box' of HRM. In this respect strength may be drawn from the humanism of an African perception of people, and to incorporate this (perhaps taking the example of Indian HRD, but in a different inflection) into people management and development approaches in Africa and other post-colonial regions.

It was therefore possible to see, within the three South African case studies presented, an interplay between two possibly conflicting requirements: the need to downsize the organizations to respond to financial constraints and commercial imperatives; and the need to respond to the social and development needs of people. The first may represent the needs of the financial stakeholders such as shareholders in the case of AECI, and also a shorter-term perspective. The second may represent the needs of the community as stakeholders: the need to skill, and re-skill, and to develop the potential of human beings as a longer-term need for the prosperity of a community. Through the extensive literacy programmes of

Table 10.1 Comparison of different organizational management systems in Africa

	Post-colonial	Post-instrumental	African renaissance	East Asian/Japanese
Main principles	Theory X Western/post-independence African Instrumental	Theory Y Western/'modern' Functionalist	Humanistic *Ubuntu* Community collectivism	Humanistic Corporate collectivism
Importance	Continuing legacy through political and economic interests	Looked to as alternative Influence from multinationals, management education and consultants	Some elements may prevail in indigenous organizations Of growing interest internationally	Developing importance through East Asian investment May be seen as alternative
Strategy	Inputs and process orientation Lack of results and objectives Risk aversive	Results and market oriented Clear objectives Calculated risk taking	Stakeholder orientation	Market and results orientation Clear objectives Low risk taking
Structure	Hierarchical Centralized	Flatter hierarchy Often decentralized	Flatter hierarchy Decentralized and closer to stakeholders	Hierarchical and conformist
Governance and decision making	Authoritarian Non-consultative	Often consultative Increasing emphasis on 'empowerment'	Participative, consensus seeking (*indaba*)	Consultative but authority from top
Control	Rule bound Lack of flexibility Outside influence or control (family, government) often seen as negative	Clear rules of action Flexible Outside government influence decreasing	Benign rules of action Outside influence (government, family) may be seen as more benign	Consensus and harmony above formal rules May lack flexibility

Character	May not act ethically towards stakeholders Not very efficient Static Probably not foreign owned	More ethically responsible Aims to be successful Change is a feature Probably foreign owned	Stakeholder interest may be more important than 'ethics' Success related to development and well-being of its people Indigenous	Harmony and face may be more important than ethics Efficiency May be slow to change
Internal policies	Discriminatory Employee policies aimed at duties rather than rights	Non-discriminatory Access to equal opportunities and clear employee policies on responsibilities and rights	Stakeholder interests Access to equal opportunities	Can be discriminatory (towards women) Employee relations may be more implicit
Internal climate	Employee alienation common Weak trade unions Inter-ethnic friction Discourages diversity of opinions Promotion by ascription	Emphasis on employee motivation Weak or cooperative unions Move towards inter-ethnic harmony Diverse opinions often encouraged Promotion based on achievement	Motivation through participation important Unions protect rights Inter-ethnic harmony taken into consideration Everyone should be able to state their opinions Promotion based on legitimization of status	Aims at employee commitment (job satisfaction may be low) Company trade unions Inter-ethnic relations may not be an issue Consensus rather than diversity of opinions stressed Promotion by seniority
External policies	Lack of customer/client policies Lack of results orientation	Clear policies on customers/clients Results orientation	A clear awareness of and articulation of stakeholder interests	A focus on business and customer networks rather than explicit policies
Management expertise	Educated management elite with low managerial expertise	High, results-oriented managerial expertise is aimed for	Management expertise based on people orientation	Management effectiveness based on collective skills
People orientation	Control orientation	People and results orientation	People and stakeholder orientation	People (in-group) orientation

217

Table 10.2 Comparison of different management attributes in Africa

	Post-colonial	Post-instrumental	African renaissance	East Asian/Japanese
Management motivators	Economic security Control	Managing uncertainty Self-enhancement Autonomy Independence Achievement	Belonging Development of person and group	Belonging Development in corporate context Elements of economic security
Management commitment	To business objectives To relatives To organization	To self To results To ethical principles To work	To group To people	To business objectives (the corporate) To results To work To relatives
Management principles	External locus of control Deontology Theory X Mistrust of human nature Status orientation	Internal locus of control Teleology Theory Y Conditional trust of human nature Achievement orientation	Internal and external locus of control Trust of human nature Status and achievement orientation	External locus of control Theory Y (in-group), theory X (out-group) Trust of in-group members Relational and relativity aspects of decision making Status through seniority
Management practices	Reliance on hierarchy Use of rank Low egalitarianism Lack of open communication Lack of open information	Some participation Mostly communicating openly Providing open information when necessary Confrontational	Participation Egalitarianism Communicating openly Providing open information	Consultative (*ringi*) Communicating and information giving to gain consensus Maintaining harmony
Main orientations	Managing process Managing power relations	Managing results (external focus) Managing people	Managing people (internal stakeholder focus) Managing results (defined by stakeholder interests)	Managing people (in-group/out-group relations) Managing results (defined by stakeholder interests)

Eskom, for example, human potential can be developed to meet the current needs of the company for skilled and technically sophisticated staff, as well as the longer-term need for social and economic development of the wider community. It is true that some foreign companies are struggling with this dilemma.

Social responsibility programmes and the case of Colgate Palmolive

A published case is that of the American company Colgate Palmolive (Beaty, 1998). Many such American companies have developed social responsibility programmes in South Africa under the guidelines of the Sullivan Code. This particular company has achieved 'an outstanding Category 1 rating' under this code (see Beaty 1998: 136–7 for a summary of the code drawn up for American multinationals operating in South Africa). Its contributions have been to fund various educational projects at schools and university (equipment, electricity, burglar-proofing of premises, supplements for teacher upgrades, outreach programmes, student bursaries, provision of career advice); and community projects (water purification and sanitation, funds for centres for the aged, road races, drug rehabilitation, mental illness, Aids). The list is very long, and includes a number of health and dental projects. The code requires that the company directs 12 per cent of its salary budget to such projects. With an annual turnover of $100 million and a workforce of 600 employees, the company had set up a $3 million Colgate Palmolive Foundation. The management and allocation of funding to projects was a responsibility of the company-appointed management rather than being carried out by representatives of the various stakeholder communities that stand to benefit from these projects. The company had been criticized by the trade union for not involving them, and at times for funding projects, for example in the area of dental care, out of enlightened self-interest rather than altruism or a sense of what is required to contribute to the development of people within the community. Many such companies have been radically downsizing, and paring down their workforce to a minimum. While Eskom, for example, has also been downsizing, it has attempted to balance the needs of developing people therefore contributing to the community rather than simply donating to worthy causes. This is an issue that is likely to continue in South Africa, and one that may be addressed by a thorough stakeholder analysis, as suggested in Chapter 9.

Questions for managers

1   Learning from some of the measures taken by Eskom, AECI and Germiston City Council, what could a foreign company like Colgate Palmolive do to contribute to the development of human potential within Africa? How could it balance this with the requirements of its shareholders, and with the contingencies of operating in a difficult social and economic environment?

2   Eskom is a state-owned enterprise that has now gone through various stages of liberalization and privatization. In view of the increased pressures to make profits and to make savings on the costs of its human resources, how can it best balance the instrumental needs of short-term competition in the global

marketplace, and the humanistic needs of developing human potential for the future well-being of South African society?

3   What can be learned from Indian HRD, and its integration of Western and non-western approaches to managing people, in order that it can be applied in African countries?

An agenda for research: post-colonialism and hybridization

Currently, management in Africa and other post-colonial societies is under-researched. There may be various reasons for this, including a lack of interest among management scholars, and a reluctance of many multinational companies to invest in regions that are seen as uncertain, unpredictable, and sometimes dangerous. Yet there are vast resources, potential and capabilities (about 80 per cent of the earth's surface regarded as 'developing') that have yet to be fully realized. Figure 10.1 points to some of the intricacies that must be taken into consideration in any research project on Africa (from Jackson, in press). The first aspect is that of changing management systems. Tables 10.1 and 10.2 illustrate three ideal types of management system that are operating in African countries (these have parallels in other post-colonial regions). It is likely that they are not

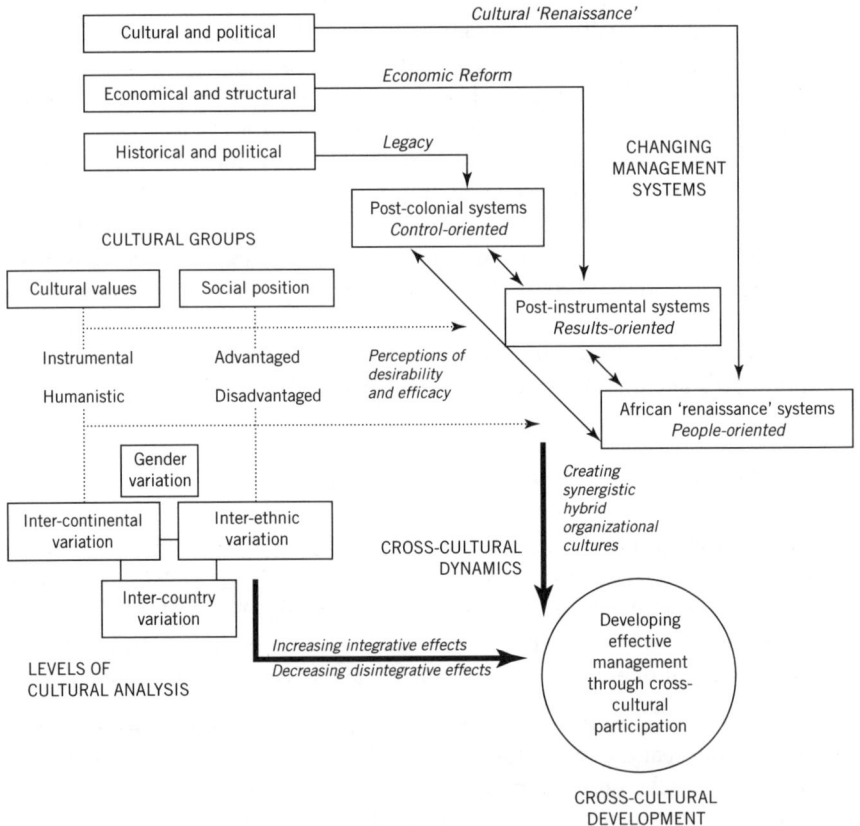

Figure 10.1 A model of cross-cultural dynamics in sub-Saharan Africa (Jackson, in press)

operating in their pure form, but in various dynamic processes, as indicated in Figure 10.1, which lead to various types of hybrid system, some highly adaptive and successful, some maladaptive. The way this is happening as a result of cultural interaction, the forms these systems are taking, and the factors leading to success and lack of success of such systems are areas ripe for research.

Cultural interactions take place at various levels: at 'inter-continental' level (African–Western: where a key factor may be the interplay of instrumental and humanistic perceptions of people), inter-country (within an economic region such as the Southern African Development Community: SADC), and inter-ethnically (within a particular country, most of which in Africa are multi-ethnic). Historical circumstances also have different cultural implications for different countries: for example, French administration would have interacted differently with the local population than would British administration; and each administration would have interacted differently among the countries that were their colonial dominions.

These dynamics are captured in Figure 10.1, and provide a starting point for research into management in Africa and other post-colonial regions. The purpose of this research should be first to understand the dynamics that create hybrid management and organizational cultures and how synergistic effects can be created through increasing integrative effects of cross-cultural working and decreasing disintegrating effects; and, secondly to use this knowledge to intervene in organizational and management development initiatives in order to develop effective management through cross-cultural participation (Figure 10.1).

Questions for researchers

1 What management systems are operating in African countries (and other post-colonial regions), in different ways in different industries and companies, and how successful are these systems in reconciling cultural differences?

2 How are instrumental and humanistic influences in organizational require-ments and management practices being managed and reconciled in post-colonial countries?

3 How are multinational companies that operate in post-colonial countries successfully adapting people management practices to local needs and expectations?

4 What are the different stakeholder needs and expectations in post-colonial countries, and how are companies identifying these, and reconciling them in their management practices?

Conclusion: the future organization

The hegemony of America and Anglo-Saxon approaches due to United States economic dominance since the Second World War may be a key factor in the preponderance of HRM practices in international management. The hunger for Western management knowledge in transitional and emerging countries is a corollary of this. There is no doubting the contributions that Western management philosophy and principles have made to wealth creation. Yet what about the many different cultural contributions that have been made, or could be made by countries as diverse as China, India, South Africa and the Czech Republic? Different concepts of organizing and managing people have arisen in cultures that are different to those of the Anglo-Saxon countries. Hegemonic tendencies have allowed little voice to be given to the so-called developing countries of the world.

Effective and appropriate management is extremely important to the welfare and prosperity of humankind throughout the world. This involves motivating people to go into work usually in medium to large goal-directed organizations that often separate them from their family, leisure and community life. Once in the organization it requires motivating people to work hard and employ skills, knowledge and attitudes that may have limited relevance and applicability outside the work context. The way this is achieved varies from culture to culture. For example, a contractual relationship may be established to reflect an instrumental regard for employees in the context of an individualistic and achievement-oriented society such as the United States. A relationship may be established in Japan that reflects an obligation of loyalty on the part of the employee to be flexible and work towards furthering the aims of the corporate collectivity. The corporation has an obligation to safeguard the person's employment and aim organizational resources at developing him or her over the longer term, as part of the collective. This may reflect a humanistic approach to viewing the value of people as an end in themselves, rather than seeing people as a means to an end. This different 'locus of human value' is important to the different cultural responses to the antithesis between life inside work organizations and life outside work.

One approach this text has taken is to look at the contributions to the management of people in international organizations that have emanated from different cultures, and to situate them firmly within their cultural contexts, but at the same time assess their value to global management. It is a problem that many countries, and therefore the cultural contributions that could be made by such countries, are in a position of relative weakness within the general power relations that exist in the world today. Contributions that could be made to global managing by a country such as Uganda are less likely to be recognized (even in

Uganda) than contributions from the United States. As a result of unequal economic standing in the world community, stakeholders' interests in post-colonial countries are less likely to be taken into account when managing the opposing influences of global integration and local differentiation. The humanistic contributions that could be made in reconciling the world outside work with that inside work organizations are often overlooked. Instrumental approaches involving calculative relations, contractual obligations, job descriptions and selection and development based on a competences approach are likely to be imported and applied in cultures with collectivistic cultures.

Western managers may take up an expatriate assignment in another country with ideas of participation and democracy in the workplace, perhaps denigrating local culture for being undemocratic, paternalistic and possibly autocratic. Yet how undemocratic and unparticipative it is to ignore local stakeholders' interests, local approaches to management, local perceptions, practices, expectations and needs. These need to be incorporated not in a simple idea of involving workers in decision making (this may simply be given lip-service) but in a thorough stakeholder analysis, a thorough investigation of local needs and culture, and an understanding of the relationship between the world of work and the world outside work.

In each chapter of this book two types of summary and conclusion have been given: the implications for managers; and an agenda for research. The purpose of this brief concluding chapter is to attempt to show the overall implications for managers, and to suggest directions for future research in this area. In doing this, it is hoped to point the way towards the future organization.

The future organization: implications for managers

One of the main tasks of successfully building appropriate management of people within the future organization is to develop both an understanding and involvement of stakeholder interests, aspirations and needs. This, it could be argued, is crucial in an increasingly globalized world where different cultural influences are daily coming into contact, interacting and melding into hybrid forms of managing through a process, not of convergence, but of cross-vergence (see for example, Priem et al., 2000).

If convergence is a movement towards one approach to managing and a universalization of principles, policies and practices, cross-vergence involves a number of different movements towards the development of new forms of managing. For example, Priem et al. (2000) assert that Hong Kong combines both Western and Chinese influences in a hybrid form of management. Yet even within this process, there is often a more dominant influence, owing to pervasive hegemonic relations (such as the influence of managers trained in the Western tradition in US business schools, and in multinational companies) or more directly to a dominant partner in international joint ventures, mergers or acquisitions. This was seen in both Chapters 8 and 9 in slightly different respects.

The problems encountered in Blue Sword in China may well have been the result of a lack of understanding of stakeholders' interests: the two parties not understanding the different expectations of each other. The Chinese partner, for example, expected to develop international standards of quality and to penetrate

European markets, the Belgians wanted access to the Chinese market at low cost. To a large extent the German (dominant) partner in the Volkswagen–Skoda venture tried to develop an understanding of the expectations of the Czech partners through attempting to develop a learning organization, and by using such methods as partnering of positions through tandem management. Again, a more thorough understanding of the needs of the main groups of stakeholders (corporate and community) would have laid the foundations for the venture, and helped to create an appropriate hybrid system of people management.

It is perhaps through this type of approach that international organizations can best manage the balance between the need for global integration (often this need reflects the perceived interests of corporate headquarters stakeholders involved in strategizing) and the need for local differentiation (often reflecting the interests of corporate and community stakeholders at local levels). One of the main tasks in assessing the requirements of corporate and community stakeholders is understanding different perceptions of the relationship between corporate life and community life. Balancing instrumental and humanistic views of the value of people in organizations is difficult without a clear understanding of such different perceptions and values. Developing an approach to managing people that is appropriate to the values and expectations of the wider community may be impossible without this type of input into management systems.

This may well be the way towards creating a true learning organization that can encompass the knowledge, know-how and values of all stakeholders. Figure 11.1 attempts to capture these elements.

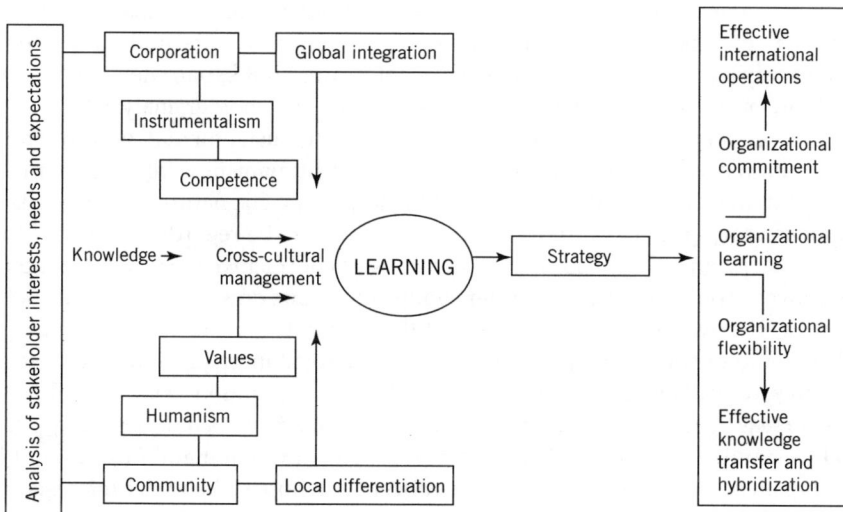

Figure 11.1
The future
organization:
process

Hence (Chapter 1) IKEA developed an approach of communicating its management philosophy to its subsidiaries, but only adapting this to local circumstances after aspects had been found to be inappropriate. For example, a requirement that training should reflect the needs of a wider community and be transferable outside IKEA was an element that could easily have been attended to at the beginning of operations in Spain. In Chapter 2, Crédit Lyonnais made little attempt to discover the needs of local managers and key employees

225

within its international operations. The main set of stakeholder interests was considered to reside in the headquarters operations, focusing on the career objectives of French managers in the context of human resource planning. Not only would an analysis of the needs of local managers have satisfied their requirements, but it would also have opened up a pool of talent for the international operation as a whole. Many organizations, such as Andersen Consultants (Chapter 3) have worked on this issue of how to deploy people from anywhere in the organization to projects and appointments anywhere in the world. Yet the competences approach used by Andersen Consultants and many international organizations, while unifying strategic intent across countries, often takes little account of local differentiation, and takes less account of the cultural values aspect of major stakeholders in local communities. The question of whether the competences approach is relevant in a particular country's culture is often not asked.

Shell is reported to have an approach to performance management that reflects a universal requirement to acknowledge individual performance in order to retain high-flying individuals. This is not negotiable. What is negotiable is the percentage of the reward package in each country that reflects this element. This is perhaps an attempt to allow for local differentiation between individualistic, high achievement societies, and collectivistic and feministic (after Hofstede, 1980a) societies. This may be the beginning of taking account of stakeholders' values and expectations.

The transfer of know-how, knowledge and values is an important element in expatriation as discussed in Chapter 4, yet often little information is available to expatriates on the results of informed stakeholder analysis. This should be a central part of the preparation for expatriate assignments (i.e. the information from such analyses) and of ongoing development throughout expatriate assignments and career development (i.e. the expertise in such stakeholder analysis).

Even Japanese corporations may act in an instrumental way in their international operations. Chapter 5 discussed the humanistic aspects of Japanese people management, but also looked at the target-specific nature of collectivism. Japanese corporations employ 'salarymen' who may be regarded as part of the collective group. They also employ numbers of contract workers. This group of employees could be used as a buffer against economic downturn, where the jobs of the collective nucleus are secure, but the contract workers are the first to go. This would enable the corporation to develop a loyal in-group at the expense of the out-group. This logic could be applied by the corporation to local employees in overseas subsidiaries. Although Japanese management techniques are applied to this group as far as possible, by developing commitment and flexibility, it is the Japanese expatriates, as part of the collective, whose stakeholder interests are uppermost. Again the extent to which a company like Chiba can transfer knowledge, values and people management techniques should also be assessed through stakeholder analysis.

The way the concept of the learning organization has often been transferred to cultures other than Anglo-Saxon ones has been through an assumption that its inherent values are universal. As was discussed in Chapter 6, the underlying values of this concept reflect an approach to learning that may not exist in other cultures. Yet an approach to developing knowledge through a stakeholder approach may well be a concept that is applicable in other cultures. Certainly developing the capability to learn through the active participation of stakeholders is not simply paying lip service to participatory management as so often multi-national companies do in other cultures. It is attempting to provide an approach to learning that is just as appropriate and important to the local community as it is to the international corporation. A stakeholder approach does not work without learning taking place. Appropriate learning cannot take place without taking account of stakeholders' interests, needs and expectations.

This of course is reflected in the need for companies not simply to manage change effectively in a rapidly changing global environment, but also to manage what was called in Chapter 7 'lateral flexibility'. Managing flexibly across cultures requires a rigorous understanding of the requirements and expectations of the different stakeholders. For example, understanding that the process of change involves high levels of uncertainty, and that according to Hofstede (1980a) different cultures respond differently to uncertainty, suggests differential manage-ment of change. A textbook approach might be to instigate communication groups in order to get people to take ownership of the changes by suggesting ways of handling this and developing solutions. The perception from a high un-certainty, high power distance culture may be, 'you are the boss and you are paid to manage, why aren't you managing?' This may also have the effect of increasing uncertainty, which may not be appropriate to a high uncertainty avoidance culture. Initial stakeholder analysis in this case would have identified such problems.

Part of the process of such stakeholder analysis would involve an identification of cultural values, and differences in cultural values among the various stakeholders. Blue Sword (Chapter 8) has already been mentioned in connection with the failure of a joint venture in China. Here there was a need to understand the respective cultural values of each stakeholder group, and how they were likely to interact. It is perhaps only in retrospect that lessons can be learned from this case. These are lessons that may be valuable in other such joint ventures where knowledge, know-how and even values are being transferred. It could be noted that not even the know-how that was being transferred from the Belgian company to China was agreed upon and needed by the Chinese partner. It was seen that the Chinese partner required the know-how to penetrate the European market. Other such problems were discussed in Chapter 8 in connection with motivational issues of Chinese employees by expatriates, where expectations were not adequately explored.

The creation of a learning organization by Volkswagen–Skoda (Chapter 9) was an altogether more positive example of an attempt to transfer knowledge and know-how. Yet this fell short of an initial and ongoing stakeholder analysis and involvement.

Finally (in Chapter 10) the three South African organizations were seen to be attempting to balance the requirements of the global market (instrumental approaches) and the community interest in developing human potential (human-istic approaches), and therefore taking account, at least partially, of the different stakeholder interests. The Indian approach to HRD was also seen as trying to balance Western and Indian approaches to people management. Colgate Palmolive, in its social responsibility efforts, could well take account of these approaches in really trying to understand the needs, aspirations and expectations of the various stakeholders involved in these efforts.

The future organization will be a stakeholder organization. By implication it is already a cross-cultural organization, which has to manage change and diversity effectively. The biggest challenge is to reconcile the two worlds: corporate and community. It could be assumed that in the advanced economies of the world this has been solved in one respect or another. In many of the post-colonial and post-Soviet countries it still has to be addressed. One of the biggest failures in post-colonial societies may be the failure of capturing the wider community collectivism within the corporation. Perhaps Japanese corporations in Japan have managed to do this. Corporations in Africa, for example, have tacked on organizational arrangements (foreign to Africa) to communities that may now be largely alienated from corporate life. The challenge for the future organization is to bring in community stakeholders, first by a rigorous stakeholder analysis, and then by involving the different stakeholders in the process of developing relevance and effective interaction among those stakeholders.

The future organization: future research

The role of research in helping to conceive and develop the future organization cannot be overstated. However, the state of research in both cross-cultural management and in the relation between cross-cultural theory and HRM/people management has still some way to go.

Chapter 1 discussed the main theories within cross-cultural management, and some of the limitations. The dominance of Hofstede's (1980a, 1991 and 2001) theory based on broad cultural value dimensions provides both benefits and problems. The theory has done much to unify efforts in this field. Replication studies abound (Sondergaard, 1994), and the dimensions are useful in providing a good first guess to the nature of national cultures, the explanation of variation in management practices among countries, and the ease of explanation of the concepts for teaching purposes (Schwartz's, 1994, cultural values do not have this same utility in teaching). The problems are that of over-simplification and stereotyping of cultures (for example Human, 1996).

The introduction of yet another dimension within the current text (instrumentalism–humanism) is not intended to replace theories or overcome the problems. It is hoped that this will add to our knowledge by focusing on a different aspect of cultural variation (locus of human value) as well as providing a concept that paints a less pejorative picture of cultures outside Western traditions (see Introduction). This has a direct bearing on the way HRM/people management is focused and formulated. It also provides an indication of contributions that post-colonial and post-Soviet societies can make to global management. As such, this is an area that needs more research.

The problems of managing people across cultures often require approaches that are more directly linked to practical application than may be provided by many cross-cultural theorists. In some ways the work of Kanungo and associates (Kanungo and Jaeger, 1990; Mendonca and Kanungo, 1994; Aycan et al., 1999) in developing links between cultural dimensions and HRM practices goes some way in meeting this more practical need (Chapter 1). Yet this does not substitute for thick cultural analysis of particular situations, to meet particular management needs. The way cultural values are manifested in particular expectations and practices in real situations is important. The way forward here may well be in stakeholder analysis. This is somewhat broader than cross-cultural analysis in some respects, but is also more specific to particular situations. Hence in areas such as international joint ventures, an approach to stakeholder analysis may provide useful and transferable results. This, together with an analysis of interaction effects between integration and differentiation of international enterprises, may go some way towards developing understanding of corporate–community interactions. The work of Rosenzweig and Nohria (1994) in focusing on the extent to which the need for internal consistency (integration) across national borders contends with forces for local isomorphism (differentiation) provides a possible starting point for this type of research. Theories can be developed about the nature of stakeholders in corporate–community relations, the factors that impact on their different expectations and actions, and their respective interests, needs and expectations.

Certainly the multicultural model of organization cannot be studied in isolation from the supranational model (Chapters 1 and 2). This juxtaposition brings into play issues of convergence and cross-vergence in relations of power across cultures. Issues of hegemony and power balances within international ventures and the balance between corporate and community groups of stakeholders are all interdependent aspects of cross-cultural research that cannot be ignored. One of the serious shortfalls of cultural value dimensions theory is its lack of dynamism. It does not tell us very much about cultures in interaction. Yet it is this aspect that is of relevance to the way management know-how and knowledge is transferred across cultures. Theories of cross-vergence are useful for this, and are a starting point in trying to develop an understanding of how hybridization works. From the discussion above on implications for managers, it is an obvious assumption that it is possible to successfully intervene in the hybridization process. This would be through active participation by the various stakeholders and an understanding of and reconciling of their different interests. In this way the results of hybridization may be altogether more appropriate to the local community and to the international corporation. This process needs investigating, and perhaps to be taken up by action research.

It is hoped that the sections in each chapter on setting an agenda for research in the particular areas will be of help in formulating research topics and research questions. It is also hoped that these few concluding remarks will help situate those particular questions within the broader conceptual and practical context of researching real management issues in real cultural contexts. In summary, the tasks ahead for research in international organization and HRM/people management are:

- developing conceptual and empirical links between theoretical formulations of cultural value dimensions and specific manifestations in HRM/people management policies and practices;

- breaking out of previously conceived and investigated cultural dimensions, to develop new concepts that are more helpful in overcoming pejorative assumptions about cultures outside Western traditions;

- investigating the cultural contributions that non-Western (particularly post-colonial and post-Soviet) approaches can make to global managing;

- advancing understanding of the interaction processes of cultures, within power relations, that give rise to successful and unsuccessful hybrid forms of managing through cross-vergence of cultures;

- developing thick cultural analysis grounded in interaction situations such as international joint ventures;

- developing the relevance of cross-cultural studies through an incorporation of stakeholder analysis of particular interaction situations;

- broadening cross-cultural analysis to include an understanding of integration–differentiation in global managing;

- developing an understanding of knowledge and know-how transfer through cultural interactions.

References

Ackenhusen, M. and Ghosal, S. (1992) *Andersen Consulting (Europe): Entering the Business of Business Integration*, reprinted in H. W. Lane and J. J. DiStefano, (eds) *International Management Behavior*, 2nd edition, Boston: PWS-Kent.

Adler, N. J. (1986–87) 'Women in international management: where are they?', *California Management Review*, 26(4): 79–85.

Adler, N. J. (1987) 'Pacific basin managers: a gaigin, not a woman', *Human Resource Management*, 26(2): 169–92.

Adler, N. J. (1991) *International Dimensions of Organizational Behaviour*, 2nd edition, Boston: PWS-Kent.

Adler, N. J. (1993) 'Competitive frontiers: women managers in the triad', *International Studies of Management and Organization*, 23(2): 2–23.

Adler, N. J. and Ghadar, F. (1990) 'Strategic human resource management: a global perspective', in R. Pieper (ed.) *Human Resource Management: An International Comparison*, Berlin: de Gruyter, pp. 235–60.

Agor, W. H. (1985) *Test Your Intuitive Powers: Agor Intuitive Management Survey*, King of Prussia, PA: Organizational Design and Development Inc.

Alderfer, C. P. (1972) *Existence, Relatedness and Growth: Human Needs in Organizational Settings*, New York: Free Press.

Allinson, C. W. and Hayes, J. (1988) 'The learning styles questionnaire: an alternative to Kolb's inventory', *Journal of Management Studies*, 25(3): 269–81.

Allinson, R. (1993) *Global Disasters: Inquiries into Management Ethics*, New York: Prentice Hall.

Argyle M. (1967) *The Psychology of Interpersonal Behaviour*, Harmondsworth: Penguin.

Argyris, C. (1992) *On Organizational Learning*, Oxford/Cambridge, MA: Blackwell.

Aycan, Z., Kanungo, R. N. and Sinha, J. B. P. (1999) 'Organizational culture and human resource management practices: the model of cultural fit', *Journal of Cross-Cultural Psychology*, 30(4): 501–26.

Bae, K. and Chung, C. (1997) 'Cultural values and work attitudes of Korean industrial workers in comparison with those of the United States and Japan', *Work and Occupations*, 24(1), pp. 80–96.

References

Barnham, K. and Oates, D. (1991) *The International Manager*, London: Business Books/The Economist Books.

Barsoux, J-L. and Lawrence, P. (1990) *Management in France*, London: Cassell.

Bartlett, C. A. and Ghoshal, S. (1989) *Managing across Borders: The Transnational Solution*, London: Hutchinson.

Beardwell, I. (1994) 'Human resource management and Japan', in I. Beardwell and L. Holden (eds) *Human Resource Management: A Contemporary Perspective*, London: Pitman.

Beaty, D. T. (1998) 'Colgate Palmolive in post-apartheid South Africa', reprinted in G. Oddou and M. Mendenhall (eds) *Cases in International Organizational Behavior*, Malden, MA: Blackwell, pp. 136–42.

Becker, B. E., Huselid, M. A., Pickus, P. S. and Spratt, M. F. (1997) 'HR as a source of shareholder value: research and recommendation', *Human Resource Management*, 36(1): 39–47.

Beer, M. and Spector, B. (1985) 'Corporate wide transformations in human resource management', in R. E. Walton and P. R. Lawrence (eds) *Human Resource Management: Trends and Challenges*, Boston, MA: Harvard Business School Press, pp.219–53.

Berry, J. W., Poortinga, Y. H., Segall, M. H. and Dasen, P. R. (1992) *Cross-cultural Psychology: Research and Application*, Cambridge: Cambridge University Press.

Bjoerkman, I. and Lu, Y. (1997) 'Human resource management practices in foreign invested enterprises in China: what has been learned?' in S. Stewart and A. Carver (eds) *Advances in Chinese Industrial Studies*, Greenwich, CT: JAI Press, Vol. 5, pp. 155–72.

Blair, M. M. (1993) *The Deal Decade: What Takeovers and Leveraged Buyouts Mean for Corporate Governance*, Washington: The Brookings Institution.

Blanchard, K. and Johnson, S. (2000) *The One Minute Manager*, New York: HarperCollins.

Blum, K. (1994) 'Managing people in Germany', Chapter 3 in T. Garrison and D. Rees (eds) *Managing People across Europe*, Oxford: Butterworth-Heinemann, pp. 40–62.

Blunt, P. and Jones, M. L. (1992) *Managing Organizations in Africa*, Berlin: Walter de Gruyter.

Blunt, P. and Jones, M. L. (1997) 'Exploring the limits of Western leadership theory in East Asia and Africa', *Personnel Review*, 26(1/2): 6–23.

Boisot, M. (1987) *Information and Organization: The Manager as Anthropologist*, London: Fontana/Collins.

Boisot, M. and Child, J. (1988) 'The iron law of fiefs: bureaucratic failure and the problem of governance in the Chinese economic reforms', *Administrative Science Quarterly*, 33: 507–27.

Bond, M. H., Fu, P. P. and Pasa, S. F. (2001) 'A declaration of independence for editing an international journal of cross cultural management', *International Journal of Cross Cultural Management*, 1(1): 24–30.

Boon, M. (1996) *The African Way: The Power of Interactive Leadership*, Johannesburg: Zebra Press.

Bovin, O. (1998) 'Towards a learning organization', in *Management Development*, Geneva: International Labour Office, pp. 357–77.

Bowman, C. and Carter, S. (1995) 'Organising for competitive advantage', *European Management Journal*, 13(4): 423–33.

Boxall, P. (1999), 'Editorial Introduction', *Asia Pacific Journal of Human Resources*, 37 (2): 1.

Boyacigiller, N. A. and Adler, N. J. (1991) 'The parochial dinosaur: organizational science in a global context', *Academy of Management Review*, 16(2): 262–90.

Boyatzis, R. E. (1982) *The Competent Manager*, New York: John Wiley.

Brady, F. N. (1990) *Ethical Management: Rules and Results*, Basingstoke: MacMillan.

Brewster, C. (1991) *The Management of Expatriates*, London: Kogan Page.

Brewster, C. (1995) 'Towards a "European" model of human resource management', *Journal of International Business Studies*, 1: 1–21.

Brewster, C., Hegewisch, A. and Holden, L. (1992) *The European Human Resource Management Guide*, London: Harcourt Brace Jovanovich.

British Petroleum (2001) www.bp.com/about_bp/ 23/05/2001.

Brown, M. B. (1995) *Africa's Choices: After Thirty Years of the World Bank*, London: Penguin.

Cassells, E. (1999) 'Building a learning organization in the offshore oil industry', *Long Range Planning*, 32(2): 245–52.

CCC (Chinese Cultural Connection) (1987) 'Chinese values and the search for culture-free dimensions of culture', *Journal of Cross-Cultural Psychology*, 18: 143–64.

Chakravarthy, B. S. and Perlmutter, H. V. (1985) 'Strategic planning for a global business', *Columbia Journal of World Business*, Summer: 5–6.

Chen, C. C., Meindl, J. R. and Hunt, R. G. (1997) 'Testing the effects of vertical and horizontal collectivism: a study of reward allocation preferences in China', *Journal of Cross-Cultural Psychology*, 28(1): 44–70.

Chen, M. (1995) *Asian Management Systems*, London/New York: Routledge.

Chevalier, F. and Segalla, M. (1996) 'Crédit Lyonnais: the internationalization of a French bank', in F. Chevalier and M. Segalla (eds) *Organizational Behaviour and Change in Europe*, London: Sage, pp. 4–36.

Child, J. (1994) *Management in China during the Age of Reform*, Cambridge: Cambridge University Press.

Child, J., Boisot, M., Ireland, J., Li, Z. and Watts, J. (1990) *The Management of Equity Joint Ventures in China*, Beijing: China–EC Management Institute.

Chimezie, A., Osigweh, Yg and Huo, Y. (1993) 'Conceptions of employee responsibility and rights in the US and People's Republic of China', *International Journal of Human Resources Management*, 4(1).

Constable, C. J. (1988) *Developing the Competent Manager in a UK Context*, Report for the Manpower Services Commission. Sheffield: Manpower Services Commission.

Constanza, J. R. (1992) *The Quantum Leap in Speed-to-Market*, Denver: Jc-I-T Institute of Technology.

Crow, J. A. (1985) *Spain: The Root and the Flower*, 3rd edition, Berkeley: University of California Press.

Cyr, D. J. and Frost, P. (1991) 'Human resources management practice in China: a future perspective', *Human Resource Management*, 30(2): 199–215.

Cyr, D. J. and Schneider, S. C. (1998) 'Creating a learning organization through HRM: a German–Czech joint venture', INSEAD case collection, and reproduced as Chapter 17 of G. Oddou and M. Mendenhall (eds) *Cases in International Organizational Behaviour*, Malden, MA: Blackwell, pp. 197–210.

Davenport, T. H. and Hansen, M. T. (1998) *Knowledge Management at Andersen Consulting*, Harvard Business School case collection, Boston, MA: Harvard Business School Publishing.

de Boer, C. (1978) 'The polls: attitudes towards work', *Public Opinion Quarterly*, 42: 414–23.

Deller, J. (1997) 'Expatriate selection: possibilities and limitations of using personality scales', in D. M. Saunders and Z. Aycan (eds) *New Approaches to Employee Management Volume 4, Expatriate Management: Theory and Research*, Greenwich, CT: JAI Press, pp. 93–116.

Derr, C. B. (1986) *Managing the New Career*, San Francisco: Jossey-Bass.

Derr, C. B. and Laurent, A. (1987) *The Internal and External Careers: A Theoretical and Cross-cultural Perspective*, working paper, University of Utah and INSEAD.

Desatnick, R. A. and Bennett, M. L. (1978) *Human Resource Management in the Multinational Company*, New York: Nichols.

Dia, M. (1996) *Africa's Management in the 1990s and Beyond*, Washington, DC: World Bank.

Diaz, A. and Miller, P. (1994) 'Managing people in Spain', in T. Garrison and D. Rees (eds) *Managing People across Europe*, Oxford: Butterworth-Heinemann, pp. 140–62.

d'Iribarne, P. (1989) *La Logique de l'honneur: gestion des entreprises et traditions Nationales*, Paris: Seuil.

d'Iribarne, P. (1997) 'The usefulness of an ethnographic approach to the comparison of organizations', *International Studies of Management and Organizations*, 26(4): 30–47.

DiStefano, J. J. (1992) 'Manners Europe', in H. W. Lane and J. J. DiStefano (eds) *International Management Behavior*, 2nd edition, Boston: PWS-Kent, pp. 278–94.

Donegan, J. (1990) 'The learning organization: lessons from British Petroleum', *European Management Journal*, 8(3): 302–12.

Dowling, P. J. and Schuler, R. S. (1990) *International Dimensions of Human Resource Management*, Boston: PWS-Kent.

Doz, Y. and Prahalad, C. K. (1986) 'Controlled variety: a challenge for human resource management in the MNC', *Human Resource Management*, 25(1): 55–71.

Dubin, R. (1970) 'Management in Britain – impressions of a visiting professor', *Journal of Management Studies*, 7, 183–98, and reproduced in D. J. Hickson (ed.) (1997) *Exploring Management Across the World*, Harmondsworth: Penguin, pp. 39–55.

Eagly, A. (1978) 'Sex differences in influenceability', *Psychological Bulletin*, 85: 85–116.

Ebster-Grosz, D. and Pugh, D. S. (1991) *Anglo-German Business Collaboration: A Report of an Empirical Study*, Open University Business School working paper, Milton Keynes.

Edmondson, A. and Moingeon, B. (1996) 'When to learn how and when to learn why: appropriate organizational learning processes as a source of competitive advantage', in B. Moingeon and A. Edmondson (eds) *Organizational Learning and Competitive Advantage*, London: Sage, pp. 17–37.

Edwards, R.W., O'Reilly, H. and Schuwwalow, P. (1997), 'Global personnel skills: a dilemma for the Karpin committee and others', *Asia Pacific Journal of Human Resources*, 35(3): 80–9.

Ehrlich, C. J. (1997) 'Human resource management: a changing script for a changing world', *Human Resource Management*, 36(1): 85–9.

EIU (1994) *Economic Intelligence Unit Quarterly Reports: China and Mongolia*, 4th Quarter.

Elizur, D., Borg, I., Hunt, R. and Beck, I. M. (1991) 'The structure of work values: a cross-cultural comparison', *Journal of Organizational Behaviour*, 12: 21–38.

Ellig, B. R. (1997) 'Is the human resource function neglecting the employees?', *Human Resource Management*, 36(1): 91–5.

Encel, S. (1970), *Equality and Authority*. Tavistock, London.

England, G. W. (1975) *The Manager and His Values: An International Perspective*, Cambridge, MA: Ballinger.

England, G.W. (1978) 'Managers and their value systems: a five country comparative study', *Columbia Journal of World Business*, 13(2): 33–44.

Etzioni, A. (1975) *A Comparative Analysis of Complex Organizations*, New York, NY: The Free Press, 1975.

Fanon, F. (1967) *The Wretched of the Earth*, Harmondsworth: Penguin.

Furness, N. and Tilton, T. (1979) *The Case for the Welfare State*, Bloomington: Indiana University Press.

Fürstenberg, F. (1998) 'Employment relations in Germany', Chapter 8 in G. J. Bamber and R. D. Lansbury (eds) *International and Comparative Employment Relations*, London, Sage, 201–33.

Galbraith, J. (1994) *Designing Complex Organizations*, Reading, MA: Addison Wesley.

Gannon, M. J. and Associates (1994) *Understanding Global Cultures: Metaphorical Journeys through 17 Countries*, Thousand Oaks, CA: Sage.

Garrison, T. (1994) 'Managing people across Europe: an introductory framework', Chapter 1 in T. Garrison, and D. Rees, *Managing People across Europe*, Oxford: Butterworth-Heinemann, pp. 1–24.

Garrison, T. and Rees, D. (eds) (1994) *Managing People across Europe*, Oxford: Butterworth-Heinemann.

Garrison, T. and Verveen, P. (1994) 'Managing people in the Netherlands', in T. Garrison and D. Rees, *Managing People across Europe*, Oxford: Butterworth-Heinemann, pp. 163–73.

Gill, R. and Wong, A. (1998) 'The cross-cultural transfer of management practices: the case of Japanese human resource management practices in Singapore', *International Journal of Human Resource Management*, 9(1).

Glenny, M. (1993) *The Rebirth of History: Eastern Europe in the Age of Democracy*, London: Penguin.

Goetschy, J. and Jobert, A. (1998) 'Employment relations in France', Chapter 7 in G. J. Bamber and R. D. Lansbury (eds) *International and Comparative Employment Relations*, London: Sage, pp. 169–200.

Goldratt, E. M. (1992) *The Goal*, New York: North River Press.

Greene, R. J. (1995) 'Cultural diversity and reward systems', *ACA Journal*, Spring: 24–33.

Grol, P., Schoch, C. and CPA (1998) 'IKEA: managing cultural diversity' [1997], in G. Oddou and M. Mendenhall (eds) *Cases in International Organizational Behaviour*, Oxford: Blackwell, pp. 88–112.

Gutmann, B. (1995) 'Tandem training: the Volkswagen-Skoda approach to know-how transfer', *Journal of European Industrial Training*, 19(4): 21–4.

Guy, V. and Mattock, J. (1991) *The New International Manager*, London: Kogan Page.

Haire, M., Ghiselli, E. and Porter, L. (1966) *Managerial Thinking: An International Study*, New York: Wiley.

Hall, E. T. (1959) *The Silent Language*, New York: Anchor Press/Doubleday.

Hamill, J. (1989) 'Expatriate policies in British multinationals', *Journal of General Management*, 14 (1): 18–33.

Hammarström, O. and Nilsson, T. (1998) 'Employment relations in Sweden', in G. J. Bamber and R. D. Lansbury (eds) *International and Comparative Employment Relations*, London: Sage, pp. 224–48.

Hammer, M. and Champy, J. (1993) *Reengineering the Corporation: A Manifesto for Business Revolution*, New York: Harper Business.

Harris, H. (1995) 'Women's role in (international) management', in A-W. K. Harzing and J. V. Ruysseveldt, *International Human Resource Management*, London: Sage, pp. 229–51.

Harris, R. P. and Moran, R. T. (1989) *Managing Cultural Differences*, Houston, TX: Gulf Publishing.

Harzing, A-W. K. (1995) 'The persistent myth of high expatriate failure rates', *International Journal of Human Resource Management*, 6(2): 458–74.

Hayes, J. and Allinson, C. W. (1988) 'Cultural differences in learning styles of managers', *Management International Review*, 28(3): 75–80.

Hazama, H. (1993) 'Trends in international business thought and literature: the recent literature of "Japanese-style" management', *International Executive*, 35(5): 461–65.

Hendry, C. and Pettigrew, A. (1990) 'Human resource management: an agenda for the 1990s', *International Journal of Human Resource Management*, 1(1): 17–44.

Hendry, J. (2000) *Shell in Nigeria*, University of Cambridge, The Judge Institute of Management Studies Case Collection, European Case Clearing House, Cranfield.

Henley, J. S. and Nyaw, M. K. (1990) 'The system of management and performance of joint ventures in China: some evidence from Shenzhen special economic zone', *Advances in Chinese Industrial Studies*, 1(B): 277–95.

Herzberg, F. (1966), *Work and the Nature of Man*, Cleveland: World Publishing Co.

Herzberg, F., Mausner, B. and Snyderman, B. (1959) *The Motivation to Work*, New York: Wiley.

Hickson, D. J. and Pugh, D. S. (1995) *Management Worldwide: The Impact of Societal Culture on Organizations around the Globe*, London: Penguin.

Hiltrop, J. M. and Janssens, M. (1990) 'Expatriation: challenges and recommendations', *European Management Journal*, 8(1): 19–26.

Hirsh, W. and Bevan, S. (1988) *What Makes a Manager*, Brighton: Institute of Manpower Studies.

Hodgetts, R. M. and Luthans, F. (1991) *International Management*, New York: McGraw-Hill.

Ho, D. Y-F. and Chiu, C-Y. (1994) 'Component ideas of individualism, collectivism and social organization: an application in the study of Chinese culture', in U. Kim et al., *Individualism and Collectivism: Theory, Method and Application*, Thousand Oaks: Sage, 137–56.

Hofstede, G. (1980a) *Culture's Consequences: International Differences in Work Related Values*, Beverly Hills, CA: Sage.

Hofstede, G. (1980b) 'Motivation, leadership and organization: do American theories apply abroad?', *Organizational Dynamics*, Summer: 42–63.

Hofstede, G. (1991) *Cultures and Organizations: Software of the Mind*, London: McGraw-Hill.

Hofstede, G. (1994) 'The business of international business is culture', *International Business Review*, 3(1): 1–14.

Hofstede, G. (2001) *Culture's Consequences: Comparing Values, Behaviors, Institutions and Organizations across Nations*, 2nd edition, Thousand Oaks, CA: Sage.

Hofstede, G. and Bond, M. (1988) 'The Confucian connection: from cultural roots to economic growth', *Organizational Dynamics*, 16(4): 4–21.

Honey, P. and Mumford, A. (1982) *The Manual of Learning Styles*, Maidenhead: Peter Honey.

Horwitz, F. M., Bowmaker-Falconer A. and Searll, P. (1996) 'Human resources development and managing diversity in South Africa', *International Journal of Manpower*, 17(4/5): 134–51.

Hughes-Weiner, G. (1986) 'The "learn-how-to-learn" approach to cross-cultural orientation', *International Journal of Intercultural Relations*, 10: 485–505.

Hui, C. H. (1988) 'Measurement of individualism–collectivism', *Journal of Research in Personality*, 22: 17–36.

Hui, C. H. (1990) 'Work attitudes, leadership styles, and managerial behaviour in different cultures', in R. W. Brislin, (ed.) *Applied Cross-Cultural Psychology*, Newbury Park, CA: Sage, pp. 186–208.

Hui, C. H. and Triandis, H. C. (1986) 'Individualism–collectivism: a study of cross-cultural researchers', *Journal of Cross-Cultural Psychology*, 17(2): 225–48.

Human, L. (1996) *Contemporary Conversations*, Dakar, Senegal: The Goree Institute.

Huo, Y. P. and von Glinow, M. A. (1995) 'On transplanting human resource practices to China: a cultural driven approach', *International Journal of Manpower*, 16(9): 3–15.

IDE (Industrial Democracy in Europe International Research Group) (1981) *Industrial Democracy in Europe*, Oxford: Clarendon Press.

Ishida, H. (1986) 'The transferability of Japanese human resource management abroad', *Human Resource Management*, 25(1): 103–20.

Jackson, S. (1992) *Chinese Enterprise Management*, New York: Walter de Gruyter.

Jackson, T. (1991) *Measuring Management Performance*, London: Kogan Page.

Jackson, T. (1993a) 'Ethics and the art of intuitive management', *European Management Journal*, special EAP 20th anniversary issue: 57–65.

Jackson, T. (1993b) 'Understanding management performance: an interpretive approach to analysis and measurement'. Unpublished PhD thesis, Henley Management College, Brunel University, UK.

Jackson, T. (1993c) *Organizational Behaviour in International Management*, Oxford: Butterworth-Heinemann.

Jackson, T. (1995) 'European management learning: a cross-cultural interpretation of Kolb's learning cycle', *Journal of Management Development*, 14(6): 42–50.

Jackson, T. (1996) 'Understanding management learning across cultures: some east–west comparisons'. Paper presented at the Academy of International Business annual meeting, Banff, Alberta, Canada, September.

Jackson, T. (1999) 'Managing change in South Africa: developing people and organizations', *International Journal of Human Resource Management*, 10(2): 306–26.

Jackson, T. (in press) 'Reframing people management in Africa: a cross-cultural perspective', *International Journal of Human Resource Management*.

Jackson, T. and Bak, M. (1998) 'Foreign companies and Chinese workers: employee motivation in the People's Republic of China', *Journal of Organizational Change Management*, 11(4): 282–300.

Jaeger, A. M. (1990) 'The applicability of Western management techniques in developing countries: a cultural perspective', in A. M. Jaeger and R. N, Kanungo (eds) *Management in Developing Countries*, London: Routledge.

Jaeger, A. M. and Kanungo, R. N. (1990) *Management in Developing Countries*, London: Routledge.

Japanese External Trade Organization (1992) *White Paper on Foreign Direct Investment*, Tokyo: JETRO.

Kanungo, R. N. and Jaeger, A. M. (1990) 'Introduction: the need for indigenous management in developing countries', in A. M. Jaeger and R. N. Kanungo (eds) *Management in Developing Countries*, London: Routledge, pp. 1–23.

Karpin, D. S. (1995) 'Enterprising nation: renewing Australia's managers to meet the challenge of the Asia-Pacific century', *Report of the Industrial Task Force on Leadership and Management Skills (Karpin Report)*, Canberra: AGPS.

Katz, F. and Kahn, R. (1978) *The Social Psychology of Organizations*, New York: Wiley.

Kedia, B. L. and Bhagat, R. S. (1988) 'Cultural constraints on transfer of technology across nations: implications for research in international and comparative management', *Academy of Management Review*, 13 (4): 559–71.

Keep, E. (1989) 'Corporate training strategies: the vital component', in J. Storey (ed.) *New Perspectives on Human Resource Management*, London: Routledge. pp. 109–25.

Kelley, L. and Shenkar, O. (eds) (1993) *International Business in China*, London: Routledge.

Kelly, L., Whatley, A. and Worthley, R. (1991) 'Self-appraisal, life goals, and national culture: an Asian–Western comparison', *Asia Pacific Journal of Management*, 7(2): 164–73.

Kendell, W. (1984) 'Why Japanese workers work', *Management Today*, January: 72–5.

Khanna, S. (1996) 'The new people economy', *Business Today* (India), 7–21 January: 12–17.

Kluckholm, F. and Strodtbeck, F. (1961) *Variations in Value Orientation*, Westport, CT: Greenwood Press.

Kolb, D. A. (1976) *The Learning Styles Inventory, and Technical Manual*, Boston, MA: McBer.

Kolb, D. A. (1984) *Experiential Learning*, Englewood Cliffs, NJ: Prentice Hall.

Kolb, D. A., Rubin, I. M. and Osland, J. S. (1991) *Organizational Behavior: An Experiential Approach*, 5th edn, Englewood Cliffs, NJ: Prentice Hall.

Koopman, A. (1991) *Transcultural Management*, Oxford: Basil Blackwell.

Kornai, J. (1992) *The Socialist System: Political Economy of Communism*, Oxford: Oxford University Press.

Kossov, V. and Gurkov, I. (1995) 'The system of management in modern Russia', *International Studies of Management and Organization*, 25(4): 9–25.

Koubek, J. and Brewster, C. (1995) 'Human resource management in turbulent times: HRM in the Czech Republic', *International Journal of Human Resource Management*, 6(2): 223–47.

Kubr, M. and Abell, D. F. (1998) 'Managers and their competences', in J. Prokopenko (ed.) *Management Development: A Guide for the Profession*, Geneva: International Labour Office, pp. 9–22.

Kuwahara, Y. (1998) 'Employment relations in Japan', in G. J. Bamber and R. D. Lansbury (eds) *International and Comparative Employment Relations*, London: Sage, pp. 249–74.

Laurent, A. (1986) 'The cross-cultural puzzle of international human resource management', *Human Resource Management*, 25(1): 91–102.

Lawrence, P. (1994) 'German management: at the interface between Eastern and Western Europe', Chapter 6 in R. Calori and P. de Woot (eds) *A European Management Model: Beyond Diversity*, London: Prentice Hall, pp. 133–64.

Lawrence, P. R. and Lorsch, W. J. (1967) *Organization and Environment*, Cambridge, MA: Harvard University Press.

Lawrence, P. R. and Spybey, T. (1986) *Management and Society in Sweden*, London: Routledge and Kegan Paul.

LCCIEB (1993) *National Vocational Qualification, Retailing Level 2*, London Chamber of Commerce and Industry Examinations Board.

Legge, K. (1989) 'Human resource management: a critical analysis', in J. Storey (ed.) *New Perspectives on Human Resource Management*, London: Routledge.

Lessem, R. (1989) *Global Management Principles*, London: Prentice-Hall.

Lessem, R. (1994) 'Four worlds: the southern African businessphere', in P. Christie, R. Lessem and L. Mbigi (eds) *African Management: Philosophy, Concepts and Applications*, Cape Town: Knowledge Resources.

Lewin, K. (1951) *Field Theory in Social Science*, London: Harper and Row.

Likert, R. (1961) *New Patterns of Management*, New York: McGraw-Hill.

Locket, M. (1987) 'China's special economic zones: the cultural and managerial challenges', *Journal of General Management*, 12(3): 21–31.

Lombardo, M. M. and McCall, M. W. Jr (1982) 'Leaders on the line: observations from a simulation of managerial work', in J. Hunt, *Leadership Beyond Establishment Views*, Carbondale: University of Illinois Press.

Lu, Y., Child, J. and Yan, Y. (1997) 'Adventuring in new terrain: managing international joint ventures in China', in S. Stewart and A. Carver (eds) *Advances in Chinese Industrial Studies*, Greenwich, CT: JAI Press, Vol. 5, pp. 103–23.

Mahieu, C. (2001) 'Management development in Royal Dutch/Shell', *Journal of Management Development*, 20(2).

Maslow, A. H. (1954) *Motivation and Personality*, New York: Harper.

May, R., Bormann Young, C. and Ledgerwood, D. (1998) 'Lessons from Russian human resource management experience', *European Management Journal*, 16(4): 447–59.

Mbigi, L. (1997) *Ubuntu: The African Dream in Management*, Randburg, RSA: Knowledge Resources.

McCalman, J. (1989) 'Performance organizations in the 1990s: flexibility for manufacturing management', *European Management Journal*, 7(3): 353–57.

McCalman, J. (1996) 'Lateral hierarchy: the case of cross-cultural management teams', *European Management Journal*, 14(5): 509–17.

McClelland, D. C. (1987) *Human Motivation*, Cambridge: Cambridge University Press.

Mendenhall, M. and Oddou, G. (1985) 'The dimensions of expatriate acculturation: a review', *Academy of Management Review*, 10: 39–47.

Mendonca, M. and Kanungo, R. N. (1994) 'Managing human resources: the issues of culture fit', *Journal of Management Inquiry*, 3(3): 198–205.

Mills, A. (1997) 'Contextual influences on human resource management in the Czech Republic', *Personnel Review*, 27(3): 177–99.

Moran, R. (1985) 'Cross-cultural contact – are women the answer to problems of culture clash?' *International Management*, 40(5): 118.

Moss Kanter, R. (1989) *When Giants Learn to Dance*, London: Routledge.

Mostert, N. (1992) *Frontiers: The Epic of South Africa's Creation and the Tragedy of the Xhosa People*, London: Pimlico.

MOW (Meaning of Working) International Research Team (1987) *The Meaning of Working*, London: Academic Press.

Mumford, A. (1988) *Developing Top Managers*, Aldershot: Gower.

Muzyka, D., de Koning, A. and Churchill, N. (1995) 'On transformation and adaptation: building the entrepreneurial corporation', *European Management Journal*, 13(4): 346–62.

Nanda, A. and Yoshino, M. (1995) *Andersen Consulting – EMEAI: Reorganization for Revitalization*, Cambridge, MA: Harvard Business School Case Collection.

National Economic Development Office/Manpower Services Commission (1984) *Competence and Competition*, London: NEDO.

Negandhi, A. R. (1987) *International Management*, Boston: Allyn and Bacon.

Nevis, E. (1983) 'Cultural assumptions and productivity: the United States and China', *Sloan Management Review*, 24: 17–29.

Niles, F. S. (1995) 'Cultural differences in learning motivation and learning strategies: a comparison of overseas and Australian students at an Australian university', *International Journal of Intercultural Relations*, 19(3): 369–85.

Nonaka, I., Toyama, R. and Konno, N. (2000) 'SECI, Ba and leadership: a unified model of dynamic knowledge creation', *Long Range Planning*, 33(1): 5–34.

Nordhaug, O. (1998) 'Competences specificities in organizations: a classificatory framework', *International Studies of Management and Organization*, 28(1): 8–29.

Ohmae, K. (1982) *The Mind of the Strategist*, Harmondsworth: Penguin.

Olie, R. (1990) 'Culture and integration problems in international mergers and acquisitions', *European Management Journal*, 8(2): 206–15.

Ouchi, W. G. (1981) *Theory Z: How American Business can meet the Japanese Challenge*, Reading, MA: Addison-Wesley.

Pareek, U. and Rao, T. V. (1992) *Designing and Managing Human Resources Systems*, New Delhi: Oxford and IBH.

Parkum, K. H. and Agersnap, F. (1994) 'Managing people in Scandinavia', in T. Garrison and D. Rees (eds) *Managing People across Europe*, Oxford: Butterworth-Heinemann, pp. 111–21.

Parson, T. and Shils, E.A. (1951) *Towards a General Theory of Action*, Cambridge, MA: Harvard University Press.

Pascale, R. T. and Athos, A. G. (1981) *The Art of Japanese Management*, New York: Simon and Schuster.

Pedler, M., Boydell, T. and Burgoyne, J. (1989) 'Towards the learning company', *Journal of the Association for Management Education and Training*, 20(1).

Peltro, P. J. (1968) 'The difference between "tight" and "loose" societies', *Transaction*, April: 37–40.

Perlmutter, H. V. (1969) 'The tortuous evolution of the multinational corporation', *Columbia Journal of World Business*, 4(1): 9–18.

Peters, T. J. (1992) *Liberation Management*, New York: Alfred A. Knopf.

Peters, T. J. and Waterman, R. H. (1982) *In Search of Excellence: Lessons from America's Best-Run Companies*, New York: Harper and Row.

Pettigrew, A., Massini, S. and Numagami, T. (2000) 'Innovative forms of organising in Europe and Japan', *European Management Journal*, 18(3): 259–73.

Phatak, A. V. (1992) *International Dimensions of Management*, 3rd edn, Boston: PWS-Kent.

Polanyi, M. (1966) *The Tacit Dimension*, New York: Doubleday.

Priem, R. L., Love, L. G. and Shaffer, M. (2000) 'Industrialization and values evolution: the case of Hong Kong and Guangzhou, China', *Asia Pacific Journal of Management*, 17(3): 473–92.

PRC (1987) 'Law of the PRC on Chinese–foreign equity joint ventures', in *The Laws of the PRC*.

Pucik, V. (1988) 'Strategic alliances, organizational learning, and competitive advantage: the HRM agenda', *Human Resource Management*, 27(1): 77–93.

Pucik, V. and Hatvany, N. (1998) 'Chiba International, Inc.', in G. Oddou and M. Mendenhall (eds) *Cases in International Organizational Behavior*, Malden, MA: Blackwell, pp. 18–32.

Pye, A. (1991) 'Management competence: "The flower in the mirror and the moon on the water"', in M. Silver (ed.) (1991) *Competent to Manage*, London: Routledge, pp. 101–17.

Quinn, J. B. (1992) *Intelligent Enterprise: A Knowledge and Service Paradigm for Industry*, New York: Free Press.

Quinn Mills, D. Q. (1991) *Rebirth of an Organization*, New York: Wiley.

Rao, T. V. (1996) *Human Resource Development: Experiences, Intervention, Strategies*, New Delhi: Sage.

Reader, J. (1997) *Africa: A Biography of the Continent*, London: Penguin.

Reading, B. (1992) *Japan – The Coming Collapse*, London: Weidenfeld and Nicholson.

Redding, S. G., Norman, A. and Schlander, A. (1994) 'The nature of individual attachment to theory: a review of East Asian variations', in H.C. Triandis, M. D. Dunnett and L. M. Hough (eds) *Handbook of Industrial and Organizational Psychology*, Palo Alto, CA: Consulting Psychologists Press, Vol. 4, pp. 674–88.

Revans, R. (1965) *Science and the Manager*, London: Macdonald.

Roethlisberger, F. J. and Dickson, W. J. (1939) *Management and the Worker*, Cambridge, MA: Harvard University Press.

Rohmetra, N. (1998) *Human Resource Development in Commercial Banks in India*, Aldershot: Ashgate.

Rosenzweig, P. M. and Nohria, N. (1994) 'Influences on human resource management practices in multinational corporations', *Journal of International Business Studies*, 25(2): 229–51.

Ross, P., Bamber, G. J. and Whitehouse, G. (1998) 'Employment, economics and industrial relations: comparative statistics', appendix in G. J. Bamber and R. D.

Lansbury (eds) *International and Comparative Employment Relations*, London: Sage, pp. 328–66.

Rotter, J. B. (1966) 'General expectancies for internal versus external control of reinforcement', *Psychological Monographs*, 80(1): Whole No. 609: 1–28.

Roussillon, S. and Bournois, F. (1997) 'Identification and development of potential for management and executive positions in France', *Career Development International*, 2(7): 341–6.

Saunders, E. (1998) 'Leadership the South African way', *People Dynamics*, February, 31–4.

Sawadogo, G. (1995) 'Training for the African mind', *International Journal of Intercultural Relations*, 19(2): 281–93.

Schein, E. H. (1985) *Organizational Culture and Leadership*, San Francisco: Jossey-Bass.

Schuler, R. S. and Rogovsky, N. (1998) 'Understanding compensation practice variation across firms: the impact of national culture', *Journal of International Business Studies*, 29(1): 159–77.

Schuler, R. S., Dowling, P. J. and De Cieri, H. (1993) 'An integrative framework of strategic international human resource management', *International Journal of Human Resource Management*, 4(4): 717–64.

Schwartz, S. (1994) 'Beyond individualism/collectivism: new cultural dimensions of values', in U. Kim, H. C. Triandis, Ç. Kâğitçibaşi, S-C. Choi and G. Yoon, (eds) *Individualism and Collectivism: Theory, Method and Application*, Beverly Hills, CA: Sage, pp. 85–119.

Scott Morton, M. (1995) 'Emerging organizational forms: work and organization in the 21st century', *European Management Journal*, 13(4): 339–45.

Scullion, H. (1991) 'Why companies prefer to use expatriates', *Personnel Management*, 23: 32–5.

Semler, R. (1994) *Maverick: The Success Story behind the World's Most Unusual Workplace*, London: Arrow.

Senge, P. (1990) *The Fifth Discipline: The Art and Practice of the Learning Organization*, London: Century Business.

Sergeant, A. and Frenkel, S. (1998) 'Managing people in China: perceptions of expatriate managers', *Journal of World Business*, 33(1): 17–33.

Shekshnia, S. (1998) 'Western multinationals' human resource practices in Russia', *European Management Journal*, 16(4): 460–5.

Silvera, D. M. (1988) *Human Resource Development: The Indian Experience*, New Delhi: New Delhi Publications.

Silverman, D. (1970) *The Theory of Organizations*, Aldershot: Gower.

Singleton, W. T., Spurgeon, P. and Stammers, R. B. (eds) (1979) *The Analysis of Social Skills*, New York: Plenum Press.

Smiley, T. (1989) 'A challenge to the human resource and organizational function in international firms', *European Management Journal*, 7(2): 189–97.

Smith, B. E. and Thomas J. M. (1972) 'Cross-cultural attitudes among managers: a case study', *Sloan Management Review*, 13(3): 35–50.

Smith, P. B., Dugan, S. and Trompenaars, F. (1996) 'National culture and the values of organizational employees: a dimensional analysis across 43 nations', *Journal of Cross-Cultural Psychology*, 27 (2): 231–64.

Snowden, D. (1999) 'Liberating knowledge', Chapter 1, in *Liberating Knowledge*, IBM Business Guides, London: Caspian Publishing, pp. 6–19.

Sondergaard, M. (1994) 'Hofstede's consequences: a study of reviews, citations and replications', *Organization Studies*, 15: 447–56.

Sparrow, P. and Budhwar, P. (1995) 'Developments in Indian HRM in the new economic environment'. Paper presented at the European Institute for Advance Studies in Management conference, Cross-cultural Perspectives: Comparative Management and Organizations, Henley Management College, UK, 10–12 November.

Srica, V. (1995) 'Managing people in Central Europe', Chapter 5 in T. Garrison and T. Rees (eds) *Managing People Across Europe*, Oxford: Butterworth-Heinemann, pp. 92–110.

Stewart, D. (1986) *The Power of People Skills*, New York: Wiley.

Storey, J. (1992) *Developments in Management of Human Resources*, Oxford: Blackwell.

Sweeney, E. (1996) 'Managing strategic change in China: the human resource paradigm', *Strategic Change*, 5(5): 331–41.

Tayeb, M. (1993) 'English culture and business organizations', in D. J. Hickson (ed.) *Management in Western Europe: Society, Culture and Organization in Twelve Nations*, Berlin: Walter de Gruyter.

Tayeb, M. H. (2000) 'The internationalisation of HRM policies and practices: the case of Japanese and French companies in Scotland', 11éme Congrés de l'AGRH, 16–17th November 2000, ESCP-EAP, Paris.

Thurley, K. and Widenius, H. (1989) *Towards European Management*, London: Pitman.

Tijmstra, S. and Casler, K. (1992) 'Management learning for Europe', *European Management Journal*, 10(1): March: 30–8.

Tixier, M. (2000) 'Communication and management styles in Australia: understanding the changing nature of its corporate affairs', *Cross Cultural Management: An International Journal*, 7(1): 12–22.

Torbiörn, I. (1982) *Living Abroad: Personal Adjustment and Personnel Policy in Overseas Settings*, New York: Wiley.

Tregaskis, O. and Dany, F. (1996) 'A comparison of HRD in France and the UK', *Journal of European Industrial Training*, 20(1): 20–30.

Triandis, H. C. (1990) 'Theoretical concepts that are applicable to the analysis of ethnocentrism', in R. W. Brislin (ed.) *Applied Cross-Cultural Psychology*, Newbury Park, CA: Sage, pp. 34–55.

Triandis, H. C., Brislin, R. and Hui, C. H. (1988) 'Cross-cultural training across the individualism–collectivism divide', *International Journal of Intercultural Relations*, 12: 269–89.

Trompenaars, F. (1993) *Riding the Waves of Culture: Understanding Cultural Diversity in Business*, London: Nicholas Brealey.

Trouvé, P. (1994) 'Managing people in France', Chapter 4 in T. Garrison and D. Rees (eds) *Managing People across Europe*, Oxford: Butterworth-Heinemann, pp. 63–91.

Tsuda, K. (1996) 'The strategy for human resources development in SMI', *International Journal of Technology Management*, special publication, 12(5/6): 534–50.

Tung, R. L. (1981) 'Selection and training of personnel for overseas assignments', *Columbia Journal of World Business*, 15: 68–78.

Turcq, D. (1995) 'The global impact of non-Japan Asia', *Long Range Planning*, 28(1): 31–40.

Turpin, D. and Hennessey, H. D. (1999) *Andersen Consulting's Global Brand Campaign*, IMD – International Institute for Management Development Case Collection, Lausanne, Switzerland.

Tyson, S. and Fell, A. (1986) *Evaluating the Personnel Function*, London: Hutchinson.

ul-Haq, R. (1995) *Strategic Alliances: Banque Nationale de Paris and Dresdner Bank*, case study of the University of Birmingham, Bedford: The European Case Clearing House.

UNCTC: United Nations Centre for Transnational Corporations (1993) *Investment Report, 1993: Transnational Corporations and Integrated International Production*, New York: UNCTC.

van Dijck, J. (1990) 'Transnational management in an evolving European context', *European Management Journal*, 8(4): 474–9.

Vaughan, E. (1994) 'The trial between sense and sentiment: a reflection on the language of HRM', *Journal of General Management* , 19: 20–32.

Vertinski, I., Tse, D.K., Wehrung, D. A. and Lee, K.-H. (1990) 'Organizational design and management norms: a comparative study of managers' perceptions in the People's Republic of China, Hong Kong and Canada', *Journal of Management*, 16(4): 853–67.

Walder, A. G. (1986) *Communist Neo-traditionalism*, Berkeley: University of California Press.

Wang, Z. M. (1992) 'Managerial psychological strategies for Chinese–foreign joint ventures', *Journal of Managerial Psychology*, 7(3): 10–16.

Wang, Z. M. and Satow, T. (1994) 'Leadership styles and organizational effectiveness in Chinese–Japanese joint ventures', *Journal of Managerial Psychology*, 9(4): 31–6.

Warner, M. (1993) 'Human resources management with Chinese characteristics', *International Journal of Human Resources Management*, 4(1): 45–65.

Warner, M. (1996a) 'Chinese enterprise reform, human resources and the 1994 Labour Law', *International Journal of Human Resource Management*, 7(4): 779–96.

Warner, M. (1996b) 'Human resources in the People's Republic of China: the "three systems" reforms', *Human Resource Management Journal*, 6(2): 32–43.

Warner, M. and Campbell, A. (1993) 'German management', Chapter 6 in D. J. Hickson (ed.) *Management in Western Europe: Society, Culture and Organizations in Twelve Nations*, Berlin: Walter de Gruyter, pp. 89–108.

Westwood, R. J. and Posner, B. Z. (1997) 'Managerial values across cultures: Australia, Hong Kong and the United States', *Asia Pacific Journal of Management*, 14: 31–66.

Wheeler, H. N. and McClendon, J. A. (1998) 'Employment relations in the United States', in G. J. Bamber and R. D. Lansbury (eds) *International and Comparative Employment Relations*, London: Sage, pp. 63–88.

Whitehill, A. M. (1991) *Japanese Management: Tradition and Transition*, London: Routledge.

Williams, J. E. and Best, D. L. (1982) *Measuring Sex Stereotypes: A Third National Study*, London: Sage.

Wolfe, A. W. (1977) 'The supranational organization of production: an evolutionary perspective', *Current Anthropology*, 18(4): 615–35.

Yoneyama, E. (1994) 'Japanese subsidiaries: strengths and weaknesses', Chapter 5 in R. Calori and P. de Woot, *A European Management Model: Beyond Diversity*, London: Prentice-Hall, pp. 112–32.

Index

Collins · *do b liantly* !

ExamPractice

ASPsychology

Exam practice at its **best**

■ **Mike Cardwell**

■ **Claire Meldrum**

■ **Jane Willson**

■ **Series Editor: Jayne de Courcy**

Contents